LAST SHIP TO FREEDOM

LAST SHIP
TO
FREEDOM

Uncovering My Grandmother's Tale
of Fleeing Post-Imperial Russia

TAMARA BUZYNA ADAMS

Last Ship to Freedom: Uncovering My Grandmother's Tale of Fleeing Post-Imperial Russia
© 2025 Tamara Buzyna Adams

Published by Thought Leader Academy Publishing
Thought Leader Academy Publishing
3901 N Kildare Ave
Chicago, Il 60641

Cover design by Claudine Mansour Design
Interior design by Liz Schreiter

Paperback ISBN: 978-1-968668-99-0
Ebook ISBN: 978-1-968668-98-3

For my grandmother, Lydia, whose courage and resilience inspired me to bring her story to life, and in memory of all those who traveled with her aboard the *Kherson* steamship.

To my mother, Helen, and my Uncle George, may this book help you see the mother you deeply adored as she once was – a young girl with hopes, dreams, and an enduring resilience, shaping the woman you knew and loved.

CONTENTS

Помни и люби!
Remember and Love!

—ZHENIA, KOLYA AND ALYOSHA ANIKEEFF

INTRODUCTION

Growing up, I was content with the little knowledge I had about my family history. I never felt the urge to dig deeper into my origins. Both sides of my family had Russian roots. While I embraced the small amount I knew, I also accepted that I would likely never learn more details about my great-grandparents, second great-grandparents, much less my third great-grandparents. I did not realize there were different types of cousins beyond just "regular" cousins. I only have five (first) cousins and never imagined it would be possible to have more, and I am the oldest cousin by three and a half years.

It's not like I wasn't exposed to my ancestral history as a kid. When we visited my paternal grandmother in Chicago, we would gather around the dining table after enjoying one of her delicious, authentic Russian meals. My father brought out the old-fashioned tape recorder, and I would hear the familiar click of the red record button. My grandmother, hesitant at first, would soon forget she was being recorded and began sharing stories of her childhood in Russia, speaking mostly in Russian with bits of English words mixed in. My mother would translate small portions at a time for me. I was fascinated by the stories, both captivating and heart-breaking at the same time.

"Babushka" was the sixth child of nine, and only one of three that survived through adulthood. She lived to the remarkable age of 98. She told stories about her grandfather being a high-ranking general, her aunt knowing the royal Romanov family, and her father's surname, Golitsyn, being associated with the famous noble family. If she were here today, I would fire countless questions at her. She had a full young adult life in Russia before immigrating to the United States in 1950 with her husband, his parents, and her two sons (one of whom is my father). But her intriguing story is for another time.

On the other side, my maternal grandmother, Lydia, spent only her first ten years in Russia. We did not have those same after-dinner discussions of her childhood. However, I distinctly remember her mentioning cousins Nyucya, Marusia, and Tanya, whom she left behind in Odessa. She kept in touch with them through letters all her life. I was, and am, impressed by their closeness, despite their distance, and how they had only known each other for 10 years as children and yet maintained such a strong bond. I felt like I did not have that kind of bond with my five cousins growing up, even though we saw each other at least once, if not twice, a year, and we lived in the same country.

I am Lydia's eldest grandchild. I always knew she was Russian and never questioned how she came to the United States. Her English sounded "American" to me, and I never detected an accent. "Grandma Frisk," as we affectionately called her, was an only child born in the beautiful coastal port town of Odessa, in pre-Revolutionary Russia. She was surrounded by a large, loving extended family there: grandparents, aunts, uncles, and cousins. She had nothing but fond memories of this time, but I do not remember any specific stories. However, my uncle and cousin from my father's side were fascinated by my grandmother's stories and frequently asked her questions about her time in Russia. As soon as these conversations began, I bolted. I thought history was boring.

Why didn't I inquire about her childhood in Russia or the harrowing journey she embarked on to reach the United States? I knew she had lived on a ship in the Black Sea, and yet did not ask about this experience. I vaguely recall hearing something about diaries she wrote from that time. She was always a very proper woman, stoic almost, and someone who rarely looked back. She was very focused on the present and never spoke of regrets about the past, at least not openly. She seemed closed off, and perhaps I was too intimidated by her to ask anything about her personal life.

Even if I had wanted to learn more, how would I ever find these details about my family in a distant country where I did not speak the language or know much about anything? To whom would I even ask my specific questions about family, anyway? All my relatives who potentially would have the answers are now long gone.

Fast forward to the year 2020. I had just turned 50 in the summer before the COVID-19 pandemic lockdown. During this midlife transition of mine, I had even more time to contemplate what I had (or had not) accomplished in my life. What was I doing with my life, and where would my life go from here? I was married with two kids, a junior in high school, and an eighth grader. For the past 20 years, my life as a wife and a mother had always been family-centered and never focused on me alone. We were a unit. I never put myself first, as wives and mothers often do. The endless time spent at home during the pandemic allowed me to truly delve into self-reflection and much-needed self-care, with my husband and kids still by my side.

Soon, I had many questions churning in my head, mostly looking into my family's past. Where did I come from? Was there a great-grandmother or great aunt I took after? Who were these mysterious ancestors living in rural European lands whose borders were constantly changing? What would it be like to live in the same place your whole life, and yet the country would have a different identity every few years or decades? Even though I did not speak the language my ancestors spoke and did not know who they were, I felt a deep connection to all of them. And I wanted to know more. I am now lucky to know the names of all 8 great-grandparents, all of whom were born in the Russian Empire. I was determined to find at least some of the answers to these questions gnawing at my core.

Little did I know that my "cousin world" would expand once I explored my ancestral roots as I got older. With the help of genealogy websites, online resources, DNA matches, and a distant relative who is conveniently located in Russia, I opened the gates to my family history and made some monumental discoveries. I found several third, fourth, and fifth cousins and now have an open invitation to visit them in Finland, Sweden, Ukraine, and Russia.

The simple joy of adding a name, even if it is only a first name, to my family tree is incredibly exhilarating. The same thrill you feel when, after working on a 1,000-piece puzzle, you finally connect the elusive piece that brings many other pieces together. This brings you one step closer to seeing the full picture. And I have always loved puzzles.

I believed I understood my own identity and family heritage from the occasional forays into the Russian language and the times we would celebrate typical Russian holidays, mostly associated with the Eastern Orthodox Church. Taking on the monumental project of researching Lydia's diaries forced me to re-examine who I thought I was. How could diaries written by an eleven-year-old one hundred years ago stimulate such critical questions inside me?

How many of us have genealogical treasures, like my grandmother's diaries? What have your ancestors left behind that encourages you to question where you come from and who you are on a personal-identity level? What memoirs, photographs, letters, or other heirlooms written centuries or even just a few decades ago await you to rediscover? Have you taken a DNA test to "just" find out your ethnicity?

My ancestry DNA tests confirmed what I knew all along, that I am 100% Eastern European (Russian, Ukrainian, Balkan, with some Finnish), but there is more to who I am than my genetic makeup. What influences did my previous ancestors have on me? What traditions were passed down to me and to my children not through DNA, but through environmental factors and experiences? And how will my experiences mold future generations?

My Great Aunt Sonya's memoirs probably deepened my obsession with genealogy. Like my grandmother Lydia, Sonya was born in pre-Revolutionary Russia, but in the beautiful city of St. Petersburg in 1902.

Unlike Lydia, she did not start writing her memoirs until she was 72 years old, many years after the fact. Having a sense that future generations would be interested in her life story, in Russia before immigrating to the United States, she would send my mother a few typewritten, single-spaced pages beginning in 1974 at my uncle's wedding. My mother was raising a family then, and did not have time to devote herself to piecing together her puzzle of a fascinating story. She would hastily read the installments and put them away, hoping to get to them later.

In 2013, a quarter of a century after Aunt Sonya died, my mother finally compiled her memoirs into a rough draft, this time with the help of a distant cousin. As if history repeated itself a generation later, I was too busy at the time to take on the project fully as I was raising a family of my own. However, I was there to support my mother in this significant endeavor.

Several years later, in 2016, I was hooked on genealogy and family history projects. I was, and am, obsessed with finding out more about myself through researching my past ancestors. Although my initial excuse not to fully engage myself with the genealogy projects with my mother was that I was busy raising my own family, I think the real reason is more likely my all-or-nothing personality. I knew that if I committed to this project, I would give it more than 110%, potentially neglecting other aspects of my life, like maintaining my home or even sacrificing personal care to spend extra hours at my computer. I have a long history of over-committing to self-inflicted projects throughout my life, such as clay bead making, scrapbooking, and card making, to name a few.

Nothing seems to have satisfied me more than the emotional wealth I have gained from my genealogical research, however, and this interest has not waned. I might even say I have become obsessed with genealogy. The more information I learn about my family, the more questions I have. Genealogy research is a continuous cycle of questions and answers with no true endpoint. It is about the process, and every discovery feels like a victory, which in turn sheds light on more mysteries waiting to be solved.

The never-ending curiosity about my ancestors makes my work that much more fulfilling.

~~~

Back to March 2020. COVID-19 shut the world down. No work. No school. No gatherings. No in-person anything. We were physically isolated from the outside world. While my family had difficulty adjusting to this new way of life, I had fully immersed myself in genealogy research, my passion! I felt the need to be "productive." Never had I *ever* had endless amounts of time free to do whatever *I* wanted. With an occasional interruption from my family (and sometimes more), I was transported to another world, all while sitting at my computer.

As I sat at home in front of my computer contemplating what genealogical project I would devote my now endless time on, I heard a "ding" coming from my phone. It was from my mother, and I knew she was rummaging through her own mother's memorabilia, as she, too, had nothing but time on her hands during COVID-19. I stopped everything and eagerly read her message; my heart fluttered at the possibility of earth-shattering news. She had made a huge discovery! I held my breath as I scanned the text. I skipped over most of the words until I read "*your grandmother's diaries.*" I knew exactly what she was talking about and couldn't help but do a happy dance at my desk.

I repeatedly expressed my elation over my mother's discovery of these diaries. As if to put a downer on my mood, my mother kept correcting me, stating, "Tamara, we have always known about the diaries; we didn't only now discover them, but we have had them all along." I felt angry, not just because I don't like being corrected by my mother, but if we had them all along, like she said, then why did we not ask her about this historic journey of hers when she was alive? My mother's response was, "I don't know." She was just as guilty as me. She even "caught" my grandmother reading these diaries when she lived in a retirement home at 90 years old, and still did not ask her about what secrets were in them. Nothing.

My grandmother lived on the steamer *Kherson* in the Black Sea for a year and a half, then another nine months living in Novi Sad, Serbia, with her family before she immigrated to the United States. The facts, as we knew them: during that time, she wrote a diary, she had extremely curly hair, her father worked on the ship, and something about how she witnessed horses running into the water after their masters who were departing on ships. Additionally, there were photographs of people aboard the ship. The unknowns: no dates for when they boarded or left the ship, no reasons why they decided to live on the ship, no clue on how they got to be on that particular vessel, and no information on who else was traveling on the ship with them.

Some answers revealed themselves on the first page of her diary, others were buried deep within the yellowed pages, and some were not in the diary at all. The first entry of her diary is dated January 29, 1921, just over a year after she had already been living on the ship. How would I discover when they departed Odessa, and what did they do for that entire year before she started writing daily entries? Why were they on the ship for so long, and how did they survive? So many questions with no answers. My understanding was that they were "just fleeing" Russia, and there would be no official documentation of their departure. What had I gotten myself into with this enormous undertaking? I took a deep breath and thought, if my grandmother could endure the conditions of living on a ship for a year and a half, certainly I could tackle this project with the same determination.

The first clue I came across was a handwritten note by my grandmother in a book her son had gifted her in 1996, titled "Black Sea"[1] which read:

"P12—General Denikin's White Army defeated by Reds
March 1920 at Novorossiysk on Black Sea - a real end of
Civil War. Baron Wrangel held out in Crimea with another

---

1   Ascherson, Neal. Black Sea: Coasts and Conquests: From Pericles to Putin. Revised edition, with updated forward. Vintage, 2007.

White Army but later was also defeated. That's when we left
Sevastopol and never returned to old Russia"

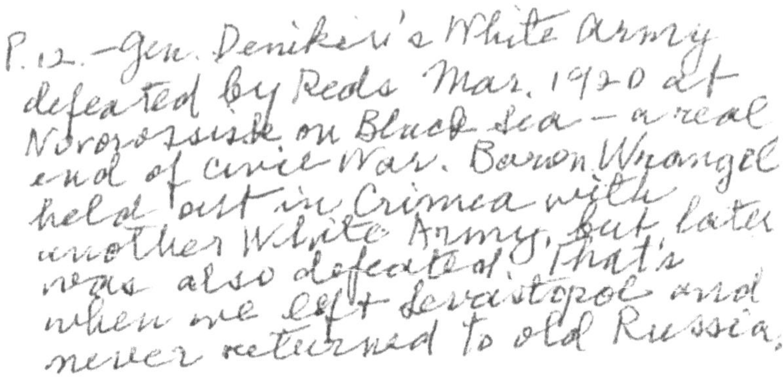

Figure 1: Handwritten note by my grandmother, Lydia.
Courtesy of the Buzyna Family.

This seemingly insignificant handwritten note verified that my grandmother, Lydia, and her family took part in the historic mass evacuation of Crimea led by White Army General Peter Wrangel in November 1920. We assumed they evacuated aboard the *Kherson* that departed on November 14 but lacked proof at the time. My jaw dropped as I learned the details. History, suddenly, became interesting to me, and I did not feel the urge to bolt when the topic arose. Over 150,000 people, only 7000 of them were children, boarded 126 vessels - anything that floated, to escape the Bolsheviks taking over their cities.

Four years after the monumental re-discovery of the diaries, we have many answers to the questions we never asked my grandmother. At the same time, we have thousands of more specific questions to ask from those answers, and we know that some of them will never get solved. When I initially embarked on this project, I did not have high expectations of discovering logistical details, much less finding any official documentation. Learning the exact date of departure and the circumstances as to why they left were a mere fantasy. Had I not taken on this project, this limited knowledge would have remained. I would not have formed the deep connection I now have with her.

Figure 2: Diary A. Courtesy of the Buzyna Family.

Figure 3: All five volumes of Lydia's Diaries dated January 29, 1921, to September 1, 1924. Courtesy of the Buzyna Family.

The Diaries

The "LDK Diaries," as we referred to them, consist of five volumes. Each volume is written in a 9¾" x 7½" wide-ruled composition book, exactly like what kids use today in school. The bindings are frayed and taped together in parts. They are labeled meticulously in her native language, Russian. They are dated Saturday, January 29, 1921, to Monday, September 1, 1924.

Diary A, as we labeled the first of five diaries, read:

Дневник (Diary)
Лидия Комаркова (Lydia Komarkova)
29 янв 1921 (29 Jan 1921)

Each entry was written with beautiful penmanship, each cursive Cyrillic letter formed with precision and purpose. When she made a mistake, she neatly crossed out the incorrect word(s) and rewrote the new word above it. Even though she wrote using "Contemporary Russian," she used "pre-revolutionary" (pre-1918) letters and spellings, or дореволюционная орфография (*dorevolyutsionnaya orfografiya*). For example, she used characters such as ѣ (called ять, yat), which are no longer in use today.

It's important to note that two calendars were used during this time period. In her diary, she recorded dates using the New (Gregorian) Calendar. The Old (Julian) Calendar, which was typically used in the Eastern Orthodox Churches up until the year 1924 and continues to be used by about half of them, is thirteen days behind the New (Gregorian) Calendar. For example, when discussing my grandmother's birthday, we would celebrate according to the Old Calendar on November 25th, but according to the New Calendar, it was December 7th. This was confusing as I was growing up.

Although only 11 years old when she started writing her diaries, there is a sense of maturity and certitude to them. She did not express much emotion in her writing; everything was a matter of fact, and *"This is how*

I spent my day," often mentioning the weather or the scenery. She often recorded the exact time she went to bed, or what time she boarded the tender to go to shore. Without going into much detail about some of her activities, you could still feel her joy when something elated her.

Her accounts of daily life on the ship were filled with excitement that could only be seen through the eyes of a child. The adults tried creating a "cloak of protection" around the children to preserve their innocence. Throughout her life, Lydia encountered many emigrants who also evacuated at the same time, but as adults in 1920, their experiences were more harrowing than hers.

PART I

The Story

CHAPTER 1

Embarking the *Kherson*

Lydia had no idea that November 14, 1920, would be the last time she would ever see her beloved homeland. Just shy of her eleventh birthday, she had already been living aboard the *Kherson* steamship with her family for eleven months. To her, life on the ship was an adventure. She had playmates, and she enjoyed traveling to various ports along the Black Sea, the coastlines of Greece, and even as far as Egypt. What an exciting life, Lydia likely thought.

Her father, Dimitri, was a merchant seaman[2] employed by the *Russian Volunteer Fleet.*[3] He was often away for long stretches, serving on ships that traveled to distant ports, Nagasaki in Japan, Vladivostok on Russia's eastern coast, and through the Suez Canal in Egypt. He would send postcards to his family urging Lydia to "be a good girl" and that he missed them.

One postcard, sent from Constantinople and addressed to Lydia in Odessa, arrived on March 22, 1912. In it, Dimitri congratulated his

---

2   A merchant seaman works on a ship usually involving trading. Dimitri worked on a ship, prior to 1920, on trade routes from Odessa to Vladivostok. This was the occupation listed on his death certificate.

3   The Russian Volunteer Fleet was also known as Dobroflot and was a ship transport company formed during the Russian Empire in 1878. Many of these ships in this service were used during the evacuation of Crimea in November 1920. The *Kherson* was part of the Volunteer Fleet.

daughter on her name day, March 23, according to the Julian (old) Calendar (April 4th, new calendar).

Figure 4: Front of postcard written to Lydia from her father. Courtesy of the Buzyna Family.

Figure 5: Back of postcard written to Lydia from her father. Courtesy of the Buzyna Family.

Translation:

My dear Lidoosya, I congratulate you on your name day. I wish you happiness and good health. Be smart, be less capricious. Goodbye, I kiss you tightly. Lovingly, your dad D.I.K.

[D.I.K. = Dimitri Ivanovich Komarkoff]

[Written at the top left:] Kiss [your] mom

Like many steamships belonging to the *Russian Volunteer Fleet,* the *Kherson* functioned as a merchant vessel during peaceful times. However, during war, it could quickly be repurposed as military transport. Many such ships were used to evacuate or repatriate Russian soldiers to safer regions. In January 1920, the *Kherson,* docked in Odessa, was scheduled for a peaceful transport voyage to Vladivostok, and Dimitri was due to report for duty.

Considering the tense political situation in Odessa, Dimitri cautiously proposed an idea to his wife, Daria:

"Do you know what? Let's go to Vladivostok, and when everything calms down here, we'll be back."

Daria agreed. In late December 1919 or early January 1920, Dimitri, Daria, and Lydia moved onto the ship and settled into their small but cozy cabin. It became their temporary home. They felt safe for the moment, but worried about their extended family remaining in Odessa.

Before departing, Lydia's parents persuaded Daria's sister, Elena, to let her youngest daughter, Tanya, come aboard with them as they prepared to leave Odessa. Lydia was thrilled – she was not just her cousin, but her closest friend. Tanya had been living with them in the family's small apartment in Odessa since Tanya's father had been killed several years before. At just five years old, Tanya witnessed his tragic murder during a robbery on a train en route to the Far East. Her two older sisters were also present, but it's unclear if they witnessed his death. Since then, Lydia's parents tried to help Elena raise Tanya, who was close in age to their own daughter.

Elena reluctantly agreed to let Tanya go. She truly believed it was for the best. After all, it wasn't like they would be gone forever. They would return as soon as the situation in Odessa stabilized. This was the only home they knew, and they never dreamed of leaving it for good.

Tanya quickly settled into the cabin with Lydia and her parents. Though the space was cramped, they did not mind. Being together was the most important thing on their minds. The girls were ecstatic, already planning the games they would play on deck with the other children. As night fell and the *Kherson* prepared for departure, excitement filled the air.

That night back at her apartment, Elena grew restless. She felt terrible guilt and had major second thoughts. "What have I done? How could I abandon my daughter? She is only 11 years old!" She tossed and turned all night, unable to sleep. Her mother's heart couldn't bear the separation from her youngest daughter. She decided that if the ship were still at the dock in the morning, she would bring Tanya home.

Elena woke as soon as the sun rose, dressed in what she wore the day before, and raced to the dock, praying the ship with her daughter had not departed. As if her prayers were answered, the ship was still there! It was delayed for repairs or some other unknown reason. She did not care what the delay was; she just wanted her daughter back. She thanked Dmitri and Daria for the kind gesture, but she admitted she simply couldn't handle being apart from her daughter, even temporarily. Devastated, the girls said their goodbyes. They clung to each other on the dock, crying uncontrollably until the adults finally had to pry them apart. That was the last time Lydia and Tanya saw each other.

Although Tanya was heartbroken to leave her cousin's family, she understood deep down that she could not leave her mother. I often wonder what might have happened if Tanya had gone with them. She remained in Odessa, eventually moving to St Petersburg, Russia. Her life was not easy. She endured the famine years in Odessa, the arrest of her first husband,[4] and ultimately the German blockade of Leningrad during the Second World War.

Lydia and Tanya continued writing letters for many years, with their correspondence only interrupted during the blockade, when it was impossible for Tanya's family to be connected with American relatives. And what if Lydia and her family *had* returned to Odessa? I, for one, would not be here telling this story...

---

4   He was arrested on March 1, 1938, and shot on May 28, 1938. (Державний архів Одеської області. Ф.8065. Оп.2. Справа 3127. Арк.24, 51/ The State Archives of Odessa Region. F.8065. Inv.2. File 3127. Pages 24, 51).

CHAPTER 2
Pre-Evacuation Aboard the *Kherson*

Ten months of chaos. The following time aboard the *Kherson* was a whirlwind of activity and a blur of constant movement. The ship made numerous stops at no fewer than six Black Sea Ports: Odessa, Sevastopol, Feodosia, Novorossiysk, Sulina, and Constantinople. Beyond these, they also docked at Famagusta (Cyprus), Piraeus (Athens, Greece), Thessaloniki (Greece), and Alexandria (Egypt). With each stop, more refugees, civilians, and military units boarded, adding to the ever-growing commotion on deck. It's important to note that these ports were not just visited once; many were revisited multiple times throughout these ten chaotic months.

A. January 1920: Departing Odessa

The original plan for Lydia's family to travel to Vladivostok was quickly abandoned as tensions on land intensified. As the Bolsheviks advanced towards the coastal cities of Russia and Crimea, the *Kherson* was redirected to Novorossiysk via Feodosia.

Lydia and her family, aboard the *Kherson* steamship, departed the port of Odessa sometime after January 3, 1920, traveling to Feodosia. Their stay here must have been short because they had already arrived in Novorossiysk by January 12th, confirmed by a telegram sent to the Volunteer Fleet Board in Feodosia on January 13, 1920, from the

Volunteer Fleet agent in Novorossiysk, Anton Ivanovich Shishkin.[5]
It read:

"THE KHERSON ARRIVED YESTERDAY."

The *Kherson* was in dire condition by the time it reached
Novorossiysk. Captain Schmelz (1) wrote a letter to his superiors urgently
requesting more coal to keep the ship operational.

A letter from Captain Schmelz to the Agent of the Volunteer Fleet in
Novorossiysk on 27 January 1920:[6]

> *The steamship "Kherson," entrusted to me, was left without
> coal on January 9. Since it was supposed to give coal to the
> "Kherson" from the "Mercedes" transport, I demanded only
> 500 poods [8.19 metric tons (1 pood = 16.38 kg = 36.11
> pounds)] of firewood for cooking for the administration and
> team. Loading of coal continues to be delayed, meanwhile
> there is no coal/fuel left due to which the temperature in liv-
> ing quarters reached 2–4 °C [+35.6 to +39.2 °F] on January
> 11 and was 0–2 °C [+32–+35,6 °F] on January 12. This
> caused increased illness among the administration and team.
> In addition, according to the statement of the Chief engineer
> [Viktor Martinovich Truen (6)], the lack of fuel due to the
> onset of frost will entail damage to boilers, machines, steam*

---

5   Российский государственный исторический архив (РГИА). Ф.98. Пароходное
    общество "Добровольный флот". Оп.6. 1878-1923. Д.196. Пароходное
    общество "Добровольный флот". Переписка с агентством Добровольного
    флота в городе Новороссийске о маршруте парохода "Иртыш" и о снабжении
    парохода "Херсон" топливом. 21 декабря 1919 г. - 2 июля 1920 г. Л.3об-4
    / The Russian State Historical Archives (RSHA). Fund 98. The Shipping
    company "Volunteer fleet". Inv.6. 1878-1923. File 196. The Shipping company
    "Volunteer fleet". Correspondence with the Volunteer Fleet agency in the city of
    Novorossiysk about the route of the steamship "Irtysh" and about the supply of
    fuel to the steamship "Kherson". December 21, 1919 - July 2, 1920. P.3back-4
    (translated from Russian).

6   Ibid. P.6 (translated from Russian).

heating and all pipelines. In this way the steamer will drop out of the number of floating ships. The 454 poods [7,44 tons] of firewood received yesterday was only enough for a day. Since coal supplies are not expected in the near future, and it is unacceptable to leave the ship without fuel, I ask you not to refuse to purchase a five-day supply of firewood in the amount of 1,500 poods [24,57 tons]. In view of the urgency of supplying the ship with fuel, it is desirable to take at least part of this amount, enough for about 2 days, in the shortest possible time. If there is a problem getting workers to cut firewood, the ship's crew can do this work for a fee.

Signed: Captain of the steamship Schmelz

Not only did the captain manage the ongoing challenges of securing coal, but he also had to contend with the disruption caused by a crew member who suffered a severe mental breakdown.[7] Yakov Byk, a helmsman, began to exhibit increasingly erratic behavior, which was recorded in the ship's logbook. The boatswain Sukovatykh (19) provided testimony regarding the incidents, which were confirmed by three other crew members: ordinary seaman Mezhero (32), able seaman Kurnosov (28), and helmsman Gorozhankin (23).

According to his fellow crew members, Byk refused to eat hot food, only ate dry bread, stated he was afraid of electric lighting, and would only handle money with his mittens on. One night, as the crew was asleep and the temperature dropped to eight degrees, he opened all the portholes in the deck crew quarters before vanishing.

The situation escalated the next day during Byk's lunch break. He threw various inventory items overboard, including a short fur coat, a weight from the deep-sea lead, one crowbar, a lower platform from the

---

7   Ibid. Inv.7. 1916-1921. File 23. Пароходное общество "Добровольный флот".
     Материалы по личному составу парохода "Херсон". 20 апреля - 8 декабря
     1920 г. Л.28-29об, 38 / The Shipping company "Volunteer fleet". Materials on the
     personnel of the ship "Kherson". April 20 - December 8, 1920. P.28-29back, 38.

ladder, an axe, three iron shovels, two caps belonging to an ordinary seaman, and firewood. After disposing of these items, he fled the steamer. He was initially dismissed on January 21 but was allowed to return to work. However, after continuing his strange behavior, he was dismissed again, this time permanently, on February 12.

On January 24, 1920, the *Kherson*, along with three other steamships (*Panama, Bruen, Empire*), transported 950 wounded and sick military men from Russia's White Army from Novorossiysk to the ports of Piraeus (Athens, Greece) and Thessaloniki (Greece). A total of 2300 people were transported via these vessels. England organized this transport and provided treatment at hospitals located in those Greek ports. I wonder if Lydia knew what was transpiring as the *Kherson* darted from port to port.

B. February 1920: Turmoil in Odessa, Reminiscing about Odessa

After January 3, 1920, Lydia never returned to Odessa. They learned that Odessa had fallen to the Bolsheviks in February 1920, which led to Lydia's hometown being evacuated. By then, the *Kherson* had already departed from Odessa and was not involved in the evacuation. There was no chance of returning anytime soon. The Komarkoff family and countless others prayed for peace in their cherished city. They thought of their families and friends being left behind, hoping they were still alive and not suffering from hardships.

Lydia had been living aboard the *Kherson* for over a month when the news of Odessa's defeat reached her. She deeply missed her aunts, cousins, and grandparents, and not a day passed without her thinking of them, especially her beloved cousin Tanya. She hoped they were safe and had not fallen victim to the Bolsheviks. Lydia faithfully recorded her family's name days and anniversaries in her diary, honoring them on the day they were celebrated.

Each day aboard the ship, Lydia followed the same routine: waking up, getting dressed, and completing her chores. She took responsibility for keeping her part of the cabin tidy and made her bed without fail. As an adult, her home in Schenectady, New York, was always impeccably neat and organized. I imagine this habit originated from her time on the ship, where maintaining an uncluttered cabin was essential due to limited space. She brought only her most treasured items along with her for the journey.

Up until she moved onto the ship, Lydia had been a student at the Mariinskaya Gymnasia[8] (also called "Odessa City First Girls' Gymnasia," which name is on Lydia's tram pass for October 1919) in Odessa. After relocating to the ship, she diligently continued her lessons independently or under the guidance of a tutor, often a crew member or passenger traveling alongside them. Her parents ensured her education continued, but Lydia was also conscientious and committed to her schoolwork.

Lydia took only her most cherished belongings on the voyage. Among them were books, a doll, and her favorite sailor's outfit.[9]

In her later years, Lydia wrote little notes in her flawless handwriting to label items she had kept with her while living on the ship. One such item is her Geography book, which is now over 100 years old. The title translated to English is *Initial Course, Geography Part II: Asia, Africa, America, Australia*. The author, G.I. Ivanov, was a teacher of the St Petersburg Second Gymnasium, and this edition is the second, revised. This is likely a book from her school in Odessa, as the title page has an "Odessa" stamp.

Curious about what pre-Revolutionary schools in Russia taught students about America, I used Google Translate to look it up. The content was written from a non-American perspective and dates to when there were only 46 states (1906). The text discusses geographical differences between North and South America and mentions that Christopher Columbus discovered America. I imagine that when Lydia was studying

---

8   This was the oldest girls' Gymnasia in Odessa.

9   Lydia is pictured on the book cover wearing this sailor outfit sitting on the deck of the Kherson in the Bay of Kotor. She also makes mention of wearing it on special occasions throughout her diary.

Figure 6: Lydia age 9 years old, from Mariinskaya Gymnasia in Odessa, 1918. Courtesy of the Buzyna Family.

Figure 7: This badge was pinned to her felt hat with a brim, from Mariinskaya Gymnasia in Odessa, 1919. Courtesy of the Buzyna Family.

Figure 8: Lydia's geography book she took with her on the Kherson, book cover. Courtesy of the Buzyna Family.

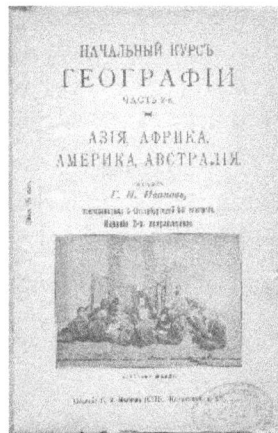

Figure 9: Lydia's geography book she took with her on the Kherson, title page. The stamp on the bottom right reads: "MYSL" (THOUGHT); Odessa, Torgovaya (St.), 20. Buying used books. Courtesy of the Buzyna Family.

about America, she had no idea that she would end up spending most of her life living there.

Another treasure Lydia kept with her in her cabin was a poetry book. It was small, with a hard cover, yellow unlined pages, and a distinct vintage scent. Some parts of the book were taped together. Inside were handwritten notes addressed to Lydia, spreading over thirteen pages. Lydia's classmates from the Mariinskaya School wrote heartwarming notes to her in this "Album of Poetry." Perhaps they wrote these messages to her just before she left, as a way to remember her school days.

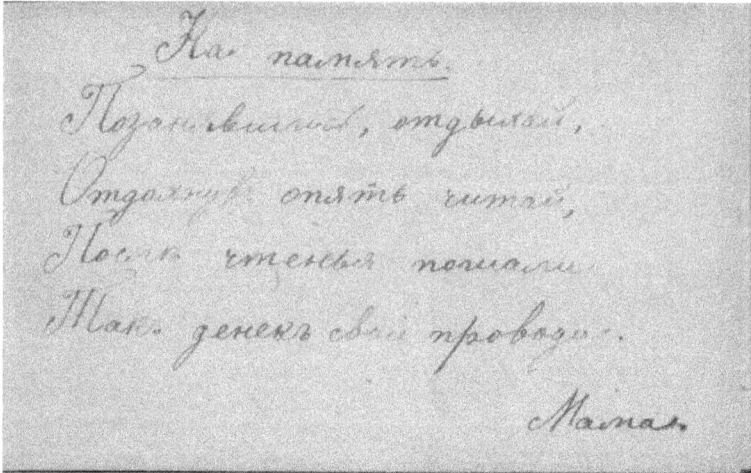

Figure 10: Lydia's mother writes in her "Album of Poetry" she took with her on the Kherson. Courtesy of the Buzyna Family.

Her mother made the first entry:

Reminder

Having done your lessons, rest.
After resting, read again.
After reading, you can play.
Always spend your day this way.

Mama

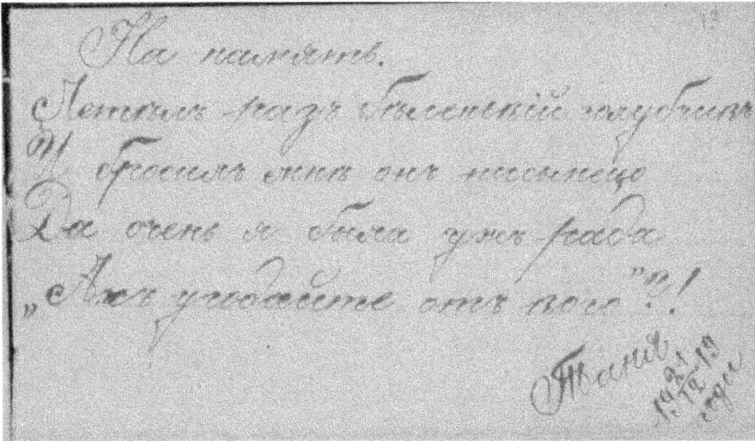

Figure 11: Lydia's cousin Tanya writes in her "Album of Poetry," which she took with her on the Kherson. Courtesy of the Buzyna Family.

On page 13 of this poetry album, there is a note from her beloved cousin Tanya, which reads:

Once a little white dove fluttered
And it brought me a letter.
That's what I was happy about:
"Argh, guess, who's the sender?!
Tanya, December 21, 1919[10]

---

10   Tanya used the old calendar date of December 21st when signing Lydia's Album of Poetry. January 3, 1920, new calendar date. This small piece of evidence confirms the Komarkoff family was still in Odessa at least up until January 3, 1920. Lydia had to have been in Odessa for Tanya to sign her poetry book.

Since Lydia did not live within walking distance of her school, she had to take the tram to school. In one of the many boxes of "Lydia's Memorabilia" carefully stored at my mother's house, there is a tram pass to the school dated 4 October 1919. The date on this tiny pass also confirms the family remained in Odessa until now.

Figure 12: Lydia's tram pass she used to take to school.
Dated October 4, 1919. Courtesy of the Buzyna Family.

C. March 1920: Evacuation of Novorossiysk

Lydia, in her elder years, recalls her time on the ship:[11]

> *...the revolution was already in full swing. And then, after Novorossiysk... in general, there were a lot of refugees on the ship, and they lived right on the deck. Well, then we went...*

---

11 Taken from the 1999 interview conducted by Dr. Valentina Pichugin who, at the time, was teaching Russian Language and Literature at Florida State University. Since 2001 she has been affiliated with the University of Chicago. The interview with Lydia was part of an academic research project about Russian language of people who belong to the first wave of Russian emigration after the revolution of 1917.

The steamer was supposed to accommodate these refugees, and, I don't know, they probably dealt with the Red Cross there, or I don't know where they got the money and all that. And we were in Constantinople, some refugees stayed there, and even there is an island not far away, Halki[12] and some of them stayed there, and then the steamer even went to Africa, to Egypt. I was in Africa, but not so wild one. In Alexandria, it's a wonderful city, Alexandria.

The *Kherson* was docked in Novorossiysk from March 4 to 6, 1920, but we do not know exactly how long it remained at port. Around mid-March 1920, the *Kherson* was used as a hospital ship to transport approximately 1042 wounded and sick people from Novorossiysk to Piraeus (Athens), Greece. On March 20, 1920, the *Kherson* brought Russian refugees to Famagusta, Cyprus, from Novorossiysk. On March 26 and 27, the *Kherson* again functioned as a hospital transport evacuating refugees from Novorossiysk.[13] Ultimately, on March 27, 1920, the White Army suffered a devastating defeat, leading to the evacuation of all ships from Novorossiysk. No White Army ships returned to this port after that date. Following the loss, General Wrangel was appointed as the new Commander in Chief of the Armed Forces of South Russia (White Army).

In Novorossiysk, we believe Lydia witnessed something so traumatic that it stayed with her the rest of her life. This story became a topic of captivating discussions at many family gatherings over the years. My uncle was especially fascinated by this story, bringing it up frequently during our visits. Even in our later years, we continue to reflect on this event's profound impact on Lydia and us.

---

12   Halki is an island that in 1912, was part of Turkey, and then was captured by Italy, and after WWI it was transferred to Greece.

13   Беляков В.В. Гости английского короля. Воспоминания генерала Ф.П.Рерберга об эвакуации беженцев в Египет // Восточный архив. 2009. № 2 (20). С.81, 82 / Belyakov V.V. Guests of the English King. Memories of General F.P. Rerberg about the evacuation of refugees to Egypt // Eastern Archive. 2009. No. 2 (20). P.81, 82.

Lydia had witnessed a harrowing scene: horses running in the sea and drowning, or something to that effect. With space on the evacuating ships limited, there was no room for horses, and the cavalrymen were ordered to leave them (the horses) behind on the shore. Unable to part with their masters who were sailing away, some horses rushed into the water, desperate to follow. Heartbreakingly, some officers shot their horses to spare them a slow and agonizing death in the unforgiving sea. Others, unable to bear the separation, chose to die alongside their loyal companions, taking their own lives.

This was considered the ultimate betrayal - Officer and horse bound together in life, unable to be separated even in death. For those officers who left their horses behind, they often swam alongside the ships, refusing to give up, until they ultimately succumbed to the elements of the sea. The loyalty of the horses and the anguish of their masters made this moment into a profound tragedy.

Today, the Monument "Exodus," erected in 2013 by sculptor Alexander Suvorov, stands on the waterfront of Novorossiysk, Russia. A powerful statue of a man leading his devoted horse was dedicated to the lives lost in this tragic defeat of the White Army on March 27, 1920. The sculptor allegedly based this statue on a scene from the film, "Two Comrades Were Serving," a Russian movie from 1968 that depicted a scene of officers leaving their horses behind in the 1920 Crimean evacuation.

I watched this film with subtitles to get a visual idea of what happened during the Crimean Evacuation. How did witnessing such an event as a ten-year-old affect Lydia? Was she scared? Did she feel safe on the ship with her parents? Did they make her go below deck so she did not see the horrors of war ashore? Looking at the photo of the monument with the beautiful scenery, it is hard to grasp that such a traumatic event occurred. I now wish I had not "bolted" when this story was told at our family gatherings. I have so many questions about what she saw and how she felt about it. I don't think anyone could leave this situation unscathed.

Figure 13: Exodus Monument in Novorossiysk, Russia. Photo by Andrey Shevchenko. Used under license from Alamy Stock Photo

A plaque located near the monument, translated into English:

And I will gather the remnant of my flock out of all the countries whither I have driven them, and will bring them again to their folds.

Book of the Prophet Jeremiah 23,3

...And so much blood has been shed here. The front has collapsed. We are rolling towards Novorossiysk... A windless, transparent night. The end of March 1920. Novorossiysk pier. We are loading onto the steamship Ekaterinodar. The officers' company rolled out machine guns for the sake of order. Officers and volunteers are loading—one o'clock in the morning. A black wall of people is moving almost silently, standing in line. At the pier - thousands of abandoned horses... From the deck to the hold, everything is packed with people, standing shoulder to shoulder... and so to the Crimea...

Officer of the Drozdovsky Regiment

My heart is unbearably sick: huge reserves have been aban-doned, all the artillery, all the horse staff. The army is bled dry...

A. I. Denikin[14]

Here the sea is in special excitement. The northeast wind is especially fierce here because the links are broken, the bridge of the dear motherland is burnt, and from here, the foreign land began, Exodus for the white warriors. They will not abandon their carbines, daring to set out on a new campaign. Oh, how many destinies are broken here, oh, the Russian schism due to sins, that it is difficult to write poetry. And where to find so much repentance, where to find so much humility to return everyone from exile mentally, and, like brothers, embrace!

V. Chizhov[15]

Lydia was on deck, trying to make sense of the commotion around her. Huge barge ships crowded the port, some departing, others preparing to leave. The decks were full of panicked people. Steam spewed out of the smokestacks, filling the sky with foghorns so loud she had to cover her ears, and in the distance on land, flames of fire and smoke engulfed buildings and warehouses. The smell of burning things. What was happening? Were they in danger? What will happen to all the people left behind? Will the Reds kill them? Her eyes widened as she spotted soldiers on horseback, rifles in hand, their faces cold and mean.

Crowds of people on the shore were desperately running in every direction, searching for family members or friends. Officers, civilians, women, and children, all caught in the chaos. Something caught Lydia's eye. Horses were wild with panic, swimming in the frigid waters,

---

14   Anton Ivanovich Denikin (1872-1947) relinquished his position as Commander-in-Chief of the Armed Forces of South Russia (the White Army) to General Peter Wrangel after the devastating defeat at Novorossiysk in March of 1920.

15   Vyacheslav Michailovich Chizhov, a Novorossiysk writer and Orthodox poet

desperate to stay with their masters. The ships were already overloaded with people and supplies, and there was no room for horses. With a heavy heart, some cavalrymen shot their horses to spare them the agony of drowning. A gentle hand touched her shoulder. She whipped her head around to see her mother, her expression both firm and tender. It was time to return to their cabin for safety.

A famous Russian poet, Nikolai Nikolayevich Turoverov,[16] also evacuated on one of the ships commanded by General Wrangel from Sevastopol, like Lydia and her family. He wrote a heartwrenching poem[17] as he left the shores of Crimea for the last time:

We were leaving the Crimea
Among the smoke and fire.
I kept shooting from the stern at my horse,
Getting past him all the time.
And he swam, exhausted,
Behind the high stern
Not believing, not knowing
That he had to bid farewell to me.
How many times being in battle,
We had expected to lie in the same grave!
The horse kept swimming, losing strength,
Believing in my devotion to him.
My batman did not miss the target -
The water turned red a little ...
I will remember forever
The disappearing coast of the Crimea.

---

16   Turoverov (1899 Russia - 1972 France) was a Don Cossack, an officer in the Russian and White Armies, and participant in the Civil War, and World Wars I and II.

17   The poem is rhyming in its original language, Russian. The original text of the poem was published in Туроверов Н.Н. Стихи: Книга пятая. Париж, 1965. C.79 / Turoverov N.N. Poems: Book Five. Paris, 1965. P.79.

Medical Crises

As if the traumatic events that occurred in Novorossiysk weren't overwhelming enough, several medical crises occurred while they remained docked there.

At 89 years old, Lydia vividly remembers a severe illness she endured while living on the ship, and how it related to her curly hair:[18]

> *Yes, I have to tell you about my curls too. And this is all on the ship, yes. Well, when we left Odessa, we were in Feodosia, and then in Novorossiysk, and I fell ill with typhus, and this was relapsing fever, it is so terrible that it's as if you are getting better, and then suddenly you get sick again. I don't know…*
>
> *And as I said, I got sick. And, obviously, I had a very high temperature, and then they said that after such a high temperature, it is better to shave off my hair.*
>
> *And so they shaved my head, and I went around with a shaved head. And that's why I had such curls.* (She meant afterwards.)

A devastating typhus epidemic swept through Russia, particularly during the evacuation of the White Army from Novorossiysk in March 1920. Due to its highly contagious nature, many refugees remained quarantined on ships for extended periods. Epidemic typhus thrives in situations like Lydia experienced: overcrowded ships, poor sanitation, and the chaos of war. The disease is transmitted through infected body lice, which likely resulted in Lydia and several other children on the ship having their heads shaved after becoming ill.

Undoubtedly, many aboard the *Kherson* contracted typhus; some managed to recover, while others succumbed to the severity of the disease.

---

18   From the interview conducted by Dr. Valentina Pichugin, at the time of the interview, was teaching Russian Language and Literature at Florida State University. Since 2001 she has been affiliated with the University of Chicago.

But illness was not the only hardship on the ship. Injuries likely occurred frequently, adding to the daily struggles of those on board. Thankfully, a medical doctor was always aboard to address any health issues that arose.

On March 1, 1920, Stoker First Class Nikita Nicholayevich Zhigulin (66),[19] began his shift at 7 a.m. and proceeded to the engine room to open the hatch and remove the upper grate over the aft (fourth) boiler room. As he lifted the iron hatch cover, he stood on the upper grate, believing it was secure. However, the grate gave way, causing him to fall with it onto the lower grate.

Zhigulin sustained multiple injuries in the fall, including a 2.76-inch-long laceration on his forehead, a 1.6-inch-long laceration on his lower back, and abrasions on his left arm and leg. Unfortunately, there were no witnesses to this incident. The cause of the fall remained unclear, as the crew described Zhigulin as an experienced and sober stoker, and the grate had always been secure in its base.

The ship's first-aid man, Boris Gavrilovich Kazantsev (17), administered the initial first aid treatment on site. Then the ship's doctor, Michael Alexandrovich Bayev (10), who started working on the *Kherson* that very day, stitched the wounds. Zhigulin was fully conscious throughout the ordeal. His stitches were removed on the fourth day, and after twelve days of bed rest, he fully recovered and resumed his duties.

D. April 1920: Feodosia

The *Kherson* was stationed in Feodosia, a city along the Crimean coast on the Black Sea, just west of Novorossiysk. Perhaps the *Kherson* was stationed here more times, but we know for sure it was at the dock sometime in April 1920.

Lydia writes next to the photo:

---

19   The Russian State Historical Archives. F.98. Inv.7. File 23. P. 31, 43-46a

Figure 14: The steamship Kherson docked in Feodosia, Crimea. Original page from Lydia's photo album, featuring her handwritten notes. Courtesy of the Buzyna Family.

Figure 15: The steamship Kherson docked in Feodosia. This version of the original photo highlights the "Papa Flag." Courtesy of the Buzyna Family.

Пар. Херсон   (Steamship Kherson)

1920 г.   (1920)

Феодосия, Россия (Feodosia, Russia)

I found the *same* photo attached to a family tree on Ancestry.com belonging to a descendant of a *Kherson* crew member. Later, I learned the owner of this duplicate photograph was Susan, the great-granddaughter of the ship's First Assistant Engineer, Mikhail Kononovich Anikeeff (7). This discovery was one of the most significant moments of my entire genealogical research project. It made me wonder how many other descendants might still be out there waiting to be found.

This image of the *Kherson* shows a very grand steamship for its time. Only two other ships around this time were similar in size, *Vladimir* and *Saratov*. Written on the side of the ship was the name - in Cyrillic, "ХЕРСОНЪ" as well as in Latin letters, "KHERSON." There are two smokestacks.[20] The *Kherson* flew two flags - one French and one Russian, the St. Andrew's Flag. The Russian flag was flown on all the White Army ships after the Russian Revolution, consisting of 2 diagonal blue lines on a white background.

In this particular photo of the *Kherson* docked in Feodosia, the Papa,[21] or the Blue Peter flag flies from the front mast. When flown at the harbor, it means that all passengers and the crew should report to the ship as the vessel is about to depart for sea. It is important to note that when this flag is flown at sea, it has a totally different meaning: the fishing net has been caught on an obstruction.

While researching Lydia's diaries, the stories she shared as an older adult, and the historical events that unfolded in the places she sailed to in 1920, this photograph from her personal album is the first that comes to mind. I picture her as one of the children on the dock running around and looking so small next to the enormous steamship. I sense her excitement about a new adventure, as well as her parents' anxiety about the unknown and whether they would ever return home. I imagine she was thrilled to be on solid ground after weeks confined to the ship.

---

20   Initially, the Kherson was built with three smokestacks, however, in 1907 the ship underwent major repairs in Copenhagen where they installed two smokestacks instead.

21   The Papa flag is a blue square with a white rectangle in the center.

In her diary entries, she frequently described the joy she felt while "strolling" through the streets of coastal towns and proudly buying postcards to remember her time spent there. Among Lydia's memorabilia collection are postcards collected as a young girl. Many of these postcards were from towns in the Crimea, including Eupatoria, Yalta, Sevastopol, Feodosia, and other nearby areas.

The *Kherson* was rapidly filling up with refugees eager to escape the turmoil in the towns. The Red Army was taking over many cities, and people feared for their lives. Lydia and her family were fortunate to have their own living quarters on the ship and were guaranteed a private stateroom because of her father's position as a crew member. One source stated the ship was originally designed to hold 74 first-class passengers, 59 third-class passengers, and 1444 emigrants.[22] Other sources claim there were 24 first-class passengers, 61 second-class passengers, 1363 third-class passengers, and a crew of 114.[23] Regardless of which number you look at, the ship was reaching maximum capacity.

The crew members whose families were on board had their own cabins. While Lydia did not describe details of their specific cabin, she mentioned they stayed together as a family. As described in the *Engineering*[24] journal article dated December 11, 1896, the

> ...*first-class passengers' sleeping cabins are on the main deck in the forward part of the ship, the modern plan of putting the best accommodation forward, so as to be away from the noise and rattle of the machinery, being followed.*

---

22   Tyne Built Ships website: https://tynebuiltships.co.uk/K-Ships/kherson1896.html

23   Other sources: https://retroflot.com/dobrovoljnyj_flot/parohodkrejser_herson .html. And Яровой В.В. Добровольный флот. СПб.: Галея-Принт, 2010. C.64 / Yarovoy Victor Veniaminovich. The Volunteer Fleet. Saint Petersburg: Galeya Print, 2010. P.64. Design Council. Engineering. London: Office for Advertisements and Publication, 1866. P.730

24   The Russian Volunteer S.S. "Kherson" / Engineering: An Illustrated Weekly Journal. Edited by W.H. Maw and J. Dredge. Vol. LXII. – From July to December 1896. London: Offices for advertisements and publication, 35 & 36. Bedford Street, Strand, W.C. 1896. P.730.

*Each cabin contains only two berths[25] with the exception
of one- or two-family cabins specially fitted. The beds are
single, Colonel Linden being strongly of the opinion that
passengers paying first-class fares should not be stacked
above one another, a view which might be more widely held
with advantage to the travelling public. The beds are made
to hinge back during the day, and when they are stowed the
cabins, which are supplied with sofas, etc., are formed into
quite comfortable sitting rooms, and have certainly far more
claim to the pretentious name of "stateroom" than those of
other well-known lines on which the expression is in vogue.
Another modern concession to the comfort of the passengers is a luggage room, which is accessible, an immense
convenience. Bathrooms, lavatories, and sanitary appliances
are fitted.*

According to this article, there were no second-class accommodations. The third-class passengers were typically emigrants, and each cabin
accommodated twelve to twenty people. The officers' quarters were on
the upper deck; the stokers slept on the main deck on the side of the
engine room. The rest of the crew sleep in beds on the upper deck towards
the front.

*...Here again, the quarters are good, there being 36 berths in
two rows, port and starboard. The beds are in a single tier,
and there is a large space between...*

The Anikeeff family owns a painting of the *Kherson* steamship created by Arseny Petrovich Sosnovskij. The artist, who resided in Herceg
Novi, Montenegro, in January 1921, painted the ship with special attention on the porthole marking the location of the Anikeeff family cabin.

Arseny Petrovich Sosnovskij was known for painting seascapes,
many of which are preserved in galleries worldwide, including the

---

25   A berth is a fixed bed or bunk on a ship, train, or other means of transportation.

Maritime Museum of Kotor, the Palace of King Nicholas in Cetinje, the Museum of Herceg Novi, galleries in Zagreb, and private collections throughout Croatia, Montenegro, Serbia, and Sweden.[26]

Figure 16: Watercolor painting of the steamship Kherson, by artist Arseny Petrovich Sosnovskij. Courtesy of the Anikeeff Family.

E. May to July 1920: Sevastopol, Drama on the *Kherson*

Sevastopol, the largest city in Crimea and a major port on the Black Sea, served as the base for the Russian Volunteer Fleet in the early 20th century.

The Anikeeff family relocated from Odessa, where all the children were born, to Sevastopol, settling in a grand house on a hill at 20 Cathedral Street (Sobornaya Street). They enjoyed stunning views of the Black Sea from their home, creating cherished memories until their fateful departure in November 1920.

---

26 https://www.russianartcollection.com/en/product/adriatic-sea-at-the-coasts-of-the -kingdom-of-serbs-croatians-and-slovenians/

Just down the road stood the beautiful Vladimir Cathedral. The family's life there was filled with many joyful moments. Watching parades that started at Cathedral Cemetery pass by their house, playing on the hillside, and admiring a stunning view that the children fondly reminisced about it well into adulthood.

In 1950, Cathedral Street was renamed Suvorova Street. The house they once lived in sadly no longer exists, and today, only a few pre-revolutionary buildings remain in the area.

The *Kherson* was stationed in Sevastopol on the dates of April 28, May 21-25, June 10, and on July 6 it left for Constantinople.[27]

At some point after June 3, 1920, Michael Anikeeff's (7) wife, Anna Ivanovna, along with their children Zhenia, Kolya, and Alyosha, joined him on the *Kherson*, a detail only recently discovered. The key to this revelation was an untranslated document that Susan re-discovered among her grandmother's things. Once translated, it revealed crucial insight, helping us narrow down the date when the rest of the Anikeeff family reunited with their patriarch, Michael, on the ship. Typically, only the captain's family could live on the ship he commanded. However, due to turbulent times, crew members were also allowed to bring their spouses and families aboard.

Translation of the document:

> *"To Mr. Captain of the steamship Kherson,*
>
> *In response to your submission of April 21 [May 4, 1920, New Calendar], in view of the difficult conditions of the transitional period, I have no obstacles to the presence of the wife of the 2nd Engineer M. K. Anikeeff on the steamship entrusted to you.*
>
> *Managing Director, signed Shtenger [Vasily Alexandrovich]*

---

27   The Russian State Historical Archives. F.98. Inv.7. File 23. P.54, 62, 68-73, 80, 82, 88

For secretary, signed Severin
With the original, correct:
Supercargo Malyavin"

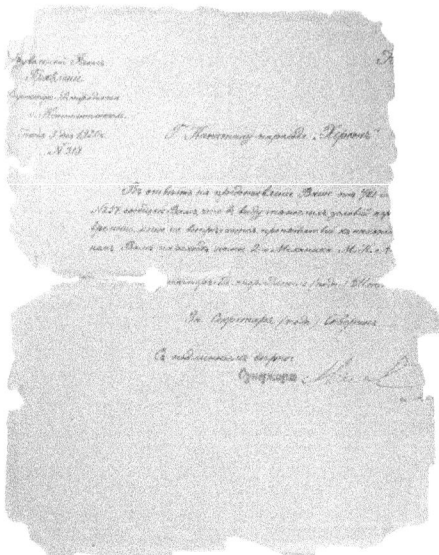

Figure 17: Document authorizing Michael Anikeeff to bring his wife and children aboard the steamship Kherson. Courtesy of the Anikeeff Family.

On May 22, 1920, at 2:30 am, an unpleasant incident occurred aboard the *Kherson* while at the Sevastopol port.[28] The following quotes are translated from Russian. Chief Mate Orest Vladimirovich Semenopulo (2) conducted an inquiry and concluded that *"...the stoker Nikifor Chernikov was sober, and [Nikolay] Burkhanov (76) was drunk. The quarrel arose over personal scores, regarding the loss of money, clothes and small things from the stokers' cockpit [...] the stoker Burkhanov suspects the stoker Chernikov in this matter."*

---

28   Ibid. P.69-73.

Testimony of Stoker 1st class Nikifor Chernikov:

"On 22 May 1920, at about 12 o'clock at night, I returned from the shore and went to bed. In our cockpit a group of stokers sat and drank vodka /[Ivan] Sinkevich (72) [Ivan] Medvedev, [Alexander] Derkachev (82), [Nikolay] Burkhanov. The stoker Burkhanov swore out loud and said that his rubber mattress was missing and threatened to kill me for this, suspecting that I had taken his mattress. Burkhanov was drunk and threatened to throw me out the porthole, got up from the table, came up to me and hit me on the side with a bottle of vodka. I was lying on the bed, Burkhanov pulled me out of the bed and called me to be reckoned with. I got up from the bunk, took a knife /small pen knife/ and stabbed him in the chest, went out onto the deck and heard Burkhanov threatening to kill me. On the deck I was arrested by the Commandant and remained in custody until the morning of May 9/22."

When the testimony was taken, S. Kornakov was present and signed for the illiterate N. Chernikov.

Testimony of the navigator's student, Evgeniy Stadnikov (13)

"On May 9/22, 1920, I, the junior navigator student of the SS "Kherson" of the Volunteer Fleet, Evgeniy Klimentievich Stadnikov, standing on watch at the gangway, heard a noise at 2:18 a.m. and the dull fall of two bodies onto the deck of the stokers' cockpit. Immediately I rushed there to find out what was happening there, where I saw the stoker Chernikov at the door of the cockpit. I asked him, "What is happening in your cockpit", but he did not answer my question and, continuing to swear, said: "I'll show you how to fight."

During this period of time, I heard noise and fuss in the cockpit, as well as excited voices: "He hit him with a knife," "Call the doctor, quickly, the doctor" and so on. Realizing that Chernikov was involved here, I ran to the gangway and warned the sentry not to let anyone ashore, since Chernikov had just at that time approached the gangway, where he stopped, swearing. From the gangway I ran back to the doors of the stokers' cockpit, where, having learned that the doctor was not yet there, I ran to the doctor's cabin and began to wake him up, saying that something was wrong with the stokers, and they needed the help of a doctor. After 3-4 minutes, the stoker Sinkevich came running there with the same purpose, but I warned him that I had already woken the doctor. He returned back to the cockpit and came back after 2-3 minutes accompanied by the wounded Burkhanov, whom he constantly advised to hold the wound with his hand. I went from the doctor's cabin and woke up the watchman's assistant V.D. Malyavin (3), to whom I reported what had happened and at the same time received from him an order to wake up Mr. commandant of the ship and report to him what was happening, so that he would order to arrest Chernikov. After which I took a lantern and, together with the commandant and the guard team of the ship, went to the poop deck, where the stoker Chernikov was found and arrested. I can't say anything more on this matter."

Junior navigator's student (signature) E. Stadnikov

Another unfortunate incident involved *Kherson* crew member Fourth Mate, Grigory Vsevolodovich Yalovikov (5).[29] This, however, was deemed an accident rather than a quarrel among crew members. Yalovikov had been appointed to this position on the *Kherson* on December 16, 1919.

---

29   Ibid. P.65, 74-76

On June 6, 1920, while the ship was docked in Sevastopol, he returned from shore with a bullet wound to his face. The bullet was lodged under the skin of his left cheek near his nose. He explained that he had been accidentally wounded at 2 am while visiting a friend's apartment of one of his friends, where a small Browning revolver discharged. Fellow crew members, Second Mate Vissarion Dimitrievich Malyavin (3) and Junior Navigator's Apprentice Evgeny Klimentievich Stadnikov (13), brought him to see Yalovikov's brother, a doctor, for the initial dressing of his wound. He was later attended to by the ship's doctor, Michael Alexandrovich Bayev (10). Due to the injury, Yalovikov was unable to perform watch duty until June 9, 1920.

The more we delved into the archival records about the steamship *Kherson*, the more we realized that life on board may not have been as calm and prosperous as Lydia makes it seem in her diaries. The older children, Lydia and Zhenia, had fond memories of their time on the ship, and it seems the parents did an excellent job of shielding them from the harsher aspects of ship life. Lydia describes her daily activities on the ship with a childlike innocence because she was a child and unaware of the challenges the adults were facing. Only a few times did she write about sailors getting drunk, but nothing inappropriate happened as she told it. She was most likely sound asleep in her cabin when an altercation occurred. While the rough sailors spent many nights drinking vodka in the salon on the ship, they still behaved decently towards the children.

The fight between Chernikov and Burkhanov was addressed immediately and set a clear precedent for unacceptable behavior. Chernikov was dismissed from the *Kherson* on May 22, 1920, the same day as the incident.[30]

---

30   Ibid. P.80

F. August 1920: Sulina, Romania

This photograph is perhaps my favorite.

Figure 18: Children seated on the deck of the steamship Kherson: Zhenia, Kolya, and Alyosha Anikeeff, Katya Malyavina, Lydia Komarkoff, Ira and Manya Semenopulo. Courtesy of the Buzyna Family.

The only evidence we have of the *Kherson* traveling to the port of Sulina in Romania is an old photograph. The photo, part of Lydia's collection, has no writing on the back besides "steamship *Kherson*" written in Russian. While I recognize it as being taken on the *Kherson* ship, I had no information about when or where it was taken. I didn't notice that most children's heads were shaved! Interestingly, the Anikeeff family has the same exact photo, but theirs includes a wealth of information on the back (pictured above). By the time I received their copy of the image, I had already successfully identified the children in the photo by first and last names. I was so proud of my sleuthing skills! How did I accomplish that without knowing any names?

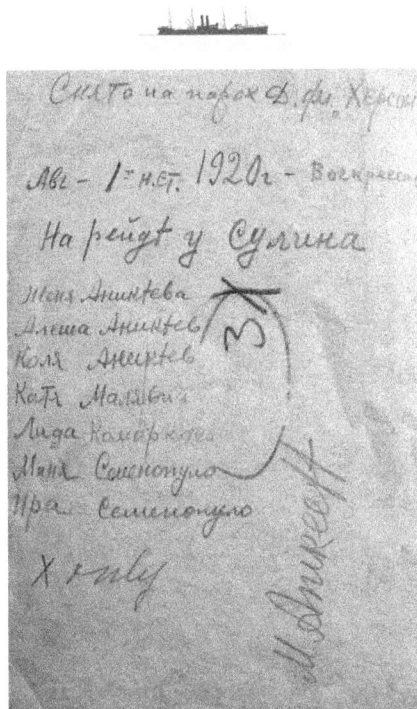

Figure 19: Inscription on the back of the photo of the children on the Kherson deck, noting their names, location, and the date it was taken. Listed on the photo: Zhenia Anikeeff, Alyosha Anikeeff, Kolya Anikeeff, Katya Malyavina, Lida Komarkoff, Manya Semenopulo, and Ira Semenopulo. Courtesy of the Anikeeff Family.

Lydia left clues for me in her daily entries, like a trail of breadcrumbs - only the crumbs were in the form of names, mainly first names or nicknames, or descriptions. She also provided hints about their ages, so I knew Alyosha was Zhenia's youngest brother of the two. The three Anikeeff children were often depicted together, and I had several photos for comparison. Despite only knowing her as an adult, I can easily point out my grandmother in all the photos. By the time we completed translating Volume A of her diaries, I was familiar with every child on the ship. Lydia focused on the children and their stories, which mattered most to her and the other children.

Perhaps the most important clue on the Anikeeff photo is the date and location:

August 1, 1920, Sunday
At the Sulina roadstead

The children are seated on a wooden bench aboard the ship, with a porthole window behind them. Despite their circumstances, they appear surprisingly happy, some more than others. My grandmother is smiling with her eyes closed, while the youngest girl, Katya Malyavina, has an infectious grin. I can't help but imagine one of the sailors making a funny face behind the camera to get the children to smile.

One striking detail that stood out upon closer examination of this priceless photograph is that Zhenia's head was not shaved like the other children's. Both of her brothers' hair appear to be cut very short but not fully shaved. This initially puzzled me, but the mystery was solved after discovering the document confirming that the Anikeeff children did not board the ship until after June 3, 1920! Since the photo was taken in August 1920, and the typhus epidemic peaked a couple of months earlier, Zhenia likely avoided both contracting typhus and the necessity of having her head shaved.

G. September, October, November 1920: Last months before Evacuation

On September 4, 1920[31] the *Kherson* was getting ready to sail Constantinople – Alexandria – Feodosia – Sevastopol, but remained in port until September 10th.

The *Kherson* made several stops in Alexandria, Egypt, in 1920 with the Komarkoffs and Anikeeffs aboard. It was at port from March 20 to 24, bringing Russian refugees from the Black Sea port cities to Alexandria. Also documented at port on October 4, 1920, it is unknown how long the ship remained there.

---

31   Ibid. P.2, 6, 30, 31, 33.

It was in Alexandria that Lydia experienced iced coffee for the first time and rather enjoyed it. She often spoke in her adult years of how beautiful she thought both Alexandria and Constantinople were.

Lydia recalls the beautiful city of Alexandria:[32]

> *In Alexandria, it's a wonderful city, Alexandria. And for the first time I ate there, as the Serbs called it, ledyana kafa, it's such iced coffee, or something like that. Well, we were in Turkey, Halki, in Africa, and then - where else? Yes, well, then...no, I think that's all.*

Alexandria was a routine stop for the Volunteer Fleet steamships, where Lydia's father, Dimitri, was employed. Among our family archives is a shark tooth[33] Dimitri brought back with "Pamyat Suez 1912" inscribed on it. We never knew the story behind it, and I could only assume it was from his travels while working aboard a ship. Thanks to the "LDK Diaries Research Project" we know for certain that Alexandria, Egypt, was part of his route.

By November 7, 1920, the *Kherson* was docked in Sevastopol, where it would remain until its final departure for evacuation.

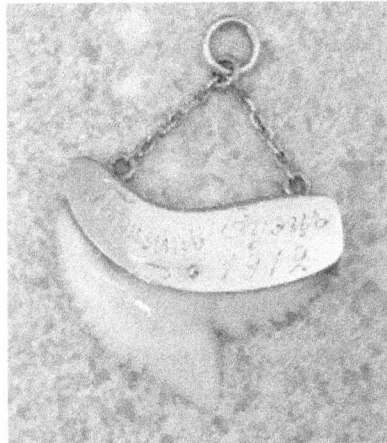

Figure 20: Dimitri Komarkoff's shark tooth souvenir from the Suez Canal, 1912. Courtesy of the Buzyna Family.

---

32 From the interview conducted by Dr. Valentina Pichugin, at the time of the interview, was teaching Russian Language and Literature at Florida State University. Since 2001 she has been affiliated with the University of Chicago.

33 "Pamyat Suez" translated means "In memory of Suez," or "Keepsake of Suez" - 1912. Dimitri acquired this shark tooth and had it inscribed on one of his work trips aboard a steamship.

CHAPTER 3
Crimean Evacuation...
Last Ship to Freedom

rimea was the final holdout of the White Army, and evacuation was inevitable. General Wrangel, the Commander-in-Chief of the Armed Forces of South Russia, had been skillfully organizing the evacuation of Crimea for some time now.

As the *Kherson* stood in Sevastopol's Kilen-Bay, Lydia and her family were aboard the ship as evacuation preparations unfolded. Prior to this, as we can assume from Michael Anikeeff's certificate, the *Kherson* was anchored at Pier #8 on the North side of Sevastopol's large bay, positioned slightly diagonally across from Kilen-Bay, on the south side of the large bay. Lydia's friend Zhenia and her family had also traveled with them on the *Kherson* during the latter part of the year. They all sensed that they might not return for a while, or perhaps ever. The Anikeeff family went ashore, frantically grabbing what they could from their large home perched on the hill in Sevastopol. They only had a few hours and needed to be quick and stealthy. How could they possibly choose what to take? Would a Red Army soldier intercept them and prevent their escape with their treasured belongings?

The Anikeeffs gathered a few precious items: a samovar, a sewing machine, icons, some family photographs, and a stash of Russian rubles. Michael and Anna Anikeeff desperately pleaded with Anna's parents and Michael's mother to join them on the ship and flee to safety. Heartbreakingly, they refused. Russia was their home, and they could not bring themselves to abandon their homeland. The Anikeeffs never heard from their parents again. The family always believed they had fallen victim to the Bolsheviks.

Just as Lydia vividly remembered the traumatic event of the horses in her later years, Zhenia also carried a sorrowful memory from her past. She often recounted the heartbreaking moment of departing Sevastopol when some were so desperate to escape that they climbed the ropes tying the ships to the dock in an attempt to board. The story, as her niece Pam remembers Zhenia's words:

> *Her voice was rich and melodious, with a lovely, slight Russian accent that strengthened as she spoke. She shared the story many times over the years, and essentially it was the same - I think she was especially touched by the sailors who in normal times would have done everything to help people reach safety, having now to cut the ropes so the ship could leave with the thousands already onboard. I think she felt their grief at having to do this, knowing the climbing men would fall into the sea.*

The story as she remembers it: *Sevastopol is a city on a hill, and everything was in flames! Fires everywhere - explosions, booms you could feel. The army was setting munition buildings on fire, destroying everything so the enemy could not use it - each time overwhelming Booms! Bright glows coated the sky, and sounds - whirling of shouts, screams, horses terrified, people trying to get on the ship. Soldiers climbing hand over hand up the ropes to reach safety onboard - Everywhere there was movement - fire - the city, our beautiful city, was only flames and noise. So many men tried to climb onto the ship that the sailors took axes and chopped the ropes - they had to do this so the ship could leave; they were probably ordered to do this, knowing the soldiers would fall into the water. There was no more room, and the ship had to leave now before the enemy came.*

Alexander Sudoplatov, who served in the regiment named after General Alexeyev, witnessed similar episodes on the steamship *Saratov*, which stood in Kilen-Bay next to the *Kherson* during loading. This is what Sudoplatov wrote (translated from Russian):[34]

> *The crowd is still loading. The ladder has already been raised. They climb the ropes, jump into the water, and approach in boats. Horses are swimming in the water. Poor animals. One is already exhausted. And the shore of the pier is made of stone and high. Hundreds of boats are sliding along the bay, and more and more approaching.*

Tragically, some who tried to escape by climbing up the ropes lost their grip and plunged into the water. The crew even cut some ropes; they could not take on more people. What fate awaited them in the soon-to-be Bolshevik-controlled town? Tales from the newly boarded people described how the Reds had already occupied Sevastopol, and drunken cavalrymen were shooting whoever was left at the pier. What a relief to be aboard an evacuating ship rather than land.

At about 2 am in the early morning of November 14, the *Kherson* left the Kilen-Bay and anchored in the outer roadstead of the Sevastopol port. Several hours later, on November 14, 1920, in the early afternoon, General Wrangel issued an order stating that no one on the evacuating ships was being held against their will. Anyone, for whatever reason, could freely disembark if they did not wish to leave Russia. He cautioned everyone that they were going into the unknown and that he had no guarantees, and to prepare to stay on the ships indefinitely. He ordered the ships to ensure enough water and food for everyone on board.

---

34 Судоплатов А. Дневник / Александр Судоплатов; вступ. статья, сост. О. Матич, подгот. текста, послесл. и коммент. Я. Тинченко. – М.: Новое литературное обозрение, 2014. С.277 / Sudoplatov A. Diary / Alexander Sudoplatov; introduction, compiled by O. Matich, text preparation, afterword and commentary by Ya. Tinchenko. – M.: New Literary Review, 2014. P.277.

Approximately 100 people, both officers and refugees, disembarked the *Kherson*. The same tender that returned people to shore, transported others from the docks to the ship, as many stood at the docks waiting for space to open on the already overcrowded vessels.[35]

Before boarding his cruiser *General Kornilov* at around 3 pm, General Wrangel sailed on a boat around the vessels waiting in the roadstead, thanking everyone for their service. In the distance, the crackling machine gun and rifle fire echoed on shore as he spoke. The *Kherson* must have been at the roadstead in sight of the Grafskaya pier,[36] because George Orlov, who was on board the *Kherson*, described in his diary how Wrangel went to the pier and how the shots were heard from shore, which means that he saw and heard it. Then Wrangel left on a boat for the *General Kornilov*. For one final time, the *General Kornilov* cruiser circled parallel to the coastline, with General Wrangel waving farewell from the ship's bridge to those who had decided to stay behind. At that moment, the *Kherson* and *General Kornilov* found themselves nearby,

---

35 From the diaries George Alekseyevich Orlov, an officer of the artillery brigade of the Drosdovskaya Rifle Division. He wrote about his experience as an evacuee on the Kherson and remained aboard until disembarking in Gallipoli: Орлов Г.А. Дневник добровольца : хроника гражданской войны 1918-1921 / Георгий Орлов; [предисловие и комментарий С. В. Волкова, доктора исторических наук]. - Москва: Посев, 2019. С.509-521 / Orlov G.A. Diary of a Volunteer: Chronicle of the Civil War 1918-1921 / Georgy Orlov; [foreword and commentary by S. V. Volkov, Doctor of Historical Sciences]. - Moscow: Posev, 2019. P.509-521.

36 There is a memorial plaque located at this pier that is dedicated to all those that left their homeland on November 14, 1920. I hope to visit this beautiful pier someday in honor of my grandmother.

and a loud "HURRAH" in heartfelt support for Wrangel was heard from the *Kherson*.[37]

After General Wrangel finished his speech and goodbyes at Sevastopol port, all 40 ships began to depart. However, the *Kherson* was delayed. The ship was already carrying 7,200 people,[38] and about 500 more were ordered to board (according to Orlov). Captain Schmelz fervently protested this order. The ship was already extremely overcrowded, with people camping out on the decks. Where would they even fit more passengers? How would they feed everyone? For Captain Schmelz, the ship's and its people's safety was his highest priority.

In response to the captain's protest, the *Kherson* took the smaller steamer *Typhoon* and an additional barge in tow. The ship carried numerous military units along with the civilians and their families. Including: The Drozdovskaya Division,[39] Markovskaya Division, many separate squads, heavy artillery batteries, part of the Samursky Regiment, the remnants of the Kuban corps and cavalry units, as well as several squads of some armored trains, to name a few, among others. The ship was dangerously overcrowded.

By 8 pm, the *Kherson*, almost the final ship to depart, according to Orlov, pulled away from the shores of Sevastopol. As the city's lights disappeared into the darkness, rifle shots could be heard across the water,

---

37 According to the memoirs of Shatilov, the chief of staff of the Russian army, who led the evacuation of Crimea: Павел Николаевич Шатилов. Памятная записка о крымской эвакуации / Севастополь. 1920. Исход. На изломе : [к 95-летней годовщине исхода Русской армии генерала П. Н. Врангеля из Крыма и Севастополя] : документальный альбом / [сост.: Вадим Николаевич Прокопенков и др.]. - Севастополь : [б. и.] ; Симферополь : Салта, 2015. С.45 / Pavel Nikolaevich Shatilov. A memo on the Crimean evacuation / Sevastopol. 1920. Exodus. At the Break: [for the 95th Anniversary of the Exodus of the Russian Army of General P. N. Wrangel from Crimea and Sevastopol]: documentary album / [compiled by: Vadim Nikolaevich Prokopenkov and others]. - Sevastopol: [publ. not spec.]; Simferopol: Salta, 2015. P.45.

38 Кузнецов Н.А. Русский флот на чужбине. Москва: Вече, 2009. С.405 / Kuznetzov N.A. Russian fleet in foreign lands. Moscow: Veche, 2009. P.405.

39 This was George Alekseyevich Orlov's unit.

a chilling reminder that the Bolsheviks had already seized control. This was the last ship to freedom.

The voyage to Constantinople was anything but easy. According to George Orlov, sometime in the night of November 14, the barge being towed by the *Kherson* was lost at sea. The next morning, the *Kherson* had to return some distance to recover it.

The steamship, designed to accommodate approximately 1,500 people comfortably, was now crammed with over 7,200 people on board. How could it possibly cross the Black Sea without capsizing or sinking? The severe overcrowding caused the ship to tilt dangerously, forcing the crew members on the captain's bridge to shout urgent commands to the passengers, "All to starboard!" or "All to port side!" in desperate attempts to balance the ship. Sleeping was nearly impossible, especially for the passengers on the deck. Lydia hardly slept and was terribly frightened. What would happen if people ignored the captain's orders? She stayed in her cabin with her mother for safety, while her father tended to his duties.

After two grueling days at sea, on November 16th, the *Kherson* finally entered the Bosporus, the narrow waterway linking the Black Sea to the Sea of Marmara. By the evening of November 17, the ship reached the crowded roadstead of Constantinople. The docks at the port were so congested with vessels that the *Kherson* was forced to anchor offshore.[40] Smaller boats weaved through the anchored boats, filled with civilians desperately trying to find friends and relatives who may have come on the latest transport.

---

40   Anchored in the waters near the coast of Constantinople.

CHAPTER 4
Safety in Constantinople

The *Kherson* was anchored at the roadstead of Constantinople from the night of November 17 to the morning of November 20.

Over the course of 4 days during this historic evacuation, some 150,000 people had descended upon Constantinople carrying Russian refugees. They were now safe from the certain death that had awaited them in Russia. One crisis averted, another created.

These people, once living a life of stability, suddenly found themselves refugees of the outcome of the Russian civil war. If they were lucky, they could bring a few pieces of clothing, essentials, and whatever special items they could carry. Many had little to no money to their name. They literally escaped with their life. In order for them to prosper in their newly given life, it was imperative that they acclimate quickly to their new surroundings in an unfamiliar country with a language they did not know. Would they succeed?

Where would they go from here? Which countries would willingly support these stateless people? Would the ships that transported them to Constantinople take them to further destinations? Who did the ships belong to, and did they need to be returned to their previously owned company or country? These were all questions that went through my head as I became familiar with this historic event. I was worried about these people, my grandmother being one of them. The refugees contemplated these questions as well, I am certain.

The answer to the question "where would the refugees go from here (Constantinople)" was complicated. General Wrangel made negotiations, mostly with Bulgaria and Yugoslavia (the Kingdom of Serbs, Croats, and Slovenes), to take in the huge number of refugees that had just fled Russia under his command. He was incredibly instrumental in taking care of his people outside of Russia. The *Kherson* was not the only ship requiring rerouting because of certain port cities' overcrowding.

While in Constantinople, Captain Schmelz of the *Kherson* wrote a letter to the director of the Volunteer Fleet notifying them of two new essential members who joined the crew on November 14, 1920, as they evacuated Crimea. He did not have time to notify the management of the Volunteer Fleet of these acquisitions until he reached safety in Constantinople.

> *To His Excellency, The Managing Director of the Volunteer Fleet,*[41]
>
> *In the city of Sevastopol on November 14 of this year [1920], according to the new calendar, one helmsman and one lacquey to the Wardroom were hired as supernumeraries. Hiring these people was extremely necessary, in view of the overcrowding of the entrusted to me steamship "Kherson" with troops and refugees during the evacuation of the city of Sevastopol and cases of illnesses subject to outpatient treatment among the crew: one of the deck crew fell ill with typhoid fever, and one lacquey scalded himself.*
>
> *... I have the honor to ask Your Excellency to approve the two positions mentioned above.*
>
> *Attached is the list of names of the ship's crew.*
> *Signed, Captain of the steamship Schmelz*

---

41   The Russian State Historical Archives. F.98. Inv.7. File 23. P.13 (translated from Russian).

On November 19th, the *Kherson* began to disembark the wounded, the sick, and anyone free of military service. Disembarkation came at a steep cost - at least 50 lira. Fewer than 200 people disembarked that day, and despite it taking all day, there still was not enough time to process everyone.

On the morning of November 20, 1920, around 10 am, the *Kherson* departed Constantinople. As the ship slowly made its way through the Dardanelles (Strait of Gallipoli), Lydia found comfort in the countless white sheets hung by Bulgarian students in Istanbul to show their sympathy and appreciation toward the defeated White Army. Despite being only eleven years old, Lydia was keenly aware of the dire situation she had just endured.

By evening, they made it to Gallipoli, a peninsula that runs into the Aegean Sea between the Dardanelles and the Gulf of Saros, and anchored away from shore at the roadstead. George Orlov, who had kept a diary of his time on the *Kherson*, finally went to shore on November 26, 1920. Many white émigré soldiers and their families evacuated to this peninsula after the Crimean Evacuation and eventually found refuge in other European countries, such as the former Yugoslavia.

After transporting these military soldiers and their families to Gallipoli, the *Kherson* returned to Constantinople and is documented as being docked at the historical Moda Pier at the port of Constantinople on December 1,[42] 4,[43] and 6–8.[44] We do not know details of why they returned to Constantinople or what they may have done there. However, they did enlist three new crew members here on December 6, 1920, including Nicholai Meldizon, Kirill Levanevsky, and Alexander Zvyagin. Despite pressure from the Volunteer Fleet to reduce the ship's crew, Captain Schmelz nevertheless enrolled the three men eager for work aboard the *Kherson*.

---

42   Ibid. P.21.

43   Ibid. P.18.

44   Ibid. P.7, 8, 9, 10, 19.

Captain Schmelz wrote a letter to the Managing Director of the Volunteer Fleet dated December 6, 1920, regarding these three new crew members:[45]

> *On December 6th of this year, by order of Your Excellency, Junker Meldizon, Cadet Levanevsky and former helmsman Zvyagin were appointed to the deck crew in addition to the complement. I can only consider these persons as part of the crew if they work equally with the others, but they will be fed, like all refugees, on the general rations.*
>
> *The crew of the steamship entrusted to me has not yet received their salary for November, and for the crew's food in December I was given only five hundred Turkish lira from the agency in Constantinople, while 2,000 Turkish liras are needed for the crew's food.*
>
> *In view of this, I consider it necessary to report to Your Excellency that I do not find it possible to feed the super- numerary employees when the regular employees do not receive their salaries.*
>
> *The Ship Captain Schmelz*

The Managing Director's response to this letter read: "*These people have been taken for the passage to Katarro. – In any case, we are obliged to feed them, since I have assigned them to the steamer.*"

---

45   Ibid. P.8 (translated from Russian).

CHAPTER 5
Nowhere to Go

Where would the *Kherson* go next? While they were safe from persecution, the pressing question now was who would take in all these refugees on the ship and provide for them?

Lydia continued her voyage from Constantinople aboard the *Kherson,* arriving in the Bay of Kotor[46] around December 23, 1920, but the steamer did not stay there. There was already an overcrowding of refugees here, and the local coastal cities refused to host more at that time. They simply had no room to house, feed, or clothe the refugees. Another pressing concern was that among the 2609 refugees aboard the ship, 77 were now infected with typhus.[47] So, the *Kherson* continued to sail north into the Adriatic Sea, eventually reaching the northernmost port town of Bakar.[48]

The *Kherson* successfully arrived at the Dalmatian coastal town of Bakar on December 31, 1920.[49] Due to the numerous refugees afflicted with typhus, the ship was not allowed to anchor close to shore and had to remain at the roadstead of the bay. No one was allowed to disembark

---

46 Previously part of Yugoslavia, today it is in the country of Montenegro.

47 Кампе, Леонид. Круги ада или прибытие белой эмиграции в Котор / Русский вестник. # 97. July 1, 2018. Адаптированный перевод: Гуля Смагулова / Kampe, Leonid. The circles of the Inferno or the arrival of the white [movement] expatriates in Kotor / Russian Herald. # 97. July 1, 2018. Adapted translation: Gulya Smagulova https://web.archive.org/web/20190128191510/http://rusvestnik. me/krugi-ada-ili-pribytie-beloj-jemigracii-v-kotor-2/

48 Formerly Yugoslavia, current day Croatia.

49 Kampe, Leonid. The circles of the Inferno or the arrival of the white [movement] expatriates in Kotor / Russian Herald. # 97. July 1, 2018.

the ship for 3 weeks. Thankfully, soup and bread were delivered to the *Kherson* from shore. However, due to poor weather that endured for several days during this time (cold, rainy, and windy, typical for this time of year), the food delivery ceased for a full two days. This made conditions even worse for the refugees on the ship. Disembarkation was finally allowed after the mandatory three-week quarantine on board the vessel. Even so, refugees, especially those who fell ill, were treated with caution once on land, keeping them in hospitals or railway cars. Fourteen people died in the railway cars of Bakar.

Mr. Karpeko, a nobleman of the Chernigov province, traveling on the *Kherson*, was one of the fourteen people who died of typhus after arriving in Bakar. Sadly, he orphaned his fourteen-year-old daughter, Olga. Thankfully, the Red Cross found her and sent her to the Kharkov Institute of Noble Maidens in Serbia,[50] and she ultimately graduated in 1924.[51] I wonder what became of her. Did she find a new life and continue on? Did she ever reconnect with her family, whom she had potentially left behind in Russia?

Another point of uncertainty was ownership of the steamer itself. Who did it belong to, and whose responsibility was it? Who was paying the crew members still working on the steamship? Debts needed to be paid off for carrying all the refugees from Russia. Somebody had to fund this massively orchestrated evacuation, transporting thousands of people to safety. So, in December 1920, the current owner of the *Kherson* steamship, the Parisian Dobroflot Board, handed the *Kherson* over to the French steamship company "Fransmar" to compensate for debts.

---

50 Краинский Дмитрий Васильевич. Записки тюремного инспектора. М.: Институт русской цивилизации, 2006. С.541, 577-578 / Krainsky Dmitry Vasilievich. Notes of a prison inspector. Moscow: Institute of Russian Civilization, 2006. P.541, 577-578.

51 https://archive-khvalin.ru/blagorodnye-3-2/

CHAPTER 6
Finding a New Home

A year had already passed while living on the steamship *Kherson* when Lydia began her diary entries on Saturday, January 29, 1921, anchored in the roadstead of Bakar. What prompted her to write about her daily life on this ship on this particular date? Was it out of obligation or custom? Had her mother kept a diary when she was younger? Did her parents encourage her? Was it self-initiated? We can only guess why. Perhaps it was the uncertainty of their future, and her parents thought it would give her some semblance of structure and stability in their immediate lives.

Lydia woke suddenly on Saturday, January 29, 1921, and scrambled to get dressed. It was already 8 am. She swung the door to her cabin open so hard that it hit the wall and made a crackling noise. Thankfully, her parents were not in the cabin to see this careless behavior she just displayed. As she raced to the deck, she heard the ship's foghorn blasting for what seemed like eternity. She momentarily stopped to cover her ears with her hands, then resumed her plan to make it to the deck before the ship departed the dock. Even though the sound was muffled, she could feel the waves shooting through her body like an electric current. Her heart was pounding from the deafening sound and running up several sets of stairs.

The large steamship had just left the dock in Bakar. She found her mother standing on deck with some other adults. Out of breath, she asked her mother in desperation,

"Mama, did Ivan Iosifovich come to bid the ship farewell?"

"No, he did not come." Her mom stared into Lydia's eyes with no emotion.

The look told her she could not show how upset she was about missing him, or learning that perhaps he did not come at all to say goodbye. Scanning the deck for the other children, she locked eyes with Zhenia. She displayed the same reserved disappointment. The two friends sauntered to Lydia's cabin, talking about how they would miss their lessons with their tutor, Ivan Iosifovich, and wondering who their new tutor would be. And would they like them?

As of this writing, we have not successfully identified exactly who the elusive Ivan Iosifovich was. We have searched many places to no avail. Our only evidence is his mention in the diaries by Lydia, a postcard written by him, and a note Lydia wrote years later describing he was her tutor.

Lydia labels her treasured postcard,

"This card was written by Lydia's tutor (Иванъ Iосифовичъ) in Jan 1921, when we were still on *Kherson* on which we left Russia."

The now 100-year-old postcard shows a scene of the Procession of the Holy Carpet on the streets of Alexandria, Egypt. On the back is a sweet message to Lydia from Ivan Iosifovich:

Figure 21: Front of a postcard sent to Lydia by her tutor, Ivan Iosifovich. Courtesy of the Buzyna Family.

Figure 22: Back of the postcard sent to Lydia by her tutor, Ivan Iosifovich, featuring his handwritten message. January 1921. Courtesy of the Buzyna Family.

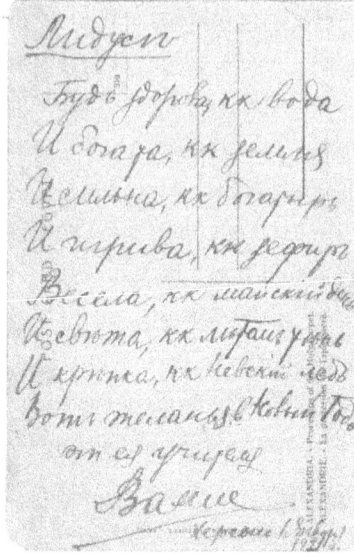

Figure 23: Many years later, Lydia jotted a note on a scrap paper identifying this postcard as a message from her tutor, Ivan Iosifovich. Courtesy of the Buzyna Family.

To Lidousya

Be as healthy as water

And as rich as the earth

And as strong as a bogatyr

And playful, like the wind (zephyr)

Happy like a Day in May

And as light as summer shadow
And strong as ice on the Neva [River in St. Petersburg]
These are wishes for the New Year
From her teacher
Vanya

Kherson 1 January 1921

Several clues indicate that Vanya, a common nickname for Ivan, perhaps wrote this note to Lydia's parents for them to give to Lydia. This was a card wishing her a happy New Year. Perhaps this is while the ship was docked at Bakar during the three-week quarantine, and he could not see her personally, so he gave the card to her parents, or someone passed it along to her family. Since Lydia was a child, she would never address an adult by their nickname, as he signed in this card. We know that Vanya is, in fact, "our" Ivan Iosifovich since Lydia labeled it as such in her later years.

The postcard sentiments give off a gentle-soul vibe from Ivan Iosifovich. No wonder she wrote so affectionately about him in her diary entries and saved this postcard years later. All the kids were so attached to him that they looked forward to their lessons with him every day. For a moment, they forgot about being away from home and that they were stateless. Their tutor had traveled on the *Kherson* alongside them, but it was time for him to depart and move on with his life. Lydia would catch up with him again, but not for well over a year.

Bay of Kotor

The *Kherson* sailed along the coast of former Yugoslavia, navigating the Adriatic Sea. The journey from Bakar to the Bay of Kotor took about two days. While the ship traveled parallel to the Dalmatian Coast, Lydia was so captivated by the breathtaking scenery that she felt compelled to describe it in her diaries. She also mentioned many times in her later years how stunning the views were.

For a child as young as eleven to remark on the scenery is impressive to me. As a kid, my family and I would take many road trips in our 1973 Volkswagen camper van. We drove all over the United States, even Alaska, one summer (from Florida). My mother would frequently point out the beautiful scenery and get frustrated if we didn't join in her admiration of the view. I would respond to this request with, "Mom, you and your mountains," and subsequently roll my eyes. I was eleven turning twelve on that Alaska trip, the same age as my grandmother on her epic journey from Russia. In retrospect, I did not display half of my grandmother's maturity at that age. I also did not witness any of the traumatic events that she did, so perhaps that contributed to her maturity at such a young age, and my lack of maturity.

Although Lydia's diary entries reflect exceptional maturity, she was just a child, longing to experience the simple joys of childhood. She often wrote about the "simple things in life" that brought her happiness. On one occasion, while the ship passed through islands en route to the Bay of Kotor, she described how elated she was that the beautiful weather outdoors allowed the children to play games on the deck. They even constructed swings from wooden boards. She exclaimed, *"...what a joyful day!"*

What child today would express such genuine excitement over something so simple? Coincidentally, as I was writing about my grandmother's admiration of the stunning Croatian scenery, my then 17-year-old daughter came rushing through the door after winter guard practice. She could not wait to tell me how they were able to practice outside because of the beautiful weather! Blue skies, spring setting in, and the perfect temperature. Could her great-grandmother from beyond have sent her some "appreciate the little things" vibes? Perhaps.

At this point in their journey, there were not as many children or families traveling on the *Kherson*, but Lydia found immense joy in playing games on the deck with those who were. After witnessing so many traumatic and historic events, she and the other children managed to embrace moments of happiness, making the most of their life aboard the ship, simply being kids. Just months earlier, their lives had been turned upside down when they left Russia for the last time. The idea of feeling happiness again had seemed impossible.

Sunday, January 30, 1921, The *Kherson* had arrived in the Bay of Kotor.

Today was very nice and all the children were outdoors on the deck as it was very warm so that all the children were only in their dresses. We were very happy, we played various games, later we made a swing out of boards and this way had a joyful day. The ship passed between islands but now here it is already 6 o'clock and we still had not arrived at Kotor. Towards 8pm we arrived.

Monday, January 31, 1921

In the morning, I did my lessons and later Katinka[52] came over and stayed with us awhile and then we went on deck to play. Today the weather is not good, there was a slight breeze, but children still played on the deck, we played very well until lunch. After lunch not all the children came out on deck, but we played happily with the mechanics, who treated us with chocolates and after that everyone went to their cabins. We were docked in Kotor Bay at Zelenika. Now I am going to read a very interesting book, Children's Encyclopedia.

---

52 Ekaterina Vissarionovna Malyavina, daughter of Second Mate Vissarion Dimitrievich Malyavin (3); "Katya"

CHAPTER 7

Everyday Life on the *Kherson*

Why was the Bay of Kotor chosen for their temporary floating home location? Perhaps because of its antiquity and rich history. Or perhaps because it was a well-protected bay of the Adriatic Sea. Most likely, however, the primary reason was the Serbian government's willingness to allow so many of the Russian émigrés to reside there temporarily.

The shoreline had little villages visible from the ship, while jagged black mountains lined the coast. If you looked closely, you could spot tiny buildings perched high on the foothills. Looking even higher, you might catch sight of a Serbian Orthodox Cross atop an onion dome in the distance.

Anchored near the coastal town of Zelenika, Lydia and her family remained on the *Kherson* for the next seven months. Despite the lingering uncertainty about the future for all the refugees aboard, the ship provided a semblance of stability for Lydia and her family during this time. Undoubtedly, this uncertainty consumed her parents' every thought. They had always believed they would return to Odessa once things got better. However, the situation in Odessa and Crimea showed no signs of improving. Now, far from their homeland and separated from their extended family, they were forced to face the reality that a happy return to Odessa was unlikely and had to come to terms with it.

Despite her parents' uncertainty about the future, Lydia writes with striking simplicity about her life on the ship. Most were happy days, even humorous, and some days she experienced sadness. She had a close-knit group of friends, and they all looked out for each other, becoming her new family. She portrayed herself as a joyful child going about life like any other kid…except she was a refugee living on a ship with nowhere to call home.

Typical days aboard the ship: January 30 to August 2, 1921

When I learned my grandmother had spent over a year living on a steamship, the first question that came to mind was, how did the children keep themselves occupied in such confined conditions? And how did they not drive their parents or the other adults on the ship crazy? The truth is, Lydia was just a typical kid and found creative ways to entertain herself.

Each morning started with her school lessons. Sometimes in her cabin alone, with other children, and occasionally with her new tutor, Vera Matveyevna Slezhinsky. As she noted in her diaries, Lydia's first day of studying with her was February 8, 1921, and she respectfully referred to her as "Madame Slezhinsky." It is possible that she was the wife of A. N. Slezhinsky (89), listed among the crew as a Stoker Second Class.

Life on the steamship *Kherson* would get monotonous, especially for the children. The adults of the ship made things interesting and entertaining for the children when possible. Surprisingly, Lydia rarely mentioned being bored. The few times she did it was usually in response to being left on the ship when others were off exploring.

One morning, when Lydia noted in her writing that *"we were bored,"* the boatswain[53] decided to entertain the restless children by taking them on the tender. Oleg[54] had promised to take them for another ride after breakfast, but the tender was already in use by then. The children had to remain on the ship; their disappointment was evident.

---

[53] Possibly Evgeniy Petrovich Sukovatykh (19), listed as the Boatswain on the crew list.

[54] Another potential crew member, though I have yet to determine their identity.

Since the steamer was anchored in the bay, a tender was necessary to travel to shore. The mechanics entertained the children by taking them for rides. Lydia proudly described how, on many occasions, she "*...rowed the entire way.*" Most of the time, an adult accompanied the children on these excursions. She specifically mentioned Oleg, Bolislav, Valya's father, Mr. Spesovsky, Uncle Seryozha, and the medical orderly among those who joined them. Even her tutor, Madame Slezhinskaya, took them out for a ride one day.

Typically reserved in her descriptions, Lydia noted that one particular tender ride was "great." This reminds me of how, as a kid, I would answer my parents' questions about my day with a simple "fine" or "great" and leave it at that. Similarly, I would stick to factual captions in my scrapbooks without sharing my feelings, much like my grandmother. In contrast, my children are far more expressive when discussing topics that matter to them. However, when they were younger, they also answered daily questions about school with a simple "fine." Now, as they have grown older, they are much more expressive than I ever was at their age.

One day, Zhenia and Lydia were given a tour of the engine room on the *Kherson,* another example of how the adults on the ship actively engaged the children. Both found the experience fascinating as they explored and observed the workings of the ship's engine, thoroughly enjoying the opportunity. On another occasion, Lydia and the other children watched coal being loaded onto the ship. Lydia stayed the entire time, captivated by the process.

Once, after an enjoyable day in town, Lydia and her friends were waiting for the tender to return them to the ship when, in her own words, "a terrible accident occurred." Although Lydia quickly reassured in her writing that everything turned out fine, there were a few frightening moments. While waiting, the children were throwing bark and coal into the water. Unnoticed by anyone, one of the children, Irochka, fell into the water. She had already disappeared twice from view before an unknown boatman saved her. Once she was pulled out of the water, Lydia compassionately offered her the underskirt she was wearing, and her brother

Shura gave her his jacket. They returned to the ship on the tender, re-telling the incident that had a fortunate ending.

Keeping Cool

The children found creative ways to escape the heat on hot summer days. They poured water over their heads on the deck, built a makeshift shower, and tried anything to cool off. But perhaps Lydia's favorite method was something she had never done – swim! On Tuesday, May 24, 1921, Lydia swam for the first time at eleven years old. In typical Lydia fashion, she described this experience in her signature straightforward manner.

I had a very happy day. Nata, Zhenia, Ira, Manya and Katya and I went ashore to swim. I swam for the first time and liked it very much.

I can vividly imagine this experience in my head, but I wish I had a photo or a video. I have so many fond memories of my grandmother swimming with my brother and me in the ocean at Panama City Beach, Florida. She would visit us at least once a year, and if it was summer, you could guarantee we were at the beach. I cannot help but wonder if she thought back to her first swim in the Bay of Kotor at age eleven each time she waded in the warm ocean water. Now, I have set a goal for myself: to swim in the Bay of Kotor on a future trip!

Lydia spent nearly every day on the ship sewing or embroidering. The day after her victorious first swim, she sewed herself a bathing suit out of an old apron! Did she have a pattern? Did she design it in her head? How did she ensure it would fit her correctly? Not only did Lydia sew this bathing suit, but she also made dresses for herself and her dolls. Undoubtedly, this skill was learned from *her* mother, who, in turn, most likely learned from *her* mother. This is a perfect example of her incredible resourcefulness.

Wednesday, May 25, 1921

I spent the day as usual; I studied and was on the deck, later read and sewed a bathing suit for myself.

Every time I read this entry, I am amazed by how nonchalant she was sewing a bathing suit!

Photos aboard the *Kherson*: Lydia wrote about how delighted she was to receive photos from her time on the ship. By reading her diaries and connecting them with these images, I better understood what life was like for her and her friends aboard the *Kherson*.

Figure 24: Lydia (center, in the white dress) with other children and several sailors aboard the steamship Kherson, anchored in the Bay of Kotor. (above) Courtesy of Buzyna Family.

Figure 25 (above): Lydia (center, in white dress) with Katya Malyavina in front of her, along with other children and a sailor aboard the steamship Kherson, anchored in the Bay of Kotor. Courtesy of the Buzyna Family.

Figure 26 (right): Lydia (center, in white dress), with Zhenia Anikeeff to her left and Katya Malyavina to her right. In front of the stairs are Kolya and Alyosha Anikeeff. Photographed on the deck of the steamship Kherson. Courtesy of the Buzyna Family.

Figure 27: Lydia wearing her favorite sailor outfit aboard the steamship Kherson, anchored in the Bay of Kotor near the shores of Zelenika, Montenegro. Courtesy of the Buzyna Family.

Figure 28: The steamship Kherson anchored near the shores of Zelenika in the Bay of Kotor. Courtesy of the Buzyna Family.

Figure 29: Lydia (tallest, on right) with the other children - possibly the photograph she refers to in her diary entry from Tuesday, May 10, 1921, noting she was "very pleased" with how it turned out. Courtesy of the Buzyna Family.

Figure 30: Children playing games on the deck of the steamship Kherson while anchored off the shores of Zelenika in the Bay of Kotor. Courtesy of the Buzyna Family.

Figure 31: Lydia stands as the tallest one, with Zhenia Anikeeff to her left and her brother Kolya beside her. Katya Malyavina stands in front, along with Alyosha Anikeeff. Two of the other girls are believed to be Manya and Ira Semenopulo. The handwritten date on the back of photo: February 6, 1921. Lydia mentions this photograph in her diary entry the following day, February 7. Courtesy of the Buzyna Family.

CHAPTER 8

Excursions

One of the greatest highlights for Lydia while living on the steamer was the opportunity to go ashore. Between Monday, January 31, 1921, and their departure on Tuesday, August 2, 1921, she documented 50 trips to shore - sometimes daily, other times several times a week, and occasionally going for a full week without leaving the ship. Each excursion was just as thrilling as the last. It was during these moments that Lydia felt truly alive and free.

Venturing into town, Lydia could experience new sights and places she had never seen. Although the *Kherson* had been anchored in the Bay of Kotor since Monday, January 31, 1921, her first trip to shore was not until two weeks later. It is unclear if the ship's inhabitants were required to quarantine for a set amount of time before disembarking, if they had to wait for the crowds of emigrants on shore to disperse, or if the delay was simply a matter of timing.

The coastal towns Lydia visited most frequently were Castelnuovo (current day Herceg Novi), Zelenika, and Tivat, all located in modern-day Montenegro.

Lydia's first trip ashore was invigorating! She woke up early to check the weather, hoping for clear skies. Thank goodness the day looked pleasant. Otherwise, she would be stuck on the ship for another day, which would be unbearable. She had anticipated this moment for days and could hardly wait to step on land, even if only for a few hours.

She skipped school lessons for the first time in a long while. She was too excited to focus on fractions anyway. At noon, they waited for the *shlyoupka*, a small tender, but the first boat was already full. Lydia squirmed impatiently, eager for the second tender to arrive and finally transport them to land, their destination: the village of Castelnuovo.

Walking alongside her parents on the paved *shossei* (highway), Lydia took in all the sights and smells surrounding her. She felt an overwhelming urge to run in every direction, pick wildflowers, and scream at the top of her lungs, but she knew better. Such behavior would not be acceptable in her parents' eyes. Instead, she composed herself, savoring the simple pleasure of walking outside on terra firma.

Soon she was distracted by the incredible views and the charming little houses lining the road. Her imagination started to take over. What if she lived in one of them? It would be wonderful to leave the ship behind, at least for a while. She pictured herself sitting in her cozy bedroom with a special spot for her doll and a bookshelf filled with as many books as possible. A warm, inviting kitchen would be filled with the aroma of a delicious feast. Outside, a swing would hang from a large tree, and a garden would bloom with never-ending flowers and vegetables. Best of all, she would sit outside sipping tea with her friends, enjoying a life of stability she longed for.

She snapped out of her daydream when something unusual caught her eye. Having only ever seen an orange tree in books, she was awestruck to see a real, live tree just a few feet away. She then noticed the towering palm trees and bay leaf trees for the first time! What a rich, beautiful land, she thought. She curiously broke off a laurel leaf twig for a closer look and ran her fingers along the veins of a leaf. The texture was intriguing, and the tactile sensation filled her with delight.

After walking for a long while, they came upon a breathtaking waterfall and paused to admire its beauty. On the way back, they ran into Zhenia, who happily joined them on their stroll. Wanting to experience the local cuisine and take a much-needed rest, Lydia and her family stopped at a restaurant. Her father ordered a beer, and Lydia and her mother enjoyed coffee. They encountered other passengers from the *Kherson* and eventually made their way to the pier, where they boarded the tender back to the ship.

Upon returning to the ship, Lydia was too excited to eat dinner, so she headed straight to the deck where the other children were playing. She couldn't wait to share her excitement about how much she preferred Castelnuovo over Buccari (present-day Bakar, Croatia). She went to bed depleted but exhilarated.

Two days later and still buzzing from her first visit, Lydia set off for Castelnuovo again.

One morning, expecting to join in games with the other children on deck, Grigory Fedorovich announced he would take her, Katya, Zhenia, and Kolya to shore. She was thrilled! But before getting even more excited, she knew she had to ask her parents' permission first. She generally did not participate in any activity without their approval, as she was expected to always ask, behave properly, and always follow instructions.

I would say this mindset carried her into adulthood. She maintained traditions of etiquette originating from the nineteenth and twentieth centuries and always had a formal and proper air about her. According to my mother, she only started wearing trousers in the 1950s and 1960s, and even then, still maintained her old-fashioned ways. She would even go camping in a dress!

Lydia's parents gave their approval for the excursion, and she giddily jumped up and down. The tender transported the enthusiastic group to shore, where they set off walking along the familiar road. Unlike her previous, reserved walk with her parents, she skipped wildly alongside Katya, Zhenia, and Kolya, picking flowers as they followed the path towards the cute town of Castelnuovo. Lydia couldn't help but think how wonderful it would be to visit this place daily. She felt so euphoric; she never wanted this feeling to fade.

Dining at a local restaurant in town was a delightful experience, and afterward, they wandered through the streets looking at the different shops and sights. All the children purchased postcards of Castelnuovo to bring back as keepsakes. Grigory Fedorovich, in need of new shoes, enlisted the kids' help in selecting a pair. After exploring more, they stopped at a pastry shop for homemade goodies and drank sweetened water. On the way back to the pier, they stopped in a grassy area to rest and pick flowers, savoring this moment.

Collecting postcards was standard for children in my grandmother's era. She often mentioned how she bought, sent, or received postcards. Some of her postcards are over 100 years old, and I have carefully preserved them, organized and stored them in a 3-ring notebook in clear, archival-safe protective sleeves. Each card has also been scanned and digitally archived. For fun, I scan them with the Google camera to see if they hold any monetary value. So far, none have any significant worth, other than priceless sentimental value.

Each trip to town typically involved enjoying a meal, sampling pastries, or having drinks at a local restaurant. Lydia's father would usually drink a beer, and, on occasion, so would Lydia and her mother. Lydia even mentioned drinking a "shot of wine." Coffee and Tea were also common choices. On one visit to town, while sitting at a restaurant with her parents, Lydia suddenly fell off the chair for no apparent reason. Was it the beer? Who knows! Everyone burst into laughter. She recorded this happy memory and said she *"...could not forget that."*

Lydia loved strolling through the town exploring the variety of shops. Sometimes she made purchases, while other times she simply enjoyed window shopping. Some common food items she and her family bought included nuts, figs, pastries, and chocolate. Other items they typically purchased were fabric for dresses, hats, and sandals, among other practical things.

Perhaps one of Lydia's favorite shore activities was picnics with her friends. One morning, Elizaveta Ivanovna, Katya's mother, surprised the children with an impromptu picnic adventure! A group of twelve gathered, and once ashore, they hiked to the waterfall. They even built a fire where they cooked scrambled eggs and boiled water for tea. Everyone enjoyed the meal, drank tea, and the children played "Cats and Mice" and picked flowers. It was a joyful day full of laughter and fun! Lydia couldn't wait to return and share the details of her excursion with her parents and Zhenia.

One of the highlights of Lydia's time on the ship was attending the Sokol Festival[55] in the medieval town of Tivat. They arrived by motor launch since it was further across the bay, which I expect to be a larger boat than the tender and with a motor. As they arrived, Anna Ivanovna (Anikeeff) was with them, and the music had already started. The gymnastics began at 5 pm and were very interesting, and there were a lot of children.

My grandmother's excursions resonate with my own love for adventure, especially on those coveted trips to the beach I took with my family. Like her, I am always eager to stay active and immerse myself in exciting new experiences. This memory takes me back to when we would motor our 25-foot cruiser across the Panama City Beach to the Shell Island channel. We would spend the day exploring, swimming, and enjoying a picnic on the boat deck or the shore. While the island had no cute towns or restaurants, its remote wilderness and endless sea oats made it a world of its own. I can imagine feeling the same joy Lydia did when she strolled down the road, searching for wildflowers, taking in the beauty that surrounded her.

---

55 The Sokol Movement was founded in Prague in 1862 and spread across all the regions populated by Slavic cultures including Croatia and Serbia. Theatrical performances and the gymnastic mass festivals were part of it. Sokol in English means falcon.

CHAPTER 9
The Importance of Faith

Having spent her early years in Odessa, Lydia was influenced by the values of her immediate and extended family and friends. As a young child, she likely attended the Preobrazhensky (Transfiguration) Orthodox Cathedral in Odessa. Her unwavering devotion to faith and family was central to her life, a theme clearly reflected in her daily entries she documented in her diaries aboard the ship.

The families aboard the *Kherson* made tremendous efforts to preserve their cherished Russian traditions and pass them down to the younger generation, despite being far from home. Upholding their cultural and religious identity was a top priority. The Church, which had been central to their lives in Russia, remained just as significant while living on the ship in a foreign land. Russian Orthodoxy played a vital role in their daily lives aboard the *Kherson* in their quest to maintain a sense of normalcy amidst an uncertain future.

Most passengers practiced Russian Orthodoxy, with only a few being Roman Catholic. Serbia had many Eastern Orthodox churches and monasteries within its borders that the passengers would attend. The inhabited towns on the Bay of Kotor were no different. Lydia describes attending church numerous times in her diaries.

In mid-March, Lydia and her fellow shipmates celebrated Maslenitsa, similar to Ash Wednesday, which is the full week before the first week of Great Lent. The celebration was filled with abundant food and lively festivities. Anna Ivanovna Anikeeff organized a special gathering, inviting all the children to the hold (the lowest part of the ship) for some singing and dancing. The following day, she and her husband, Michael, took the children to a nearby field to continue the festivities.

Everyone attended the Serbian Orthodox church in town and *"...stood a bit,"* according to Lydia. In traditional Eastern Orthodox Churches, pews are absent, as it is customary and expected for the worshippers to assume the conventional praying posture of standing for the duration of the service. Services typically last an hour and a half. However, chairs are sometimes placed along the edges of the church for the elderly or those unable to stand for extended periods.

After church, Lydia and her friends wove wreaths with flowers they found in the field. Each person had their own wreath and proudly wore it while enthusiastically dancing around the church grounds. The festivities continued into the evening, filled with more food, flowing wine, and lively singing. As they made their way to the tender, they continued to sing Russian folk songs boisterously, and they returned to the ship with a full belly and a smile on their faces.

In the days leading up to *Pascha*, or Eastern Orthodox Easter, Lydia accompanied her father to town to gather necessary items for the celebration. They attended a bustling bazaar, purchasing meat, egg dye, and an assortment of sweets to make this holiday extra special. As customary, Lydia and her father enjoyed coffee and beer during their outing. A ride on the tender ended her day. At the close of her entry for this day in particular, she veers from her typical closing sentence of *"...and this is how I spent the day,"* to *"...and that is how I very happily spent the day."*

The day before Easter, Lydia and her mother went to confession and communion at the church in town. This is a common practice prior to Easter for many Orthodox Christians, including me. Along with Uncle Skochemaro (50) and Zhenia, Lydia bought flowers for Easter. She stayed up late coloring eggs with the other children.

In her Easter entry, she specifically noted that no school lessons were completed because of the holiday. I chuckled to myself - she was so detail-oriented that she needed to document this fact. It seemed obvious that no school would take place on a holiday such as Easter. This meticulous record-keeping perfectly reflects the structured and disciplined personality I was familiar with from her later years. It is almost as if she needed to reassure herself that skipping her daily schoolwork was truly justified.

Easter was a joyous occasion; everyone wore their holiday dresses, exchanging personal greetings and congratulating one another. Customary Easter greetings for Russian Orthodox Christians are as follows:

> *The greeter exclaims,*
> *"Kristos Voskres!" (Христос Воскрес!) meaning "Christ*
> *is Risen!"*
> *The response by the other person is:*
> *"Voistinu Voskres!" (Воистину Воскрес) meaning, "Truly*
> *He is Risen!"*

I grew up participating in this responsive greeting and can recite it in English, Russian, and Greek. Many Russian traditions were passed down to me, including this one, for which I am grateful. However, one tradition that was not preserved was the Russian language. Even though both my parents are fluent, I can only engage in elementary conversations and read Cyrillic by sounding out each letter, and I am not fluent.

There was no "Easter Bunny" in Russian Easter traditions. However, it was customary to exchange small gifts among fellow Russians during the holiday. During Easter of 1921, while still living aboard the ship, Lydia was delighted to receive a ring from her tutor, Vera Matveyevna, perfume and soap from Dyadya[56] Vanya, and some chocolate from Dyadya Kolya.

Easter aboard the *Kherson* was celebrated on May 1, 1921. This photo captures the children in their holiday best, accompanied by several

---

56   Dyadya in Russian means Uncle. In Russian culture it was customary for children to address family friends and close acquaintances as "Uncle" before their first name, as a sign of respect and formality. They were not related to her.

adults, standing on the deck of the ship with the mountains of Zelenika in the background. Their expressions exude happiness and contentment. The exchange of these special greetings extended for several days after Easter Sunday.

Figure 32: Easter Sunday, May 1, 1921. Lydia, the tallest girl dressed in white, stands with Zhenia Anikeeff to her right. The little girl held by a sailor is Katya Malyavina, and the other two girls are believed to be Manya and Ira Semenopulo. Courtesy of the Buzyna Family.

After Easter,[57] weddings among the passengers began. In May alone, three weddings took place, and Lydia participated in each of them. Lydia and Zhenia even had the honor of serving as bridesmaids.

In preparation for these weddings, Lydia eagerly helped the adults select flowers for the nuptials. The process involved taking the tender to town, followed by a train ride to a special flower shop. Sometimes, Lydia would even pick flowers to add a personal touch to the bouquets. Lydia's focus during the wedding preparations seemed to be the flowers and her role as a bridesmaid, proudly standing alongside the bride and groom.

---

57 In the Eastern Orthodox Church, weddings cannot be performed during the week before Great Lent, Great Lent and Great Week (a total of 56 days before Easter).

It was heartwarming to see how the adults encouraged the children to participate actively in these traditional rituals, fostering a sense of unity between the children, adults, and everyone involved.

The first wedding was Nata's, short for Natalia. Lydia did not mention who the groom was but noted that she and Zhenia were chosen to be bridesmaids on Nata's special day. Lydia's best men were Slobodianik (85) and Derkachev (82). Zhenia's best men were Tokarev (87) and Sazanovich (86). In her diary, she simply referred to them by their last names when retelling this experience. Thanks to the documented crew list, we now know their full names.

Lydia and Zhenia transported the flowers they purchased for the wedding in a carriage. I can't help but imagine a horse-drawn, Cinderella-style carriage, decorated with flowers that Lydia arranged herself. After the bride and groom were married, the celebration party continued at the restaurant, where Lydia met up with her parents. She mentions being photographed during the events of the day, but unfortunately, no photos survived. The festivities went well into the night, and Lydia did not return to the ship until after one in the morning!

The second wedding that took place among the passengers was Aunt Liza's wedding (Elizaveta, or Elizabeth). This time, Lydia's mother, Daria Pavlovna, was the sponsoring mother (witness), and Orest Vladimirovich Semenopulo (2) was the sponsoring father (witness). Once again, Lydia and Zhenia happily served as bridesmaids to the wedding.

By 2:30 in the afternoon, all the guests from the ship were ready to go ashore. After arriving on shore by tender, they boarded the train heading to the restaurant in the town. While waiting for the guests to arrive, Lydia indulged in ice cream and pastries. She then accompanied Uncle Skochemaro (50) and Uncle Vanya (possibly Kruchik (52) and Uncle Kolya (Nicolai, but unsure of his exact identity) to purchase flowers for the wedding. From there, she traveled to the church by carriage.

Following the wedding, Lydia and all the guests returned to the *Kherson*, where one of the guests entertained her and Zhenia with some magic tricks that she described as *"...very interesting."* Yet another late night for Lydia - 11 pm to be exact.

Another wedding occurred just two days later; this time, Lydia Stepanovna and Sinkevich (72) were married. Once again, Lydia and Zhenia enthusiastically embraced their roles as bridesmaids. Selecting bouquets was once more an essential wedding preparation task. They performed their duties with a sense of importance and pride.

Uncle Skochemaro once again served as Lydia's best man, and he, along with Lydia's mother, were the first to leave the ship to purchase flowers. After buying the flowers, they headed to the church for the wedding. The restaurant reception was a lively celebration. Lydia described it as *"...very joyous and everyone drank champagne, wine and beer and ate ice cream."* Later, she went to the ship via tender, accompanied by her mother, the doctor, Aunt Liza, Constantine, and Uncle Kolya.

Lydia did not participate in the fourth and final wedding, as she stayed back with Katya so that her mother could attend the celebrations. The wedding was between Elizaveta V. and Grigory Fedorovich.

The following day, Katya and Lydia met Katya's mother at the restaurant where the wedding celebrations had taken place the night before. They lingered there for quite a long time and did not return to the ship until late. Upon their return to the ship, her father punished her for staying out too long, and she spent the rest of the day confined in the cabin. Lydia did not appear to regret her behavior, nor did she protest the punishment, simply noting that she was "punished."

If my grandmother were alive today and I asked her about this incident, I have no doubt she would say "...it was just the way it was," offering no further explanation or questioning the reason behind the punishment. That was how she saw the world, accepting things as they were without complaint.

It appeared the children had so much freedom both on the ship and on land that I was surprised to learn that Lydia was punished for returning so late. I wonder what the exact circumstances were that led her father to punish Lydia.

Her son, George, remembers his mother as warm, loving, and caring, but also firm. When she was displeased with his behavior, she made it known verbally, and he never felt like he was being punished but knew he was expected to behave appropriately.

Several other religious holidays were celebrated among the passengers. Typically, they would attend church and have a picnic in a field or enjoy meals in a restaurant. These were always joyous occasions, and Lydia full-heartedly participated in these events.

On *Trinity Day*, or *Day of Pentecost*, Lydia visited the Monastery that I believe to be the Savina Monastery, located near Herceg Novi, Montenegro. While exploring the grounds, Lydia picked mulberries in a field and even came across a dead snake! Later, she joined the other parishioners in lively singing and dancing, an experience she truly enjoyed. Three churches are located on the Savina Monastery grounds, one originating from the year 1030. This church, as you can imagine, was renovated several times. Another church was built from 1777 to 1799, and represents several architectural styles: Romanesque, Gothic, and Byzantine with elements of Orthodox Baroque. Today, the monastery continues to be functional and includes a winery.

I have since added this monastery to my bucket list of locations to visit when I retrace her journey. I cannot help but wonder if any archival records exist from her time in the area, perhaps even marriage documents from the weddings Lydia attended. How amazing it would be to uncover a paper trail of these religious sacraments that took place so many, many years ago.

St. Vitus Day, or *Vidovdan*, is a Serbian National and Religious holiday observed annually on June 28th. Having never heard of this holiday before, I looked it up and discovered that the date aligned exactly with Lydia's diary entry. This is yet another confirmation of her meticulous record-keeping, and I am in awe, especially considering she was only eleven years old at the time.

According to the Serbian Orthodox Church, this holiday honors St. Prince Lazar and the Serbian holy martyrs who perished in the 1389

Battle of Kosovo against the Ottoman Empire. In celebration, flags were displayed across the ship, and the shores were illuminated with countless lights, creating a beautiful scene from the ship's deck.

A few weeks later, on Tuesday, July 12, 1921, Lydia participated in celebrations for the Holiday of Peter and Paul. Apparently, it is a holiday celebrated by both Russians and Serbs. There were many fireworks and lights on display. Rockets were even shot off the *Kherson,* which was fun to see. Flags were displayed on the *Kherson,* but much to the crew's disappointment, no Russian flags were flown. Lydia wrote in a small script that everyone was disappointed by this. Even at just eleven years old, she felt a deep connection to her homeland of Russia, which remained strong despite being so far away.

Lydia's Name Day Celebration

In the Eastern Orthodox tradition, Name Days hold greater significance and joy than birthdays. Lydia celebrated her Name Day aboard the *Kherson* surrounded by family and friends on Tuesday, April 5, 1921.

Katya was the first to visit Lydia's cabin that morning, bringing her a gift of figs. Shortly after, Zhenia presented her with a portrait of herself. After the early morning excitement, Lydia made her way to the deck where she received even more gifts - Elizaveta Ivanovna[58] gave her beads, Elizaveta Vasilievna offered her a pastry, and Maria Aleksandrovna gifted her a napkin, Manya brought cocoa, and Vera Matveyevna gave her chocolate. To top it all off, Lydia Pavlovna[59] treated the children to a homemade torte.

Lydia diligently recorded the Name Days for her family back in Odessa in her diary, marking each occasion with a prayer and often celebrating with a pastry or a shot of wine in their honor. She frequently expressed how much she missed her relatives and wished she could

---

58   Elizaveta Ivanovna Malyavina, wife to second mate Vissarion Dmitrievich Malyavin (3)

59   Lydia Pavlovna Schmelz nee Kolosova, wife of Captain Viktor Franzevich Schmelz (1)

celebrate with them in person. She often noted how they observed these special days according to the old calendar, continuing to maintain their traditions away from home.

CHAPTER 10

Back to Normalcy

In addition to the religious celebrations, Lydia participated in other festive events while living aboard the *Kherson*. Several stick out so vividly in her mind that she recorded them in her diaries. There was always something or someone to celebrate!

Shortly after they arrived at the Bay of Kotor, the crew celebrated to honor a fellow member, Chief Engineer Alfred Victor Martinovich Truen (6). Despite the poor weather on Wednesday, February 2, 1921, Lydia was ecstatic to be invited for breakfast in the wardroom (officer's mess on the ship) to celebrate Truen's 25 years of service for the Russian Volunteer Fleet. He had just turned 62 years old and was likely to be nearing retirement. The festivities continued in the salon where everyone played games, danced, and enjoyed the lively atmosphere. After the arduous departure from Sevastopol and the long journey that followed, the crew and their families were long overdue for a celebration.

Another activity that helped restore a sense of normalcy, though not exactly fun, was tending to necessary medical or dental issues on shore. Often, these doctor offices were located in the doctor's home, and if they were lucky, the doctor would be home and available to see patients. Lydia described several visits to the dentist, recounting her fear and anxiety each time. Over a time span of six months, Lydia visited the dentist seven times in Castelnuovo. On three of those visits, the dentist was not home, forcing her to return another day.

One day in March, Lydia accompanied her parents to shore to visit the dentist. While her mother went shopping, her father took her to the dentist's office. This time, the dentist was home and free to see Lydia. However, when he suggested pulling her tooth out, she refused. Later, she returned with her mother and finally allowed the dentist to extract her tooth.

Lydia expressed bravery despite feeling scared during the painful procedure:

> *...when we came out of the [dental] office we met up with my mama and I went with her to the dentist, regardless of how afraid I was, he pulled out my tooth. It was very painful, and I cried.*

To my surprise, the next line of her journal casually moves on to the next activity, as if nothing traumatic had happened at the dentist.

> *Eventually we went to the tender, having arrived on the ship, I fished with a fishing pole but caught nothing, and that's how I spent my day.*

Another dental procedure Lydia had to endure was what I would guess was a root canal. She did not specifically write "root canal," but I believe this is what took place. On two occasions, Lydia states how afraid she was to go to the dentist again because she did not want another tooth pulled. Instead, the dentist *"...took a nerve from another tooth and it was very painful."* She and Zhenia sometimes traveled to the dentist together, and while Lydia had another nerve removed, Zhenia had a tooth removed and *"...cried a lot."* After the nerve removal, a man she called Uncle Petya (Peter) drew a picture of her, perhaps to distract her from the pain.

Lydia's matter-of-fact mindset defined her entire life, calmly accepting events as "just how it is," no matter how difficult. This pragmatic outlook shaped her whole personality and response to hardship. A heartbreaking example came in 1960 when her husband suffered a fatal stroke and was hospitalized. My mother was a freshman in college, and her brother was only 14. When my mother asked if she should come home, her mother told her not to. He passed away shortly after, but her reaction remained consistent with her stoic approach to life.

Living in such close quarters, passengers frequently contracted contagious illnesses. In early July of 1921, Lydia contracted what appeared to be a viral or bacterial infection. The doctor was called and, upon physical examination, found her glands swollen. She experienced a headache, a "severe temperature," and felt "wilted." Her mother rubbed iodine on her, a typical home remedy at the time. A few days later, her doctor treated a rash in her mouth by administering medicine, while the assistant applied a compress to her neck, likely to reduce the fever. Her spirits lifted when the other children visited her in her cabin. Perhaps she had the flu or strep throat? No diagnosis or treatment was mentioned, other than home remedies.

When the doctor permitted the compress to be removed the following day, Lydia was cleared to go up to the deck. However, her mother, worried she might "catch a chill," kept her in the cabin. Unfortunately, Lydia remained isolated there for another day.

Lydia's parents insisted she take castor oil as another home remedy, although they did not specify the reason for it. Lydia strongly disliked taking it and initially refused, but eventually gave in and took it with some tea. The mere thought of castor oil afterward made her feel nauseous. This experience with castor oil undoubtedly left a lasting impression on her for the rest of her life.

Although I do not remember any home remedies used when I was growing up, my mother introduced one I recall in particular when my kids were young. She cracked an egg yolk into a small glass, added sugar, mixed the solution until it was light yellow, and said, "Drink this, it will help with your cough." I had never heard of such a remedy before, and the thought of it was completely unappealing. She called it "Gogol-Mogol" and explained how her mother would give her this concoction when she was sick.

CHAPTER 11
Departing the *Kherson*

After 18 months, the Komarkoff family's time on the *Kherson* steamship had finally come to an end. They officially moved off on Tuesday, August 2, 1921. After going to the doctor with her mother, Lydia watched a cable lower their luggage from the ship to shore. She was hoping nothing would fall into the water.

With a heavy heart, Lydia said goodbye to everyone on the ship. Anton, Pavel, and Nikolai transported her family to shore in the tender. They proceeded to find a hotel in Castelnuovo called Jadran. Lydia had nothing favorable to say about their new hotel, describing it as "alright." The family had a solemn evening walking about the town and had dinner. Back at the hotel, her mother made a delicious Kisel with dewberries. This dish made Lydia feel at home and made at least some of the sadness go away. I never realized my grandmother knew how to make this, one of my favorite Russian dishes of all time! Had I known, I would have requested this each time I saw her!

Kisel is a cold dish eaten in a small bowl, having the consistency of a thick gel, but not solid. Like Jell-O, but not quite. A little more liquid-like, but not quite. The flavor was typically some sort of berry and usually red in color. Sometimes tiny tapioca pearls were added for texture. My heart feels warm thinking of this dish, bringing me back to my childhood, visiting my paternal grandmother. Kisel was one of many requests I would present to my Russian Babushka on my father's side each time we visited.

It was my absolute favorite Russian dish she made, and to this day, I can't figure out how to make it like she did.

Soon after their nightcap of coffee, they went to bed exhausted and unsure of what the future held for them. Almost immediately, their skin crawled with little bed bugs maliciously biting them. They slept on the floor for the remainder of the night. What an awful experience for them. Luckily, the next day her father found a much nicer room at the Savina Hotel, perhaps near the Savina Monastery.

Over the next few days, the Komarkoff family continued to stay local in Castelnuovo. They ran errands, went to the dentist, and spent time with their friends from the *Kherson*. Time spent with them was bittersweet as Lydia knew they would leave soon and permanently. She cherished this time very much.

During this short time, Lydia spent quite a bit of time with little Katya. One night, she even spent the night in her hotel. Eating ice cream, picking flowers, and running around outside. They would also travel together for dental visits. No more teeth pulling, thankfully for Lydia.

Lydia spoke about visiting Anton[60] in the town. She never wrote his patronymic or surname, so his identity is a mystery. If he were a crew member of the ship, then perhaps he, like Lydia and her family, would have moved off the ship. Traveling to Anton's house, the road was very bad, and they became very tired, and it was so hot out. Unfortunately, they did not stay long because they needed to return and catch the train. Lydia and her parents drank some cold beer on their way home.

Lydia ate ice cream with her parents at the "Amerikan Bar" and then met Elizaveta Ivanovna and Katya (Malyavina) at her hotel. Katya again spent the night with Lydia in her hotel room. They enjoyed each other's company, listened to music in town, then went to bed at a decent hour. The following day, Lydia returned to the ship with Katya via motorboat. Lydia happily played with the children on the deck one last time.

---

60   This could be the pot cleaner Anton Augustinovich Bolchunas (109), or the lacquey Anton Aloisovich Lipnitsky (103). Lydia mentioned (Uncle) Anton 14 times in her Diary Volume A.

While waiting for the train back on shore, Lydia picked blackberries with Zhenia and Nata. They also spent time together on the scenic seashore. The train finally arrived at *"...ten minutes after three."* Along with her parents, Lydia returned to their hotel. That evening, she took a walk with her parents, and they unexpectedly found themselves in the village of Igalo, a small town just west of Castelnuovo (Herceg Novi). Once again, they enjoyed a beer before returning to their hotel.

It was finally time for them to pack up their things. Once they were packed, they attended a lovely concert which was very *"interesting."* They went to bed tired and ready for their next adventure.

Thursday, August 11, 1921. The Komarkoff family packed their things for transport to the train station. Lydia's father wheeled the heavier items on a wagon while Lydia and her mother took a boat to the town of Zeleniki to meet her father. Lydia was touched by the large crowd bidding them farewell at the train station. It was a bittersweet moment filled with emotion. When would she see these familiar faces again? Would she ever? Hugs were exchanged, tears shed, and heartfelt goodbyes were shared. As Lydia parted ways with the friends with whom she shared a life-altering experience, she also said goodbye to the way of life as she knew it, living aboard the *Kherson*.

Once they boarded the train, it left quickly. The route was beautiful. The train climbed an incline, and then down the hill. The coastal shoreline was lined with tall mountains and hills, and to reach inland, the train needed to go over or through the hills to get to the other side. After traveling approximately 253 kilometers (157 miles), they arrived at the train station in Uskoplje, Bosnia and Herzegovina (now named Gornji Vakuf-Uskoplje). At 10 pm, they transferred to another train and continued on their train journey. Lydia did not sleep well on the train at all.

The train route led them through similar scenery to the day before, including many villages and tunnels. By 10 am the next day, they arrived in Sarajevo after riding another 100 km. They waited in the train station until their next train left at 11 pm. This time, Lydia effortlessly slept on the train despite being very crowded.

After traveling another 213 km, they arrived at 11 am the next morning at the station in Bosnin Brod (now called Brod) in Bosnia and Herzegovina. Still, they had to wait until 8 pm when the train actually left the station. Lydia was so exhausted and again had no problem falling asleep on the train. Brod to Indija, Serbia was another 200 km, and they made their final transfer here. A short train ride of 35 km led them to their last stop.

After a grueling, three-day trip riding multiple trains, the family arrived in their final-for-now destination of Novi Sad, Serbia. Sunday, August 14, 1921.

CHAPTER 12
Life in Serbia:
A New Normal

Now that Lydia and her family were adjusting to their new life as refugees in the Kingdom of Serbs, Croats and Slovenes (Yugoslavia, Serbia), they encountered an entirely new set of challenges. The most urgent issues that required immediate attention would be living accommodations, employment, and whether they would remain in Serbia or move elsewhere. What were their options? Another question looming in their minds: was life improving in Odessa, and should they return? The thought of returning to Odessa was heavy on their minds, although it was unclear if they seriously considered it. I know they hoped to return and longed to reunite with their extended family more than anything.

What led the Komarkoffs to choose Novi Sad? Why did they not remain aboard the *Kherson* like other crew members who continued to Malta? Novi Sad and its surrounding areas had the second highest population of Russian refugees, as well as a strong Orthodox community, which might have influenced their decision. The only larger population of Russian refugees in Serbia was in Belgrade. Serbia had agreed to take in approximately 20,000 Russian refugees who evacuated with General Wrangel during the mass exodus from Crimea in 1920. Wrangel was instrumental in establishing organizations to help these stateless refugees rebuild their lives and find a safe haven, where they were met with acceptance rather than discrimination.

Lydia mentions visiting the "Russian colony" in Novi Sad multiple times in her diary. However, she does not elaborate on what they did there. She does drop a few clues about the colony on November 17, 1921:

Today in the morning at 10 o'clock I went to town with mama, to the colony for produce. There I met a girl from my third class and a boy from the preparatory class. We received the produce very quickly, coming home it rained. On the way home we bought postcards and Turkish coffee. When we returned home, we looked over the items that had been allotted to me, there was cocoa, flour, sugar, beans, conserved canned milk and rice.

Since Serbia and Yugoslavia welcomed the white emigres displaced from their homeland, small Russian communities emerged after the Russian Revolution. I believe the Russian Colony Lydia mentions was one of these settlements. Lydia and her friends likely gathered essential food staples from these colonies through local residents and humanitarian organizations.

This colony likely also served as a gathering place where fellow Russians could connect, support each other, and rebuild their lives in exile. It would have been a center for sharing resources, finding employment, and preserving their cultural and religious traditions in a foreign land. Dimitri, Lydia's father, most likely was employed by a local restaurant, possibly through connections within the Russian colony in Novi Sad.

Living Arrangements

When they arrived in Novi Sad, it appeared they had connections within the city who helped them find a place to stay. Whether these contacts were acquaintances from before or people they met along the way is unclear. They seemed familiar with them, but without the last names, I cannot confirm if they were also aboard the *Kherson*. Some names she mentioned: Udavichenko,[61] Uncle Anton, Ivan, Mikhail Dimitirievich, Maria Leonidovna, and Tanyusha.

Despite frequently moving around during their year and a half on the ship, one constant remained - their cabin. No matter where they were in the world, they always had that personal space to call home. Now that they were in unfamiliar territory, they had to find a new place to call home. Would they be able to find stability and settle in?

They initially took over the apartment in Sremska Kamenica[62] that Udavichenko and Tanyusha occupied, as they were leaving. Several days later, Ivan woke them up at 4 am to inform them they should move to another apartment. Despite all the relocations and disruptions, they remained calm during it all.

Everyday Life in Novi Sad, Chores

One recurring theme in her diaries was that, regardless of where they were, Lydia was always expected to help with chores. She fulfilled these tasks without complaining and even enjoyed a few of them. Her father once bought her a small iron that uses hot coals, and she happily spent nearly an entire day ironing clothes! As she often expressed, "*...and I was very pleased.*" Although I do not iron much, I find it surprisingly satisfying.

Another day, she purchased a wooden darning mushroom for mending socks and seemed to enjoy this task. I wonder if her mother encouraged her to take on these projects or if she pursued them on her own initiative. She seemed to enjoy embroidery as well. Was she expected to do this craft like her mother?

Lydia liked to sew, embroider, and knit, and would occupy much of her time doing this when she had downtime or was bored. She even

---

61   Stoker Second Class M. D. Udovichenko (94), crew member from the *Kherson*. Perhaps this is who Lydia describes? Could he have departed from the *Kherson* sometime before the Komarkoffs left the ship and were scheduled to meet him in Novi Sad to help them look for a place to live?

62   Sremska Kamenica is a town in the urban neighborhood of Novi Sad, Serbia. Lydia often refers to this location as Kamenitsa.

took apart her father's scarf and knitted a new one! She also liked to sew clothes for her doll and "put her in order."

Plums were plentiful in Novi Sad, as Lydia would pick them off the trees or the ground as she walked by with her new friends. Perhaps they were in season. Lydia's mother made a delicious plum jam that she sampled with hot tea one afternoon. They would visit a vineyard nearby, and they even got to see how wine was made!

Lydia was expected to help in the kitchen, which I believe she found fulfilling. It created a bond with her mother and gave them something to do together. Peeling potatoes, grinding up crumbs, and rubbing tomatoes through a sieve were typical tasks she was asked to do in the kitchen. They made traditional Russian and Ukrainian dishes such as Pirog, Korzhiki, Kisel, and Kotlety.

I do not recall my grandmother making many of the typical Russian dishes while I was growing up. However, one dish that sticks out to me is Kotlety, a fried meat patty. It was a recipe passed down to my mother, and I remember her making it when I was younger. My mother also made Beef Stroganoff, but I don't know if her mother ever prepared that dish.

Transportation to various places was often on the motor launch boat down the Danube River. She frequently would take this alone on her way to and from school. Although the boat seemed to be her preferred method of transportation within the city, she would occasionally opt for the tram in the busy streets.

Lydia frequently mentioned visiting the "banya," or public bath, during their time in Novi Sad. Perhaps this was necessary if their living quarters lacked a bathtub or shower. It was a ritual she and her mother shared, though it did not always go smoothly. On one occasion, the bathhouse was so crowded that they waited over an hour to take their turn in the bath. But the real adventure began on their trip home.

Feeling refreshed, they were met with a torrential downpour as they stepped out of the banya. Seeking refuge in the awnings of the nearby Catholic church, they huddled together, hoping the rain would pass. Once they realized the rain was not letting up, they returned via motorboat launch, rather than braving the drenched streets on foot. This, however, required patience as they waited another hour and a half to board the boat home, shivering in their damp clothes. Thankfully, her father greeted them with their much-needed galoshes, listening intently as they told him about their unexpected adventure.

A Source of Income

Dimitri, Lydia's father, worked at "our" restaurant, as she describes, in Petrovaradin.[63] It is unclear whether Dimitri owned the restaurant or simply worked there, but I imagine he was an employee rather than the owner. Preserved in our family archive are numerous postcards and letters. Many are addressed to a restaurant that undoubtedly Dimitri worked at. Lydia and her mother would often meet at the restaurant after school and have a meal there.

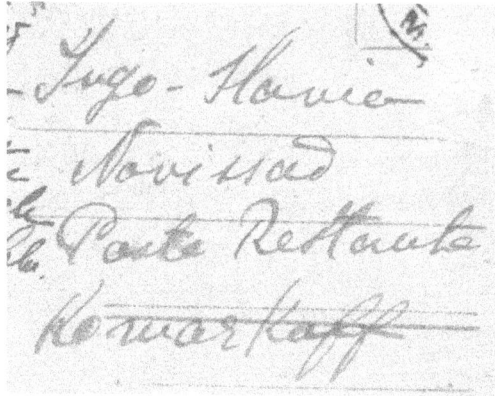

Figure 33: Postcard addressed to the Komarkoff family at their mail drop in Novi Sad, Yugoslavia: Poste Restante, Novi Sad, Yugo-Slavia, Komarkoff. Courtesy of the Buzyna Family.

While in Novi Sad, Lydia celebrated holidays to create an atmosphere of normalcy. Daria and Dimitri continued to practice their Russian culture and religious traditions with their daughter Lydia, just as they did while

---

63   Petrovaradin is a town just southeast of Novi Sad on the Danube River

living on the *Kherson*. Reading Lydia's descriptions of these events filled me with a sense of "home" and "warmth," as these are the same values passed down to me by my mother during my childhood in Tallahassee, Florida. Celebrating Orthodox holidays outside of Russia formed an inseparable bond between Lydia, her family, and their community. I feel deeply connected to my Russian roots because of the traditions my grandmother preserved and passed down to me.

I found it intriguing that Lydia remembered and documented the Name Day for the former heir to the throne, Alexei (Czar Nicholas' son), even posthumously. Perhaps she thought of others named Alexei in her community as well.

Lydia celebrated her twelfth birthday on December 8, 1921. This entry was one of her more detailed writings:

> *Today is my birthday [25 November, Old Style calendar] and when I awoke I saw presents that were on the table. Papa gave me a portrait of me and mama, an album, pastries and apples. I was very, very pleased and grateful to mama and papa. But in spite of it all, I went to study and we studied with V. F. [Vera Fedorovna] as always. Today I did not stay at Barkovsky's but came home soon. When we had dinner, we drank wine and I served everyone wine and pastries. In the evening mama, Uncle Jakov and I played this new interesting game, and we laughed a lot. Afterwards mama and I had supper, drank tea, I sat a bit more and went to bed.*

On Sunday, March 5, 1922, Lydia attended the Serbian Orthodox Church because it was the first week of Lent, and they wanted to go to confession and communion. She was very impressed that, despite the priest being Serbian, he conducted the confession like in Russia.

Easter was always one of my favorite holidays growing up. In her diaries, Lydia emphasized the many holidays celebrated in the Eastern Orthodox Church. Even if she did not go into a detailed description of each holiday, she made sure to mention which holiday it was, and funnily enough wrote that "of course" she did not do her lessons that day. She also mentioned Serbian holidays, even if she did not celebrate, because they always affected what she was doing or unable to do that day. She was acutely aware of traditions, whether those she practiced or those that surrounded her.

Sunday, April 16, 1922:

> *Today according to the old-style calendar, it is Easter for Russians and Serbs (Eastern Orthodox), and I think for Hungarians according to the new style [calendar]. When I got up in the morning I put on a new pink dress, wished mama and papa Christ is Risen [Happy Easter] and mama and papa together gave me a red satin pisanka[64] on which is a pretty rooster and inside are chocolate candies. First, we celebrated breaking our fast and ate very delicious cheese Pascha that mama made.*

For every Easter I remember, my mother would painstakingly make Pascha. It was always an incredibly arduous process that required her to special-order the Farmers Cheese and assemble a multi-dimensional wooden mold. I looked forward to this delicious treat during our annual Easter celebrations. She made sure to continue the tradition with her grandchildren.

Until I read this entry, I had not realized that Daria, my great-grandmother, also made Easter cheese, Pascha. Could my mother's desire to continue this tradition come from knowing her grandmother made it too? Or was it to feel closer to her Russian roots? I wonder how many generations of women in our family have passed down this recipe tradition. While I have never done this, I appreciated my mother's efforts. Now that I know this tradition goes back further than my mother, perhaps I will try making it with her this year and fully immersing myself in the experience.

---

64   Pisanka is an Easter Egg

As we prepare it, I will reflect on Daria making it in their home in Novi Sad, wondering where life would take them next.

CHAPTER 13

Life in Serbia:
Lydia goes to School

Now that Lydia was somewhat settled in a new place, she was thrilled about the prospect of attending a traditional school with a fixed location, unlike her previous schooling aboard the *Kherson*, where she had worked sporadically with tutors and studied independently. However, schooling in Novi Sad proved to have its own unexpected challenges. But Lydia accepted them with a calm attitude, simply thinking, "That is just the way it is."

On Tuesday, August 23, 1921, Lydia learned that she would start gymnasia.[65] Her mother apparently spoke with the director, and they admitted her even without an evaluation. She expressed herself in her diaries as being "*...very pleased*" with this scenario. She craved structure and truly enjoyed learning, plus she would meet other children her age. She reminisced about her lessons on the *Kherson* with her various tutors. She hadn't attended school in an actual building since she left Odessa in January 1920. The daily routine would be welcome, even though she missed her friends from the ship terribly.

Wednesday, August 24, 1921, was her first day in the new school:

Today I got up at 6 o'clock in the morning, got ready, drank tea and went with my mother on a [small] boat to

---

65   Gymnasia, or Gymnasium, was a term used for schools in European countries.

the gymnasia [school]. Having arrived there, I became acquainted with the children and we played in the yard [playground]. Later we went to prayer [session], and after class for lessons. I was called on in several subjects. Today we had very interesting gymnastics. At half past 2 I went home with Yuna,[66] having returned [home] I told everything [that happened that day at school] to mama. In the evening, we drank tea and then went to bed.

When she returned home from school daily, she would describe her day to her mother. I wonder if she used more descriptive words than she wrote in her diary entries. They would often talk while she would help her mother make dinner or do other chores.

After only a few days in her new school, she learned the location would be in a different building the following week. Over the course of her nine months living there, her school location would be moved numerous times, sometimes not finding out until she showed up at the empty area. Lydia would wander by herself, or if other children were around, searching for the teachers and school kids. Perhaps they were only allowed to use buildings that were not already occupied with other things going on.

Her new school location was now at Koupatinsky Park. There was no building, and the classes were conducted on the benches in the park. She describes this experience:

Wednesday, August 31, 1921

Today when I arrived at the gymnasia all the children were led in pairs [that is, two by two] to Koupatinsky Park [in small letters above the normal script:] because there is no school building. There were only benches on which we wrote somehow as best we could, we also played various games and Cossacks – Robbers, since the park is very large

---

66   Yuna, or Juna is the nickname for Junia

it was interesting to play [there]. After the lessons every-
one departed, and I went to the motor launch. After having
returned home I read and helped mama, in the evening we
drank tea, and I went to bed.

Often, when Lydia arrived at school, regardless of location, there
were not always enough teachers to conduct lessons or enough children
to form classes. As a result, they would only have a particular subject that
day or play if no teachers showed up. Lydia mentions the game "Cossacks
and Robbers," perhaps the Russian version of "Cops and Robbers." Often,
the lessons would be shortened because of the cold, since her classes
would be held at outdoor parks.

On September 7, 1921, Lydia learned from a girl in town that the new
location was a Shanuar Garden, and she was glad to study there since
they had tables.

Lydia was used to moving around and seemed to make friends easily.
No matter what she and her friends played, Cossacks and Robbers, Flags,
or played ball, they always managed to have a good time. Going to the
local movie theater was another favorite activity of Lydia's. She also
mentions seeing the opera "Tosca" shown on the movie screen in Novi
Sad. She clearly had an interest in the arts, and I can't help but believe
her parents nurtured that passion.

One of her most frequent activities to do with friends was playing
outside in the local park. One day, they found a small snake and were
"*...very frightened and took another route.*" She would also visit her
friends' houses, and they would come to her place. One day, when she
visited Yuna, she remarked on how wine was made from grapes.

Lydia expected to do well in her classes, and for the most part, she
did. She received a "two" mark (possibly out of 5?) for her Russian
Dictation assignment and came home very disappointed, sharing her frustration with her mother. On these rare occasions she received poor marks,
she would express her distress over the grade. She never mentioned her

parents reprimanding her for bad grades, it was always her own disappointment that stood out.

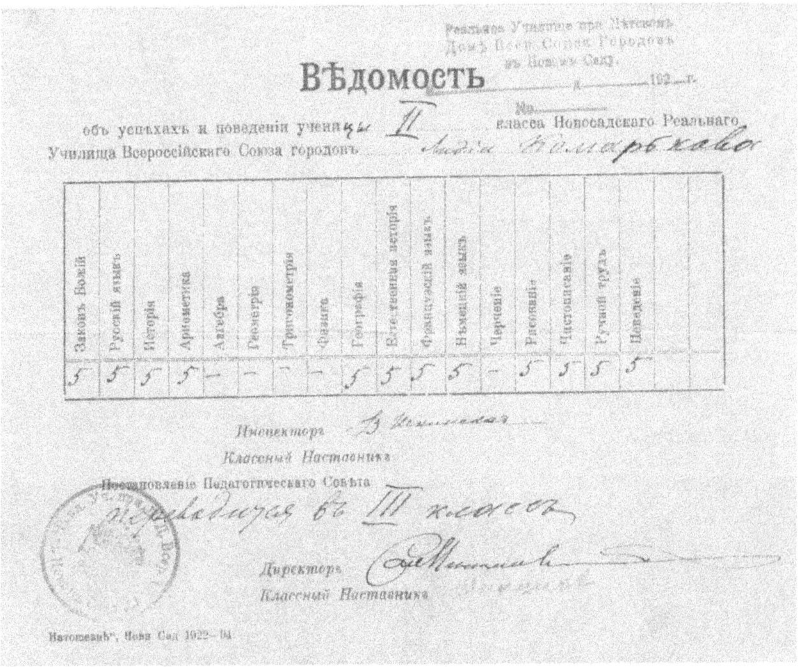
Реальное Училище при Дѣтскомъ
Домѣ Всер. Союза Городовъ
въ Новомъ Садѣ.

ВѢДОМОСТЬ

д ______ 192__ г.

№ ______

объ успѣхахъ и поведеніи ученицы II класса Новосадскаго Реальнаго Училища Всероссійскаго Союза городовъ

Законъ Божій	Русскій языкъ	Исторія	Ариѳметика	Алгебра	Геометрія	Тригонометрія	Физика	Географія	Естественная исторія	Французскій языкъ	Нѣмецкій языкъ	Черченіе	Рисованіе	Чистописаніе	Ручной трудъ	Поведеніе		
5	5	5	5	–	–	–	–	5	5	5	5	–	5	5	5	5		

Инспекторъ

Классный Наставникъ

Постановленіе Педагогическаго Совѣта

переводится въ III классъ

Директоръ

Классный Наставникъ

Figure 34: School document from Lydia's time in Novi Sad.
Courtesy of the Buzyna Family.

This document was one of her report cards from the "Realschule in Novi Sad at the Orphanage of the All-Russia Union of Cities." This school was in existence in Novi Sad from 1921 to 1938. Sergei Rudolfovich Mintslov was the principal of the school, and his signature is the one second from the bottom. Vera Fedorovna Shkinskaya, whom Lydia mentions in her diaries, signs as the "Inspector" on this report card, first signature under the chart.

A translation of her grades from the report card:

God's Law	5
The Russian Language	5
History	5
Arithmetics	5

Algebra	-
Geometry	-
Trigonometry	-
Physics	-
Geography	5
Natural History	5
The French Language	5
The German Language	5
Technical Drawing	-
Drawing	5
Calligraphy	5
Manual Labor	5
Behavior	

Figure 35: Lydia (middle row, third from left) with her classmates in Novi Sad. October 12, 1921. Courtesy of the Buzyna Family.

Lydia described this class photo in her diary and documented that it cost 3 dinars[67] to purchase the photo. She was thrilled when her mother permitted her to buy this priceless photo.

On October 31, 1921, Lydia was alerted that the gymnasia would be closed for two weeks due to a Scarlet Fever outbreak. I am sure Lydia and the other children were disappointed. Nevertheless, Lydia kept herself busy going to town, playing with her friends, doing tasks at home, and reading. Her teacher, Vera Fedorovna, came to bring her lessons during this break from school and informed her that she would go to the Barkovskys' house on Monday to study.

Vera Fedorovna brought a book for Lydia to read called *The Silver Prince*, by Tolstoy, and she finished it two days later. Even while on the *Kherson*, Lydia read books. My grandmother always liked to read. She even kept a handwritten list of all the books she read when she was older.

Lydia became close friends with Konstantin and Kirill Barkovsky and often studied at their house. Sometimes Vera Fedorovna would conduct a lesson or two there as well. They enjoyed each other's company so much that one time, when Lydia was at their house, the boys would not let her leave and locked the door. They liked playing cards, looking at books, and even exploring their incredible stamp collection for an afternoon!

During bad weather, like a snowstorm or hazardous conditions due to thick mud from the melting snow, Lydia's mother frequently did not allow her to go to school. Although she would be terribly disappointed, she acquiesced and realized she could not argue with her mother. Her friends would bring her assignments, and she would happily complete them at home. She would complain how bored she was when she was not allowed to attend school. I do not know if other children were allowed to go to school in these conditions, or if it was just Lydia's parents who were possibly overly cautious.

For a short duration, when the Danube River had chunks of frozen ice floating in it, the boats were not running, and Lydia had to walk about

---

67   The dinar was introduced in 1920 in the Kingdom of the Serbs, Croats and Slovenes, the state that preceded the formation of the Republic of Yugoslavia.

an hour to get to school. Again, she was not allowed to go to school if the weather was bad.

At one point, she was scheduled to perform with her school group in a rhythmic gymnastics performance, called *Pierrot and Pierrette,* but the weather worsened even more than in previous days. Her friend Maya came to her house to report that Vera Fedorovna and all the children were *absolutely asking* if her mother would allow her to attend the rehearsal the next day for the performance. They suggested that Lydia stay the night at Barkovsky's house, probably closer to the school, to ensure her participation in this important event.

After several days stuck at home, Lydia was overjoyed that her mother agreed to the earlier plan. Her mother immediately started sewing the little shoes and a costume for Lydia to participate in the show. Everyone was so happy, and Lydia went to bed dreaming of her upcoming dancing recital.

When Lydia was not allowed to go to school or stay home for any reason, she often complained of boredom. I noticed this as she got older, like any teenager, although she was only 12. One day in late April, when the weather was so stormy outside that she stayed in her room all day, she contemplated her situation. She tried to keep herself busy with drawing or knitting, but these activities could not get her to stop thinking about her friends she missed from the *Kherson.* Like any teenager, she wished to be anywhere but where she was.

Thursday, April 20, 1922

The weather today is not good, it was about to rain and there was no sun. I stayed in the room all day. At first I was making order in the drawer, then I was drawing and knitting - all little by little. I kept thinking about the Kherson and would have liked to be there again. I am very bored without the children! I would very much like to be in Odessa, Zagreb, on the Kherson or in America. In the evening, I was reading a book by Dostoevsky and went to bed at 9 o'clock.

CHAPTER 14
Life in Serbia: Impactful Events

General Wrangel Visits Lydia's Classroom

A pivotal event occurred on Saturday, March 8, 1922. A story that Lydia told throughout her adult life and left a lasting impression, especially with my uncle and cousin, and anyone familiar with Russian history. At the time, I didn't fully grasp its significance. I was unfamiliar with General Wrangel or his crucial role in my grandmother's evacuation from Russia. If I had the opportunity to hear her tell this story today, I would be completely captivated.

> *I was told that General Wrangel was supposed to come to our classroom, so everyone was awaiting his arrival. After class III, a car drove up to the gymnasia, Wrangel was sitting in one of them and in the other his adjutants. Wrangel walked around all the classes and when he came into ours, everyone said "Good Day, Your Excellency," he stood around a little and afterwards went to the other classes, when he was leaving the gymnasia, the children were bidding him farewell at the car and were crying "hoorah", the crowd was terrible. After that we were released. I was able to make it onto the 1 o'clock motor launch and having come home I told Mama about everything. Later I read and knit.*

My cousin Len vividly remembers this story from when my grand-mother told it. Although he recalled her tale about the horses in the Black Sea, her encounter with General Wrangel left the most significant impression on him. Lydia mentioned there was a specific way you were expected to respond to General Wrangel, using the phrase "Rad starat'sya," which translates to "glad to try my best (do my utmost)." It was the formal response given by the person speaking with General Wrangel if he (the General) had praised the person before this. This is exactly how Russian Imperial and White army soldiers responded to praise from officers. Len likened it to how American soldiers respond to their superiors with "Sir, yes, sir" when given orders. That was the impression he got from her when they discussed the moment.

General Peter Nicholayevich Wrangel (August 27, 1878 – April 25, 1928), also known as the "Black Baron," lived in Sremski Karlovci,[68] Serbia, in exile, where he was head of all the White Russian refugees.

Earthquake

This "major event," as Lydia described it, took place during school hours on Friday, March 24, 1922. I can only imagine how frightening this experience must have been, especially for a young girl away from the comfort and reassurance of her parents.

> *Today at the gymnasia we had a major event. During the history class, it was V class, we felt ourselves swaying as if rolling from a wave when on a ship. Everyone, of course, was frightened but did not know what it was. But it immediately stopped. When everyone left to go home, we found out that this was an earthquake. When I came home mama told me that it also took place in Kamenitsa. After dinner I went to the park since I thought there would be violets but there were none and we returned home.*

---

68   12 km, or 7.5 miles, from Novi Sad

The Serbian King Alexander I and the Romanian Queen Maria pass by in their Car

Lydia describes the thrilling experience of watching the Serbian King and Romanian Queen, along with their entourage, pass by in their cars as she left her school in Novi Sad. Technically, when Lydia witnessed this event, Maria was a Princess until she married King Alexander I in Belgrade on June 8, 1922, when she earned the title of Queen.

On Tuesday, April 4, 1922, Lydia writes:

When I came from the gymnasia to Kamenitsa I saw that the streets were decorated with Serbian and Romanian flags and there was a huge crowd of people. I found out that the Serbian King and Romanian Queen will be passing through. Of course, I stayed and waited. Automobiles quickly appeared and I saw the King and Queen, and everyone was shouting "long live." And I was happy with this. When I came home, I told mama about this. Since papa went to Belgrade today, I was only with mama and it was lonely.

King Alexander I of Yugoslavia (December 16, 1888 - October 9, 1934) was highly regarded by Russians living in exile, like my grandmother, as he welcomed and supported them into his country, providing refuge and assistance during their displacement. So, for Lydia, witnessing King Alexander I pass by was a moment of great honor and excitement. He had been newly crowned King in August 1921 and was deeply appreciated among the Russian emigre community.

House Burned Down

For the first time in her diaries, Lydia devoted two full pages to describing the fire that destroyed their rental house in Novi Sad. Her level of detail reveals how truly impactful this experience was for her.

Even though they recovered all their belongings and were unharmed, the emotional toll of losing the house, a symbol of stability, must have been significant. For Lydia, already living in the uncertainty of exile, this event undoubtedly intensified her and her parents' fear of the unknown.

Sunday, April 30, 1922

Today there was a big unfortunate event in Kamenitsa. In the morning after we drank coffee, papa went outside to the yard and saw smoke, he came inside immediately into the room and said that there is a fire and I, of course, was very frightened, and papa and mama began packing our things, our landlord was afraid for his house. When I went outside to the yard sparks were already flying. Finally, our things were not all put together, only by papa, I helped carry them [out]; We cried out and did not know what to do. As soon as we had taken our things out to the yard, the house caught on fire, and we went with our things to some garden…I was so frightened I cried. The crowd was pouring water from barrels onto the houses, later the police helped and saved our things, even the small miscellaneous ones. Finally, the fire was out and I went with papa to see our house which burned completely to the ground. After this papa found a room in Ripario Hotel and we moved there. Later Lena stopped for me and we went to the park and later looked at the burned down houses and there were all of 7. I came home as it was getting dark. Our room was quite nice. When I was going to bed, I was thinking all the time that there would be a fire. And this way the day was very bad.

CHAPTER 15
Journey to America

On September 16, 1921, the Komarkoffs received a letter from Uncle Kostya, in which he suggested they come to the United States. Unfortunately, this letter was not preserved. I would have loved to have read the exact wording of this suggestion.

Possibly in anticipation of eventually moving to America, Lydia mentions having their photographs taken soon after their arrival in Novi Sad. Could her parents have been thinking ahead and considering a more permanent move to the United States at that time?

Figure 36: Lydia's portrait taken in Novi Sad while preparing immigration paperwork to the United States. Courtesy of the Buzyna Family.

Figure 37: The Komarkoff family – Daria, Lydia, and Dimitri – photographed for immigration paperwork to the United States. Daria, Lydia, Dimitri Komarkoff. Courtesy of the Buzyna Family.

Friday, November 11, 1921, was a significant day for Lydia. Not only did it snow (is this where I get my love of snow from?), but the family received several letters: Uncle Kostya[69] in America, Katya in Malta, and Uncle Anton. She had been eagerly awaiting letters from family and friends for some time now and would remark with disappointment that no letters were waiting for them at the post office.

Uncle Kostya's letter expressed his sorrow that the Komarkoffs had decided *not* to come to America. Sometime between September 16 and November 11, they must have written him a letter with their refusal to his New York City proposal.

Lydia seemed disappointed by this news. She mentioned that she was excited to get a letter from New York. Perhaps she was secretly wishing to go to America?

> *Having come home I read the letter again and wrote a letter*
> *again to Uncle Kostya. I was so happy that mama and papa*
> *agreed to travel to Kostya's. Papa will send a telegram and*
> *a letter.*

Did Lydia play a role in convincing her parents to move to the United States? What were the reasons they did *not* want to come? What were the reasons they *did* want to come? Were they still holding out hope for the possibility of returning to Odessa? At times like these, I wish Lydia had expanded on her feelings about the situation.

Dmitry traveled to Belgrade on several occasions - to receive money sent by Uncle Kostya, and to apply for passports and visas to travel to America.

On Sunday, February 19, 1922, the Komarkoffs received letters with good news from Odessa. Here, Lydia expresses probably the most emotion I have seen in her writing:

---

69 Constantine Pavlovich Vertsinsky was Lydia's uncle (her mother Daria's brother), who had already come to the United States.

Today was a very joyous day. First, papa came and even better that we received letters from Odessa. Oh Lord! How happy we were that all of them [in Odessa] are alive and healthy, we cried all day and rejoiced. Papa brought drawings that Ivan Iosifovich had drawn very well; Papa also brought postcards. We were very happy all day rereading the letters. In the evening, I prepared my lessons and went to bed.

Dimitri had returned from business in Belgrade on February 19, and Lydia and her mother missed him deeply. He most likely was applying for their passports.

On Monday, April 24, 1922, they unexpectedly received a letter from Uncle Kostya stating he had sent them money and that they *"...should come [to America] quickly."* Dimitri brought home a beautiful bouquet of lilacs in celebration of the news. Lydia excitedly thought about her future travels:

After dinner I reviewed my lessons, and I was thinking about our travel and how at last we will arrive in "America." [She placed the quotation marks around America.]

On May 6, 1922, Dimitri received Uncle Kostya's check and traveled to Belgrade for several days to process the necessary paperwork for their journey to America. When I examined their immigration documents that my grandmother saved, there were numerous stamps in various languages, including French, English, and Russian. Several stamps were dated May 8, 1922, correlating perfectly with Lydia's account of her father visiting Belgrade.

On Lydia's last day at gymnasia, her mother accompanied her to bid farewell to her classmates and teacher Vera Fedorovna, where she was presented with a big bouquet of flowers, and was *"...very pleased."* She spent her final night at the Barkovskys' for dinner, where her parents and other friends joined in the festivities.

Finally, on Friday, May 12, 1922, the Komarkoff family embarked on their lengthy journey to America:

Today papa packed all our things, put them on a wagon and with our former landlord went to the railroad station, and mama and I went to the babushka to say farewell and then came home. At half past 9 Mama and I went to the railroad station. On the way we left our letters at the post office, then sat down in the tram and went to the railroad station. While we were riding [on the tram], we saw the II and III classes coming two by two with Vera Fedorovna [Shkinskaya], I, of course, was very happy that they came to bid me a farewell and as soon as the tram arrived, I ran to meet them. They gave me very many flowers and asked that I write to them and send them stamps. Papa treated all of them to pastries and we went to the platform. Soon after, Vera Fedorovna came there also and told me that since I did not say good-bye to the director, that I should write to him; I was given a piece of paper, Vera Fedorovna dictated and I wrote this:

Very Respected Sergei Rudolfovich (Mintslov)[70] I wish you the best, I will never forget you. Lydia Komarkova, student III class.

In a little while the train arrived and everyone went into the [train] car but I still stood with the children. Finally, Papa and mama came for me and we said farewell and as soon as we approached the train, it started moving, papa and I jumped on, mama was afraid but somehow jumped on, we had seats so we were able to sit.

Their train journey continues:

---

70   Lydia penciled in his last name years later, in parentheses above his patronym

The way to Belgrade was not very pretty, mostly pastures. We ate on the train and sat all the way and did not do anything. We arrived in Belgrade at 3:35 in the afternoon. Papa left our luggage in a safe storage area, and we went into town. Mama, papa and I went to a pastry shop and mama and I had "iced coffee" and papa drank tea, after that we went to the main street, onto the boulevard, we saw the palace of King Alexander and generally looked around the town, but I very much did not like it because it was dirty, many houses under construction and there are no nice streets except the main one. Since we were supposed to leave for Zagreb at 7 o'clock, after buying some groceries, we went to the railroad station.

After leaving Belgrade, they proceeded to Zagreb, where they stayed in a hotel for a few nights. During their stay, they were happy to reunite with Ivan Iosifovich, Lydia's former tutor from the *Kherson*, ate at the Moscow Restaurant in town, and did a little shopping. From Zagreb, they traveled by train through the stunning landscapes of Switzerland. Lydia embraced this experience by purchasing postcards displaying the beautiful scenery at each town where they transferred trains.

At one stop, a doctor inspected them, and everything went smoothly. A Serbian agent then escorted them to a hotel in Buchs, Switzerland. The next day, they took the train to Basel and saw Lake Geneva from the windows, another spectacular view. Lydia counted how many tunnels they passed through - 12 in total - and noted one was so long it took fifteen minutes before reaching the other side!

When they arrived in Paris, they managed to walk around the city briefly. Lydia's impression of Paris was that the streets were chaotic, noisy, and filled with so many cars that she was frightened to cross the street! She really hoped to see the Eiffel Tower. She was disappointed there was not enough time, as they needed to board the train to Le Havre,

France, where they were required to undergo a mandatory seven-day quarantine, before their voyage across the Atlantic Ocean.

Another agent greeted them at the train station in Le Havre and took them, along with their luggage, to a huge building where they would stay for the duration of their time before heading to America. The women and children slept separately from the men. Lydia and her mother shared a bunk bed - she was on the top and her mother on the bottom. Lydia remarked that her mother "...*made the bed like it should be.*"

They ate all their meals in a common area, and Lydia remarked that the dinner was *"fairly good"* on that first night: pea soup with rice, fish, potatoes with meat, cheese, and wine. Entertainment was provided in the spacious dining hall, where music was played in the evening. Lydia enjoyed playing games with the other children and even watched a movie later. Although Lydia found most days rather dull, the occasional opportunity to explore the town helped break up the monotonous days of waiting to board their ship. Lydia quickly adapted to the situation, befriending two girls, Anyuta[71] and Rosa, with whom she mostly *"played billiards and ball."*

Each day in quarantine, they followed the same routine. However, they were allowed to wander about the nearby town. There were many interesting sights, and they enjoyed exploring the wide streets and many stores. One day, they even got lost returning to the building. Walking along the seashore, they were struck by its beauty and found a garden with swans gliding in a lake nearby. They also took a walk to the pier where they would board the ship later that week, and even attended the circus for entertainment one afternoon.

The day was finally here! They were going to America! On Saturday, May 27, 1922, it was time to board the massive steamer, the *SS La Savoie*.

I did not ever expect that the ship "Savoie" would be so big!

---

71   Anyuta is a nickname for Anna

Figure 38: Postcard purchased by Lydia aboard the La Savoie during her journey to the United States. Courtesy of the Buzyna Family.

As excited as she was to come to America, the journey on the *SS La Savoie* was miserable. She vividly described her first impressions:

They took us to the stern, the very lowest deck of the ship in 3rd class and gave us a totally small room [cabin] but we would have settled in it well, were it not for 2 more people who also came in with us, since there were 5 cots in the cabin, it was very tight in our cabin but we could do nothing about it. The ship was supposed to leave at 9 o'clock and it was only 6 o'clock. At 7 o'clock everyone was called to supper. In our dining area it is truly dirty and, as a matter of fact, that area is not really meant for a dining room. The supper was even worse than in Le Havre. The 1st course was soup, God knows what kind, the 2nd an unpalatable sauce, and for the 3rd [course] potatoes, the same. I ate almost nothing. After supper papa, mama and I went to the deck, which is on the bottom, it is the dirtiest, and we were not allowed up to a higher deck than the 3rd class [area]. The ship left only at 9:30 in the evening. It was pulled by 2 motor launches [tugboats], and when it left the harbor, it went on its own. I stood with mama and papa on the deck until Le Havre was not completely visible and then we went to the cabin. Papa arranged our bed to be softer and mama and I went to bed on the same cot.

Since their cabin was in the stern at the bottom of the vessel, they felt every movement, and the ship rocked violently. For nearly two full days, Lydia and her mother remained in the same cot in their cabin, unable to walk or even sit comfortably due to the constant rocking. At night, the rocking was even worse, and Lydia was very frightened. They even missed their meals, and on one occasion, the motion was so bad that Lydia vomited.

Wednesday, May 31, 1922:

Today at 10 o'clock in the evening we were at the halfway mark so that we have only 4 more days [on the ship].

I admire Lydia's meticulous nature; she even recorded the precise time they reached their halfway point on their ocean voyage. This is something I can see myself doing. Her attention to detail is truly remarkable, and through this project, I am more certain than ever that I inherited this trait from my maternal grandmother. To me, it is both a blessing and a curse. The satisfaction of making a major discovery is immense, but I often can't move forward without first finding the exact information I am after.

Midway through their trip, the weather finally improved, calming the rough seas and allowing them to explore the ship more freely. One day, while they were on the deck, Lydia and the other passengers spotted what appeared to be a whale! She further described the sight as a "...*spout of water and something black in the water.*"

Excitement grew among the passengers as they approached New York on June 4. Lydia purchased souvenirs being sold by a man walking around the ship, including a postcard of the *La Savoie* and a flower pin with a miniature view of the ship encased in glass. After the last day's fog, it had finally lifted, heightening the anticipation. Lydia even thought she had spotted the shore, but was disappointed to find out they were still relatively far away. Around 9 pm, Lydia saw a lighthouse, and everyone gathered on deck, hoping to get a glimpse of the big city lights. A tugboat met the pilot ship and began to guide it steadily into the harbor. A *"mass of lights"* then came into view, almost glowing. Lydia's heart raced with excitement! Unfortunately, all the passengers were soon instructed to return to their cabins, as they would need to wake at four in the morning to begin the disembarkation process.

On June 5, 1922, they arrived in New York City!

Today was such a happy one for me that I cannot describe it.

After many inspections and delays, they were allowed to disembark at Ellis Island, and after an inspection by the doctor, they were allowed to leave. This is where Uncle Kostya met them, and they took a motor launch together to New York City. I never realized that Lydia probably had never met her Uncle Kostya before, or if she had, she was very young. Her first impressions of him:

> *I expected Uncle Kostya to be completely different from what I imagined: he had no mustache and he is completely American.*

Constantine, or Uncle Kostya, immigrated to the United States in October 1912 aboard the *SS Birma,* which sailed from Libau, Russian Empire (present day Liepāja, Latvia), and had been living in Manhattan ever since. Unlike Lydia's family, he returned for a visit to Odessa in 1929. Despite her uncle's visit, it remains unclear why Lydia never returned to Odessa.

Lydia's diaries continue until September 1, 1924, with her entries becoming slightly more detailed and expressive compared to her earlier entries. She even integrated English words as she learned the language. She fully embraced her new life in New York City and never once regretted leaving Odessa. While she missed her extended family there terribly, I do not believe she ever considered returning. Lydia was never to return to the Russia she had once called home.

PART II

Malta

CHAPTER 16

Troubles in Malta

When starting this project, one of the burning questions was: What happened to the *Kherson* and its inhabitants after the Komarkoffs left the ship? Truthfully, I did not expect to find those answers. However, I soon learned that the ship sailed to Malta and that the Anikeeff family spent time there. This newly gained information sparked my curiosity, leaving me with far more questions than I had before.

Since departing Crimea on November 14, 1920, the *Kherson* had been plagued with severe financial difficulties. In the Bay of Kotor in March 1921,[72] the ship accumulated a debt of 100,000 dinars[73] for provisions - essential items such as food, water, and supplies needed to

---

72   Государственный архив Российской Федерации (ГАРФ). Ф. Р-6817. Русский Военно-Морской агент в Королевстве Сербов, Хорватов и Словенцев. Белград. Оп.1. Русский военно-морской агент в КСХС. Белград. Д.3. Переписка с комендантом парохода белогвардейского добровольческого флота «Херсон», с белогвардейским военным агентом в Королевстве С. Х. С. и другими о прибытии пароходов в заграничные порты и отправке их с военными грузами в Крым для белогвардейской армии ген. Врангеля. 1920-1922. Л.27 / The State Archives of the Russian Federation (SARF, Moscow). Fund P-6817. The Russian Naval Agent in the Kingdom of Serbs, Croats and Slovenes. Belgrade. Inv.1. Russian naval agent in the KSCS. Belgrade. File 3. Correspondence with the commandant of the White Guard Volunteer Fleet steamship "Kherson", with the White Guard military agent in the Kingdom of S.C.S. and others about the arrival of steamships in foreign ports and their dispatch with military cargo to the Crimea for the White Guard army of General Wrangel. 1920-1922. P.27.

73   Approximately $2000 at the time, if the exchange rate at the time was about 50 dinars per US dollar.

maintain the ship's operation. The ship lacked the necessary funds to pay the suppliers in Zelenika to receive these items.

On April 14, 1921, the situation was so dire that the crew refused to work unless they were given food. Captain Schmelz wrote a letter, out of extreme desperation, to the Managing Director of the Volunteer Fleet:[74]

Today the supplier stopped delivering food. There is nothing to feed the crew.

The deck and engine crews refused to perform ship work due to lack of food.

The elected representatives of the crew declare that they will continue working if they are given food until May 6th, and on the days when food is given, they will work. The crew requests that the maintenance due to them for six months be paid by May 6, or they will be forced to finally stop all work.

Reporting the above, I ask you to petition the Board to send an authorized member of the Board to meet all the needs of the crew of the steamship, which is currently in a dire situation.

The steamship captain Schmelz

The *Kherson* was transferred from the Volunteer Fleet to the English company, London Steamship and Trading Company, at the end of April

---

74   The State Archives of the Russian Federation. F. P-6817. Inv.1. File 3. P.6.
(translated from Russian)

1921,[75] which was a conditional sale.[76] It flew under the English flag and was renamed *"Raetoria"* on June 15, 1921. Lydia writes an entry in her diary on this date further confirming this.

Wednesday, June 15, 1921

Today I was on the deck until breakfast. After breakfast it rained and I went into the cabin, and I read, sewed, and helped mama. And that is how I spent a boring day. Today an English flag was hung. Kherson is now called Raetoria.

In Figure 39, the lifebuoy reflects the name change from *Kherson* to *Raetoria*, indicating that the photo was taken after June 15, 1921, when the ship was renamed. Michael Anikeeff (7) is seated in white, wearing a white hat and holding a young child. To his left is Chief Engineer Truen (6). The slightly blurred little girl standing, I believe, is Katya. The man sitting on the deck to the left of the *Raetoria* lifebuoy, wearing a suit, is possibly the artist Arseny Petrovich Sosnovskij. This identification is based on a comparison with another known photo of him, though it remains a guess. If it is, in fact, him, I would guess the time frame to be between June 15 and October 6, 1921, while the ship was still anchored in the Bay of Kotor, as he was documented living in Herceg Novi in Montenegro. Many of the men in this photo appear in other photographs we have; however, their identities remain uncertain. I hope to discover who the rest of these sailors are one day!

---

75 Российский государственный исторический архив. Ф.98. Оп.6. Д.353. Пароходное общество "Добровольный флот". Переписка с Лондонской пароходной и торговой корпорацией по эксплуатации пароходов "Тверь", "Херсон", "Саратов". Том 3 и последний. 17-30 ноября 1921 г. Л.98 / The Russian State Historical Archives. F.98. Inv.6. File 353. The Steamship company "Volunteer fleet". Correspondence with the London Steamship and Trading Corporation on the operation of steamships "Tver", "Kherson", "Saratov". Volume 3, the last one. November 17-30, 1921. P.98.

76 The State Archives of the Russian Federation. F. P-6817. Inv.1. File 3. P.20-20back.

Figure 39: Crew members of the Raetoria (formerly the Kherson) on deck.
Courtesy of the Anikeeff Family.

On July 30, 1921, Lydia noted that her father was finally paid, just days before they departed the *Kherson* permanently. That money was essential for them to survive.

> *Today papa, thank God, received his salary and we were*
> *very happy.*

Lydia never wrote about the financial struggles the *Kherson* experienced. It is unclear if she was kept in the dark about these challenges or if she simply chose not to mention them. I feel the adults shielded the children from the hardships to protect their innocence. She mentioned on several occasions that her father went ashore to purchase supplies, which suggests that it may have been one of his roles on the ship.

The *Kherson/Raetoria* continued to experience financial disputes and negotiations through September 1921, with no end in sight. Due to insufficient funds, the ship could not release the 25 crew members it was trying to discharge. Among them, Chief Mate Semenopulo (2) and Third

Assistant Engineer Guibner (9) had to continue to Malta, despite wanting to stay behind in Zelenika.[77]

Initially slated to leave the Bay of Kotor on Thursday, September 15, 1921,[78] the ship's departure date was now delayed until October 6, 1921, due to disputes over the crew's wages. An agreement was made between the crew and the British company that upon arrival in Malta, the sailors would finally receive their overdue wages.

Previously holding a high rank in the Russian Navy, and later commandant of the *Kherson* from December 6, 1920, until October 1921, Viktor Borsuk documented the struggles of the Russian officers of the ship by writing letters to the Russian Naval Agent in the Kingdom of Serbs, Croats, and Slovenes. He viewed the ship's sale to the English firm skeptically, deemed it controversial, and believed it was part of a "dirty, dark transaction." While attempting to safeguard Russian interests, he faced resistance from the crew aboard, including Captain Schmelz.

He was excluded from the crew list, denied food provisions, and ultimately lost control of the ship. When the *Kherson/Raetoria* sailed to Malta, he was forced to go ashore in Zelenika. He lamented its departure:

On October 6, at 2 pm, the former Kherson, now Raetoria–
Russia plunged into darkness – set out to sea.

—Captain 1st Rank V. Borsuk[79]

---

77 Российский государственный исторический архив. Ф.98. Оп.6. Д.351. Пароходное общество "Добровольный флот". Переписка с Лондонской пароходной и торговой корпорацией по эксплуатации пароходов "Тверь", "Херсон", "Саратов". Том 1. 28 июля - 23 сентября 1921 г. Л.77 / The Russian State Historical Archives. F.98. Inv.6. File 351. The Steamship company "Volunteer fleet". Correspondence with the London Steamship and Trading Corporation on the operation of steamships "Tver", "Kherson", "Saratov". Volume 1. July 28 – September 23, 1921. P.77.

78 The Russian State Historical Archives. F.98. Inv.6. File 351. P.79.

79 The State Archives of the Russian Federation. F. P-6817. Inv.1. File 3. P.5-7back.

On October 27, 1921, having arrived in Malta, the situation escalated further. The British Company was unable to fulfill its promise of paying the sailors, and by November 30, 1921, things were still not resolved. The captain and the crew took legal action and sued the London Steamship and Trading Corporation for not paying them.[80] By February 13, 1922, the court ruled in favor of the *Kherson/Raetoria* crew and issued an order for the sale of the ship.

After many negotiations between various organizations, the Maltese government, out of humanitarian concern, provided the temporary assistance to these Russian sailors and their families, which consisted of 62 officers and sailors, 17 wives and children.[81]

As of this writing, we do not know the exact date when the *Kherson/Raetoria* was sold, because we could not access the final documents of this sale. However, a crucial clue about the sale of the ship was discovered in a postcard sent by Elizaveta Ivanovna Malyavina to the Komarkoffs in Novi Sad, revealing that the auction for the vessel was scheduled for April 24, 1922.

---

80 The Russian State Historical Archives. F.98. Inv.6. File 353. P.31, 109; Appropriation Books (Malta): https://www.crewlist.org.uk/data/vesselsnum? officialnumber=137746&submit=searchb https://www.crewlist.org.uk/data/ appropriation?officialnumber=137746 (in the bottom)

81 Malta and Russia: Journey through the centuries: Hist. discoveries in Russo - Maltese relations / Comp. a. ed. with introd. by Elizaveta Zolina. - [Valetta], Cop. 2002 / Путешествие через века : исторические открытия в российско-мальтийских отношениях : [перевод с английского] / сост., ред. и авт. предисл.: Елизавета Золина. - Москва : ЦГО, 2005. P.226-227.

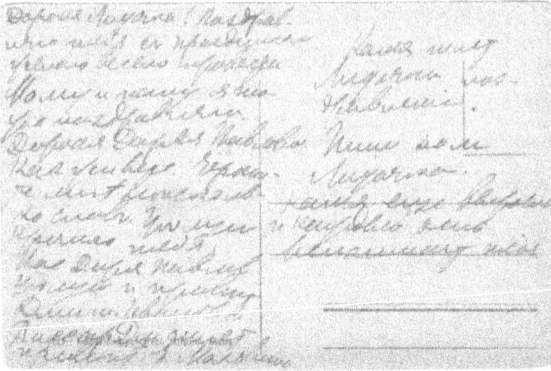

Figure 40: Back of a postcard featuring a message from the Malyavina family to Lydia's mother, Daria. Courtesy of the Buzyna Family.

Figure 41: Front of a postcard from the Malyavina family to Lydia's mother, Daria. Courtesy of the Buzyna Family.

Translation of this postcard:

Dear Daria Pavlovna

Christ is Risen!

Have a good Easter. We are still out of money. It is unknown when the end will be. The auction is scheduled for April 24. I have news from Odessa: ours are all healthy. Write. I kiss you tightly.

Greetings from Vissarion Dmitrievich to you and Dmitry Ivanovich.

As of January 1923, only seven members of the crew remained in Malta,[82] Michael Anikeeff was one of them, and they all planned to leave soon.

At some point in 1923, the *Kherson/Raetoria* was sold to the Italian mechanical manufacturing company, Societa Italiana Ernesto Breda, in Milan, and in 1924, the ship was dismantled and scrapped for metal in Venice.[83]

Did the crew receive the wages they deserved? And those who left Malta, where did they go? Many questions still remain. Perhaps, in time, the missing details will emerge, allowing us to complete this intricate puzzle.

---

82 Malta and Russia… / Путешествие через века… 2005. P.227.

83 Яровой В.В. Добровольный флот. СПб.: Галея-Принт, 2010. С.66 / Yarovoy V. V. The Volunteer Fleet. Saint Petersburg: Galeya Print, 2010. P.66.

CHAPTER 17

The *Kherson* Families in Malta

Another question emerged: Now that we know how many crew members were in Malta, who specifically were they? How would I figure this out without a documented list? Reviewing the information from the Komarkoff and Anikeeff families, I can confidently start making my own list, though it will be very short.

Lydia kept cherished postcards from her *Kherson* friends confirming that Zhenia, Katya, and Uncle Skochemaro (50) spent time in Malta. The Anikeeff family preserved many photos from their time in Malta, having spent nearly two years there. While Michael continued to attend to his duties related to the *Kherson* and the turmoil surrounding it, his family endured another period of exile, much like Lydia and her family in Yugoslavia, but instead on the small, British-controlled island of Malta, which may explain why the *Kherson* ultimately ended up there.

Perhaps this photo (Figure 43) was taken at the refugee barracks where they stayed, or perhaps they stayed aboard the ship while it was still docked in the harbor. The Anikeeff Family is pictured here with other crew members of the ship. From left to right, the three children in the front are Kolya, Alyosha, and Zhenia. I do not know who the little girl with the hat is, or the lady who is holding her hand. Standing against the railing are Michael and his wife, Anna Ivanovna. I recognize the other two men, but cannot confidently identify them.

Figure 42: Postcard depicting the port of Valletta, Malta.
Courtesy of the Anikeeff Family.

Figure 43: The Anikeeff children standing in front, left to right: Kolya,
Alyosha, and Zhenia. At the top left is Michael Anikeeff with his wife Anna
Ivanovna. The man on the far right is possibly Vissarian Malyavin. Malta,
circa 1921-1922. Courtesy of the Anikeeff Family.

Postcards sent to family members often contain valuable clues about their lives, leaving it up to us to decipher these hidden nuggets of information. Lydia received several postcards from her *Kherson* friends staying in Malta. A postcard from Zhenia, sent to Lydia in Novi Sad:

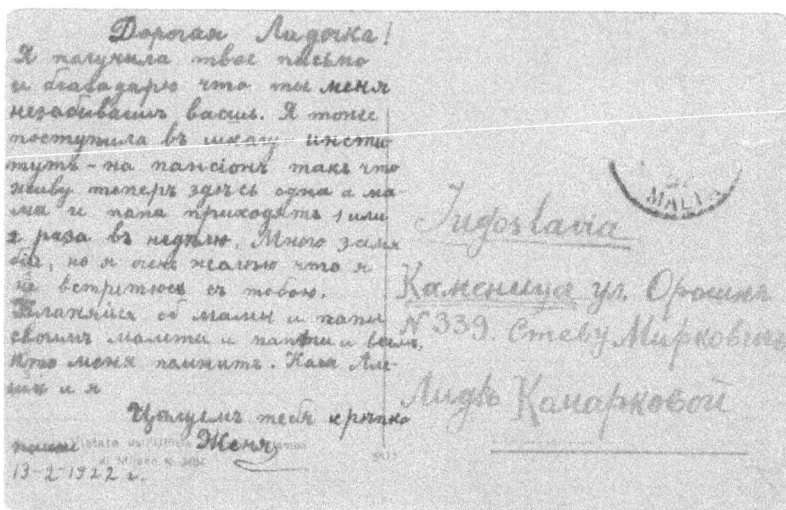

Figure 44 (above): Back of a postcard from Zhenia to Lydia, dated February 13, 1922. Courtesy of the Buzyna Family.

Figure 45 (right): Front of a postcard featuring a handwritten message from Zhenia to Lydia, February 13, 1922. Courtesy of the Buzyna Family.

Translation:

Dear Lidochka!

I've received your letter, and I thank you for not forgetting me. I've also entered a boarding school, so now I live here alone,

*and my mom and dad come (to me) 1 or 2 times a week.
There are a lot of classes [at school], but I really regret that
I won't meet you. From my mom and dad, bow to your mom
and dad and everyone who remembers me.*

Kolya, Alyosha and I kiss you warmly. Write. Zhenia

February 13, 1922

The most interesting detail extracted from this postcard is the address, which pinpoints where the Komarkoffs lived in Novi Sad. Unfortunately, the street name must have been changed, making it challenging to find the current location. To uncover its exact location, I may need to travel to Sremska Kamenica and consult with the local archives for records of the Oroshitch street—another location to add to my bucket list.

While in Malta, Zhenia attended a local Roman Catholic boarding school, while her brothers were enrolled at the British Boys' School. It is unclear why the children attended boarding schools during their stay. Did their parents remain on the ship? Were they housed in the refugee barracks or the naval dockyard facilities? A visit to the archives in Valletta may provide more answers to these lingering questions.

This postcard (Figure 46, 47), of the Anikeeff children, sent from Malta to Lydia in the United States, is dated December 21, 1922. They are dressed in elegant sailor suits, similar to the one Lydia cherished.

Through my newfound connection with the Anikeeff descendants, I discovered that one of the crew members, Electrician Nicholai Vladimir Pavlovich Gazenbush (63), passed away in Malta at age sixty. Zhenia's granddaughter, Susan, held onto these photographs for years, unsure of their location - possibly Malta, she thought - and whose grave was this? The tombstone inscription was in Russian, which she could not read. When she shared these photos with me, I eagerly put on my detective hat and used my Russian knowledge to decipher the name on the gravesite, which led me to an incredible discovery!

Figure 46 (left): Left to right: Alyosha, Zhenia, and Kolya Anikeeff. Postcard sent from the Anikeeff children in Malta to Lydia. Courtesy of the Buzyna Family.

Figure 47 (below): Back of the postcard featuring the Anikeeff children, with a short note on the right side that reads, "Remember and Love!" Courtesy of the Buzyna Family.

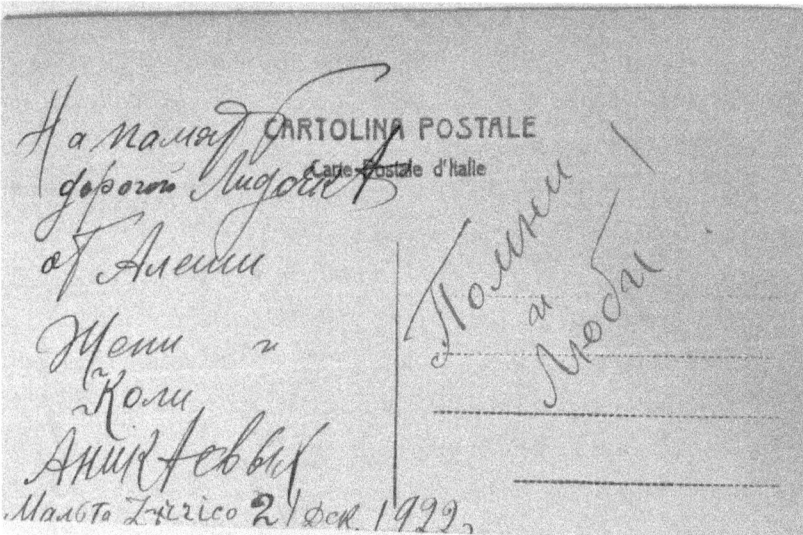

I instantly read the name, Gazenbush, and soon found a more recent photograph of the same tombstone on the Find-a-Grave website. This discovery led me to connect with the person overseeing the graves at the Ta'Braxia Cemetery in Valletta, Malta, where he is buried. She shared additional details and photographs about the gravesite and cemetery, and how it was recently cleaned up. In 2015, a memorial regatta was held. Gazenbush was honored by a flower laying ceremony at his grave, and then later an emotional lowering of wreaths into the ocean commemorating all the fallen sailors.

Figure 48 (above): Crews members attend the funeral of fellow Kherson crew member Nicholai Vladimir Pavlovich Gazenbush (63). Malta, March 1922. Courtesy of the Anikeeff Family.

Figure 49 (right): Gravestone of Nicholai Vladimir Pavlovich Gazenbush (63). Courtesy of the Anikeeff Family.

A photo (Figure 48) of his burial shows what is unmistakably the remaining crew members of the *Kherson* gathered by his gravesite.

Translation of the tombstone (Figure 49):

In Memory of
Nikolai Vladimir Pavlovich
GAZENBUSH
Born 4 December 1862
Died 3 March 1922
Who served as a mine warfare specialist on the ships of the
Russian
Volunteer Navy from 1891 to 1922
From the crew of the Volunteer Fleet ship
"KHERSON"
"PEACE TO YOUR ASHES"

Gazenbush continued his service aboard the steamship *Kherson* after it departed the Bay of Kotor on October 6, 1921, until it arrived in Malta on October 27, 1921. He died on March 3, 1922.

Compiling a list of crew members in Malta will be a task for another time. Like all genealogy projects, they are never truly complete.

PART III

Research

CHAPTER 18
Why Research?

Why research your family history? For me, exploring my genealogy has been a deeply rewarding experience of self-discovery. Learning about my ancestors has helped me understand who I am, offering a sense of identity and belonging. It has grounded me and given me more confidence in the person I am today.

My research has strengthened my connection to my Russian, Ukrainian, and Finnish roots. I have developed a greater appreciation for the cultures and traditions that shaped my family. The stories passed down by my grandparents are treasures, and I feel a responsibility to preserve them so that future generations can understand where they come from, long after I am gone. I often wonder, will any of my children, nieces, or nephews one day feel this same passion for our family's past?

How do you decide where to begin? With so many possible directions, it often comes down to what resonates most with you. Maybe you have an ancestor who was forced to flee their beloved homeland during wartime? Or perhaps a relative whose courage in overcoming immense challenges helped shape your family's identity? You might notice personality traits or behaviors that echo across generations? Or maybe you're starting from scratch, with just a name on a document, unsure where it will lead.

What began for me as an effort to write a book based on my grandmother's diaries became something much greater. Lydia's story is not only a family legacy but a powerful narrative of survival, freedom, and resilience. While her diaries were fascinating from a historical standpoint, I was also drawn to this research because I never felt particularly close to Lydia. I often felt so different from her. I hoped that by delving into her story, I might challenge, or even debunk, those assumptions.

As I explored, I reflected on the immense struggles my grandparents, my great-grandparents, and their families endured during the Russian Revolution, World War I, and World War II. Lydia always embodied remarkable steadiness and strength, which likely came down generations before her and passed down like heirlooms.

On my father's side, the story is equally powerful. He and his family fled Russia during World War II on what was literally the last train out of their village in what is now western Ukraine. His fate could have been drastically different. Their train passed by Auschwitz, almost stopping. Instead, they were brought to a displaced persons camp in Ingolstadt, Germany, where they lived for five years. At age twelve, my father immigrated to the United States, not speaking English or knowing anything about American culture. His persistence and strong work ethic, most likely inherited from his ancestors, carried him through. He earned a PhD in mechanical engineering and served as a university professor for many years. Like Lydia, he, too, exudes stability and determination. I cannot help but wonder if anyone on my father's side kept a diary? Is there a written record waiting to be uncovered?

Researching these stories has helped me feel closer to those who came before me. If you embark on your own family history journey, be prepared for the unexpected; you never know what stories will be revealed.

The incredible journey of researching my grandmother's life through her diaries has been filled with profound discoveries, meaningful challenges, and surprises I never could have predicted. Join me as I share the highs and lows of what I found.

CHAPTER 19
Research Team

What happens once you have identified the family history project that you want to pursue? How do you approach a task that can feel both daunting and overwhelming?

Researching your family history is an emotional whirlwind – tedious, fascinating, frustrating, gratifying, heartwarming, heartbreaking, time-consuming, exhaustive, nostalgic, and ultimately, transformative. Over the past 25 years of diving into my family's past, I have experienced every one of these emotions, and then some!

Before going any further, you must realize it cannot be done alone. Assembling a research team is essential to uncovering and preserving your own family story. Before reaching out to potential collaborators, clarify your project's goals. What do you hope to achieve? What do you want to discover? What is the end result you envision? These are just a few questions I ask myself at the start of any new research endeavor.

Where do you find a team of researchers? Start with your own family. Look for relatives who are already curious or might be intrigued if you share an exciting discovery. Don't be discouraged if no one shows interest initially – sometimes all it takes is one compelling story to spark someone's curiosity. Once they get a glimpse of the richness of your family history, they might become just as invested as you are!

But don't stop at your family. Your local library, genealogy societies, or even online communities can be tremendous resources. One of my favorite tools has been Facebook groups. There's a group for nearly every area of genealogy research. Chances are, someone else is working through the same challenges as you are. I've not only received invaluable advice in these groups, but I've also made some wonderful friends along the way.

I often think of myself as the CEO of this significant family history project. My research team consists of my mother, Helen, a distant relative who contributed valuable archival research, and later, Susan, granddaughter of Lydia's best friend on the *Kherson*. Each of us brings our own specialized skills and dedication. While we haven't yet hired a professional genealogist to assist with our research, we're open to doing so if we hit a major roadblock. For now, our amateur efforts have taken us surprisingly far!

If we ever need professional help, it's easy to find. Ancestry.com, for instance, has a green button labeled "Hire an Expert" option that connects you with skilled professionals through their AncestryProGenealogists website. Thanks to my involvement in various Facebook genealogy groups, I also have contacts I could call upon if more help is needed.

The Research Team Broken Down: Tamara - Granddaughter of Lydia

For the past 25 years, I have been the driving force behind many of our family history projects, having taken over the research from my mother. We work closely together, exchanging every detail of our discoveries, and I can always count on her to share the excitement of our findings. As a largely self-taught genealogist, I have made some remarkable break-throughs in our family history. Still, none of it would be possible without the support of my dedicated team. Being my mother's daughter, following in her footsteps came naturally. Going "down the rabbit hole" into the depths of our ancestry is something we genuinely bond over, and it has only strengthened our relationship.

I was born and raised in Tallahassee, Florida. Thanks to my parents and grandparents, I grew up deeply connected to my Russian heritage, culture, and religion. My family was slightly larger than my mother's, including five first cousins, two aunts, two uncles, and three grandparents. My immediate family consisted of my mother, my father George, and my younger brother Peter. We visited with our grandparents regularly, all of whom were of Russian or Ukrainian heritage.

With my grandmother Lydia, we primarily spoke English, and I never detected an accent, but others did. Her devotion to the Russian Orthodox faith ran deep, and attending church together with her was expected. Her home was filled with icons, trinkets, and memorabilia that reflected her heritage.

She lost her husband, my maternal grandfather, to a fatal stroke 20 years after they married in 1940. I was born nine years later and never saw her openly grieve. To me, she always maintained a stoic and resilient demeanor. It wasn't until I read a letter she wrote two months after his passing that I saw a more vulnerable side. "I am behaving well, and sometimes out of nowhere I start to cry, then I feel better," she confessed. It was a rare and unexpected glimpse into her inner world.

As I grew older, like my mother before me, I became increasingly curious about our ancestors from Russia and Eastern Europe. I never imagined that one day I would have 1095 names in my family tree!

My spark for genealogy ignited unexpectedly. In December 2004, at my husband's paternal grandfather's funeral, I spoke with one of my husband's uncles about their parents' immigration from Europe. I was fascinated by their story and came home determined to trace their family's roots. His Eastern Slavic grandparents were also Eastern (Russian) Orthodox and had attended the Orthodox Church of America (OCA) in Stamford, Connecticut. His family had been in the United States longer than mine, and there were quite a few of them, so I thought researching his family would be "easier" and less complicated than researching my family.

At the time, I had a toddler and little free time, but I still managed to carve out moments to dive into my husband's Carpatho-Rusyn lineage. When I first met Melania, my husband's grandmother, in 1999, she hugged me warmly, smiled, and said, "You are one of us." That simple gesture meant everything. Our shared faith and cultural traditions created an immediate bond. It felt like meeting a long-lost relative.

Although the connection was not biological, the emotional tie was undeniable. However, I couldn't help feeling like something was missing. There is a unique sense of fulfillment that comes from knowing you are connected to someone through shared bloodlines. That depth of identity and belonging can't be fully replicated.

I met many of my husband's distant cousins, many of them fellow genealogy enthusiasts, through Facebook groups. I even met a fifth cousin in person when she visited Tallahassee! Thanks to their guidance, I soaked up everything I could about research techniques: how to read Latin church records, trace family trees, and identify a Most Recent Common Ancestor (MRCA).

I had nearly given up on researching my own bloodline. Exploring my husband's family helped satisfy that itch to piece together a larger story. I would give my mother daily updates, gushing about my discoveries, even though they weren't from my side of the family. Being straightforward like her mother, my mother finally asked, "When are you going to start researching *our* family?"

And thus began my quest to discover *my* ancestral roots…

Helen - Lydia's Daughter; and My Mother

My mother, Helen, was born in New York City in 1941 and grew up in a two-story beige house on Regent Street in Schenectady, New York. A prominent brick chimney at the front of the house is a detail that has stayed with me since my childhood visits.

Her paternal grandparents, George and Anna, lived nearby until they died in 1945 and 1946. Her maternal grandparents, Dmitri and Daria, lived in New York City until old age made independent living impossible, passing in 1957 and 1959. Her father, Vladimir Georgievich, studied at the Institute of Ways and Means of Transport Communication (Ingenerov

Putei Soobshcheniya) in St. Petersburg, Russia, and immigrated to the United States from Finland in 1923. He worked as an engineer at General Electric until his sudden death in 1960. His younger sister Sonya immigrated from Finland two years after him, in 1925, accompanied by their mother Anna. Their father, George, immigrated in 1929. Her brother, also named George, was born five years after her. Together, they formed the small but close family she knew.

That core family was expanded by a tight-knit community of Russian immigrants, many of whom also worked at General Electric. Among them were the Diakoffs, one of many connections we would later realize ran deeper than expected. As I immersed myself in Lydia's diary research, I uncovered an astonishing fact: Alexis Ivanovich Diakoff, the husband of Lydia's best friend in Schenectady, had also evacuated from Sevastopol on the same historic day – November 14, 1920. His son Harry and I still marvel over this mind-blowing coincidence.

My mother played a crucial role in this entire research process. As Lydia's daughter, she had unique insight and direct access to documents, photographs, and treasured mementos her mother left behind. Though she was raising a family and working full-time, she still took the time to organize everything with care and intention. She may not have had the bandwidth to dive deeply into genealogy research then, but thanks to her thoroughness, I had a solid foundation to build upon.

As I explained DNA matches and cousin terminology to my mother, like "third cousin twice removed," my mother admitted she had never known any cousins. Her mother was an only child (we later discovered that Lydia may have had a half-sibling from her father's first marriage), and her father's only sibling never married or had children. For Helen, cousins were a mystery; if any existed, they were likely far beyond her reach in Finland, Russia, or Ukraine. How would she ever find them? And if she did, she would be eager to meet them!

As DNA matches began to surface from those regions, mostly third to fifth cousins, she often reflected on how much she had longed for a bigger family. She was grateful for her close-knit upbringing, but always wished for cousins to play with.

One of her earliest steps in this research process was reaching out to older relatives who might remember "the old times." A simple question, like asking an elder family member, "What village did my great-great-grandparents come from?" can be key to locating vital records in an archive. With help from her mother, who still had old addresses, my mother mailed a handwritten family tree to a first cousin once removed (her mother's first cousin) she had never met, in the 1990s. He returned it by snail mail, updated with names and notes, an old-school collaboration that marked the beginning of something much bigger.

That effort came full circle in 1999 when, at age 58, my mother finally fulfilled a lifelong dream of meeting her bloodline cousins for the first time! It was a powerful, emotional trip. She even met the very cousin who had helped expand the family tree.

Her connection to Russian History and Culture has remained strong throughout her life. She didn't speak English until kindergarten and still speaks fluent Russian today. She earned a Bachelor of Fine Arts in Russian Language and Literature from Connecticut College with a minor in art. Later, she completed a Master of Fine Arts in graphic design at Yale.

Between those two degrees, she had an experience that profoundly shaped her life and deepened her connection with her roots. From September 1963 to May 1964, she participated in the United States Information Agency traveling graphic arts exhibit traveling through the former Soviet Union, spending two to three months in each city: Alma-Ata, Moscow, Yerevan, and Leningrad (current day St. Petersburg). She had to write a letter of qualification and pass a panel interview to be selected. At just 22 years old, she represented American fine and commercial art and answered questions from the curious Soviet visitors.

One of the most unforgettable moments of that trip was working alongside none other than American painter Norman Rockwell, who joined the exhibit in Moscow for three weeks. My mother described him as humble and down-to-earth. She often translated questions from the

Soviet visitors for him, like, "How much do you get paid for a painting?" She recalls him politely asking to borrow a pencil or wondering if she minded where he set up his easel.

One day, he asked her to model for him, and within half an hour, he captured her likeness in a beautiful portrait. The painting shows her in profile wearing a soft green sweater, her expression serene and thoughtful. With its warm tones and delicate brushstrokes, the piece hung in our home for many years and is now part of a cherished family collection. After returning to the United States, he called her mother, Lydia, to ask where he should send the portrait of her. Caught off guard, it took her a moment to realize it was *the* Norman Rockwell on the phone!

After completing her nine-month assignment in the Soviet Union in May 1964, my mother did not head straight home like the others. True to her independent spirit, she traveled solo through Scandinavia for several months. She eagerly exchanged her return flight for a ticket aboard the "world's fastest ocean liner," the *SS United States.* She boarded in Le Havre, France, and arrived in New York City five days later. This wasn't just on a whim; it was a deliberate choice to mirror her mother's immigration voyage from 1922. The decision perfectly captivated her character: adventurous, independent, deeply connected to her heritage – qualities I also recognize in myself. It's deeply reassuring to understand where that drive comes from.

Growing up, my mother often heard Lydia's stories about the *Kherson,* the *La Savoie*, and life in Novi Sad, Serbia. By age thirteen, Lydia had already lived through more adventures than many do in a lifetime. My mother inherited that same thirst for discovery. She didn't just welcome opportunity, she sought it out. Now in her 80s, she can honestly say she has "traveled the world." Like her mother, she lived a life full of meaningful and unforgettable adventures. And that same enduring spirit lives on in her, and in me.

Susan - Granddaughter of Lydia's best friend on the *Kherson*

Connecting with Susan was one of those unexpected gems that emerged from my research of Lydia's diaries. She is the granddaughter of Zhenia Anikeeff, Lydia's closest friend aboard the *Kherson*, and the great-grand-daughter of Zhenia's father, Michael Anikeeff, who served as one of the ship's crew members. The bond between Lydia and Zhenia made the connection between their granddaughters feel almost destined.

We did not meet in person until April 2022. On a whim, I decided to reach out while planning a trip to my daughter's winter guard competition. I had emailed Susan just a few days before, letting her know that my daughter, her friend, her mother, and I would be driving through her area. I suggested we meet for lunch or dinner. Without hesitation, Susan replied with warmth and generosity: "You are invited for dinner at our home and to spend the night, your friend and daughter as well." Despite never having met in person and only having known each other through emails and phone calls for two years, her invitation felt like one from a long-lost relative. I graciously accepted immediately.

That visit was more than just a meal or stopover – it was a moment of profound connection. Susan and I bonded instantly, our conversations filled with stories, discoveries, and a shared sense of wonder about our grandmothers' lives. We quickly realized that what connected us wasn't just family history but also a mutual passion for preserving and under-standing it. It felt as if Lydia and Zhenia guided us, communicating through their granddaughters to ensure their stories would be remembered.

Although the descendants of the Anikeeff family did not preserve the Russian Language, they upheld their Russian heritage through the arts, particularly dance. The newly immigrated Anikeeffs found joy and iden-tity in performing traditional Russian folk dances. Adorning colorful and ornate traditional costumes, Zhenia performed with the Russian Dance Troupe in Detroit, Michigan, during the 1920s and early 1930s. Through those performances, she passed down a sense of cultural pride that still echoes in the family today.

Susan became the Anikeeff family's historian and was the guardian of many priceless photographs, documents, and memories of her grandmother's journey. She had carefully saved these treasures for decades but hadn't fully explored their meaning. When I reached out in 2020, those long-preserved items suddenly came alive again, becoming essential puzzle pieces in our efforts to reconstruct life aboard the *Kherson*.

Wanting to ensure these materials were preserved and easily accessible, I meticulously organized Susan's documents into a three-ring binder with page protectors, scanned each document and photo, and uploaded them to the cloud. Seeing photographs I had never seen before was nothing short of exhilarating for both of us.

As we reflected on our grandmothers' shared journey aboard the *Kherson*, it struck us: *exactly* 100 years had passed since their final departure from Russia and the rediscovery of Lydia's diaries. This didn't feel like a coincidence, but a calling. Their voices had waited patiently to be heard again.

Figure 50: Susan with Tamara in New York City, November 2024. Tamara gave a presentation to 14 descendants of the Anikeeff family – whose relatives were aboard the Kherson with her grandmother. Courtesy of the Adams Family.

In November 2024, we gathered in New York City with other descendants of the Anikeeff family. As we stood in Times Square beneath the giant digital billboard featuring the cover of *Last Ship to Freedom*, we were overwhelmed with emotion. (Figure 51).

Figure 51: Three generations of Anikeeff descendants in Times Square as Tamara's book cover is displayed. Left to right: Nate, Pam, Susan, Tamara, Leslie, Tess, and Michael. Courtesy of Hannah Duncan Photography.

CHAPTER 20

Coming up with a Timeline of Events

Once my research team was in place, we set out to reconstruct a timeline of our ancestors' journey aboard the *Kherson*. How did I piece together all this information when Lydia didn't even begin her diaries until after she had already spent a whole year aboard the *Kherson*? It took relentless effort – sweat, tears, and plenty of digging! There were more questions than answers in the beginning, but persistence gradually revealed the story hidden between the lines.

It is almost impossible to grasp just how little we initially knew about their time on the *Kherson*, and how far we've come since then. Before translating even the first page of the LDK Diaries, this was all we knew:

What my family knew:

- Lydia lived on the steamship *Kherson* in the Black Sea for a year
- She wrote a diary
- She had extremely curly hair
- She witnessed horses swimming into the sea
- Her father worked on a ship as a purser and often traveled to the Far East

What the Anikeeff family knew:

- Michael Anikeeff and crew stole the steamship *Kherson* from the Russian Navy
- They had two hours to gather their belongings

- They took their Singer sewing machine, samovar, and icons
- Survived using British coins, Michael earned from his Navy days
- They lived in Malta before eventually immigrating to the United States

Our Initial Unknowns:

- What were the specific dates they lived on the *Kherson*?
- Why did they leave Russia? What were their circumstances?
- Why were they on this particular vessel?
- Who else was traveling with them?
- When were the Anikeeffs in Malta? And Why Malta?
- What happened to the *Kherson* after everyone left?

Determining when and where the Komarkoff family boarded the ship seemed like the most logical place to start. We suspected they boarded in Odessa, but it was only a guess. And what about the Anikeeff family? When and where did they board the *Kherson*? Did Dimitri Komarkoff and Michael Anikeeff know each other before their time spent on the *Kherson*? Susan and I are convinced they did.

This uncertainty is difficult for me to accept. My perfectionist brain craves precise dates and tidy chronological sequences. Then another realization struck me: the date they boarded the *Kherson* might not align with the date it departed Odessa. I also wondered whether they remained on the same ship the entire time or initially evacuated on another vessel before transferring to the *Kherson* later. I suspected they had stayed on one ship throughout, but had no evidence to support this. The questions swirled in my mind like a whirling dervish, persistent and endless.

How would I ever find the answers?

In moments like these, it's easy to get caught up in dwelling on what's missing. But I've learned to refocus on what we *do* have. We are incredibly fortunate that my grandmother meticulously saved so many documents, letters, photos, and, of course, her diaries. I often wish I could go back in time and ask my grandmother questions about that time in her life while the memories were fresh in her mind. Lucky for me, and for this project, someone had already done that. She had, in fact, been interviewed. It wasn't by me, but at that point, I wouldn't be picky. I embraced this unexpected gift like a giddy schoolgirl.

Although I wasn't present for the interview, I could easily imagine the dusty brown tape recorder I had come to associate with conversations like these. Decades later, I found this very audio tape, carefully labeled and stored amongst other tapes in a small, clear container with a pink lid. As soon as I saw it, I felt a wave of anticipation. I could hardly wait to have it translated. Lydia had spoken in her native Russian, and I wondered which of my lingering questions she might have answered. Hearing her beautiful voice again was deeply emotional. With my heart pounding, I began to analyze every word as though my life depended on it, because in many ways, it did.

The contents of that interview, combined with documents from her memorabilia boxes, confirmed that Lydia and her family had, in fact, boarded the *Kherson* in Odessa. They had lived on the *Kherson* from the beginning and had been a part of the historic Crimean Evacuation led by General Wrangel. That interview was only the tip of the iceberg. The clues weren't always obvious, and I found myself reviewing the tape and a small, torn piece of paper with Lydia's handwritten notes multiple times before I could confirm even a few facts.

Know your history. Once I verified the Komarkoff family's connection to the Crimean Evacuation, I devoured everything I could find on the subject. Understanding the historical context helped explain why my family and many others spent over a year aboard a ship to escape the advancing Bolsheviks. Their prolonged time on the *Kherson* would have made little sense without this background knowledge.

Learning that General Peter Wrangel was the Commander-in-Chief who orchestrated the evacuation was a key discovery. I can't recall exactly how I stumbled across his memoirs,[84] but once I did, I read sections of them to understand the gravity of the situation better. His firsthand account provided essential depth to my research.

First-person accounts like his are a gold mine for genealogy and historical research. I found several memoirs online from individuals who had sailed on the *Kherson* or similar ships during the evacuation. Even a single sentence describing their experience held more emotional weight than reading an entire history textbook.

By connecting my family's story to these significant historical events, I was able to narrow in on specific record collections related to the evacuation. However, accessing those records wasn't easy, as they are stored in the Russian Archives, and viewing them required an in-person visit to their reading rooms. Thankfully, a distant relative of mine could access them on my behalf and discovered key information that helped us reconstruct that year aboard the *Kherson*, before Lydia's diaries even began.

Another valuable source was immigration records. If your ancestor arrived in the United States through Ellis Island, you could search its extensive database for passenger lists. I found multiple ship manifests, not only for the Komarkoffs and the Anikeeffs, but also for many of the *Kherson* crew members who eventually made their way to America.

Online Search Engines for Research:

The real research began once I had extracted every possible clue from Lydia's diaries and our family memorabilia. I developed a well-oiled system, meticulously investigating each name, location, or event mentioned in her writing. My go-to online research tools, used in this order, are Ancestry, MyHeritage, Family Search, and Google. Additionally, I used Newspapers, Genealogy Bank, Find-A-Grave, Find My Past, and Google Maps, among others.

---

84   Wrangel, Pyotr. Always with Honor. Edited by Alexandr Vatlin, translated by
      Sophie Lund, Russian Liberation Movement Historical Society, 1957.

I shared my grandmother's unyielding perseverance as I followed the small breadcrumbs she left behind in her carefully chosen words. I refused to give up, even when the odds were against me. Every few months, I revisited sources I had already combed through, hoping new information might have surfaced. Maybe, just maybe, this time I would finally discover that critical clue I had been searching for all along.

Case in point: I had developed a bit of an obsession with checking FamilySearch for newly updated records. One day in 2022, on a whim, I searched Lydia's mother's family name in its original Cyrillic spelling, "just for fun," something I had done countless times before. I slowly and carefully typed each letter, double-checking to ensure accuracy. With a deep breath, I clicked "search" and waited in suspense. Would this be the time something new appeared? Fingers crossed.

And there it was, a result I had never seen before. My heart pounded as I clicked on the listing for "Pavel Osipovich Vertsinsky." Could this record reveal the secrets of *my* second great-grandfather, Lydia's grandfather? I held my breath as the record loaded.

A basic translated summary of the record stared back at me on my computer screen. Could I view the full document, or was it only an index? I always hold my breath when clicking "view image of record," knowing full well it might be unavailable or require a trip to the nearest FamilySearch Center[85] to view it. For this record, I would have climbed mountains if I had to. Luckily, the image was viewable instantly from my desktop computer. Now came the real challenge: could I decipher a document written over 100 years ago in pre-Revolutionary Cyrillic script? To my amazement, the answer was a resounding yes.

This document turned out to be from the newly released 1897 Odessa Census. I had recently taught myself how to read Cyrillic cursive, an effort that paid off tremendously as I examined the beautifully

---

85 FamilySearch has libraries located throughout the country where you can conduct your own genealogy research on their computers and assistance from a volunteer if needed. These are associated with the main FamilySearch Library in Salt Lake City.

handwritten entries. I knew just enough Russian to confirm that this was indeed my family, but I had to rely on my native speaking relative to help interpret the finer details.

There she was, my great-grandmother Daria (Lydia's mother), 18 years old, living with her father, her mother, and two siblings. Not only did the census confirm their address, which corresponded with what we had, but it also revealed something extraordinary. Daria's father[86] was Catholic and had been born in Poland. Even more remarkably, the record specified the exact village in Poland from which he came from. This was both shocking and exhilarating.

As I processed this new evidence, my mind immediately started planning the next research project phase. I haven't ventured down that rabbit hole yet, but I am confident I'll be able to uncover his birth record if it's out there.

This particular FamilySearch collection became an invaluable resource for the LDK Diaries Research Project. I returned to the 1897 Odessa census records repeatedly, searching for any trace of people associated with the *Kherson*. Could these records contain more hidden details about those we knew so little about?

By cross-referencing names from the *Kherson* crew list, I found several men who also appeared in this census. That discovery allowed me to learn more about their lives in pre-Revolutionary Russia, painting a fuller picture of the world that Lydia came from.

Researching genealogy in a country with a complicated history like Russia often feels like searching for a needle in a haystack. Honestly, sometimes I think finding the needle might be easier!

---

86   The rest of Daria's family was Russian Orthodox, and we assumed he was as well. However, this record proved this theory wrong - another unexpected discovery

CHAPTER 21

My #1 Top Research Tips

Whenever someone asks me how to begin their genealogy research, my answer is simple: start with what you already have. Before diving headfirst into archives and online databases, carefully analyze, extract, and organize the documents, photos, and memorabilia already in your possession. You might be surprised by how much you can learn from taking a closer look.

Many people often feel overwhelmed by shoeboxes or large bins stuffed with scattered family keepsakes. If that's you, not to worry! Start small. Begin sorting items into categories by person, surname, or document type. For example, gather all materials related to a particular ancestor or surname and group them together—alternatively, separate birth certificates, marriage records, and photos into different piles. Once divided, you can further organize by date or family branch.

Personally, I prefer to organize my hard copy documents and photos into three-ring binders by surname and in chronological order. One of my four-inch-thick binders is devoted solely to my grandmother Lydia, the author of the diaries who inspired my research. This treasure trove holds priceless baby photos of her as a baby, pre-Revolutionary photos from Odessa, and even a photo featuring a "mystery" person whose identity still eludes us.

For the LDK Diaries project, I have crammed seven binders with relevant research information. Maybe I've gone a bit overboard, but at least I can usually find what I need, whether it's filed neatly in the correct notebook or sitting on my desk in a messy pile. One binder is solely dedicated to the ship's crew members. I arranged the crew lists chronologically at the front, followed by detailed information on individuals, all alphabetized and color-coded with pocket dividers.

Of course, organizing isn't just for physical documents. Files on your computer need backing up, and digitizing your collection is critical. On my computer, everything is stored in folders by surname and individual, then sorted by date, from oldest to newest.

Early in the research process, I spent significant time scanning all photos, documents, and keepsakes related to the diaries. These had been tucked away for decades in clear plastic boxes with handwritten labels made by my mother, forgotten until rediscovered during the early days of COVID-19. This rediscovery was nothing short of transformative – it brought Lydia's world to life and connected her legacy to mine.

Sometimes the answers to your questions are right under your nose. I have often found myself puzzled over an ancestor, only to realize later the key details were hidden in a document I had all along. Revisiting familiar records with fresh eyes, especially after learning something new from another source, can suddenly make overlooked details come into focus.

And don't forget to search your surroundings – literally! Look around your home (or your relatives' homes) for anything connected to the ancestor you are researching. The hunt for clues can be both exciting and rewarding. I've found treasures rummaging through closets at my parents' house – on nearly every visit, I'd find something "new." That's how I came across Lydia's childhood geography book and little album of poetry, both of which had traveled with her on the *Kherson*. These keepsakes added valuable information to my grandmother's story aboard the *Kherson*.

Some potential sources to explore include old photographs, letters, postcards, official documents (such as birth, marriage, and death certificates, passports, or any other official records), family Bibles or religious items (like icons), cookbooks, audio or video recordings.

Old Photographs: When examining old photographs, always check the front and back for names, dates, locations, or embossed studio markings. A hidden name or studio location can open new doors. In one case, I didn't notice the subtly positioned embossed date on Lydia's mother's portrait until years later.

Lydia carefully preserved her photos from her time on the *Kherson* by mounting them in an album with black construction paper pages, labeling each one. Unfortunately, while she meticulously recorded the location and year, she rarely identified the people in the images. So, when Susan recovered her old family photos, my first question was, "Is there any writing on the back?" A perfect example is the now familiar "shaved head" photo (Figure 18) of the children sitting on the ship deck – names revealed in Zhenia's handwriting, hidden in plain sight.

Letters and Postcards: Written correspondence can be goldmines for clues about relationships, locations, and historical context. Examine the handwriting, return addresses, and even how the person signed their name. I always plug the addresses into Google Maps – sometimes the homes still stand. Remember, Europeans typically write the day before the month on dates.

Lydia faithfully saved her letters and postcards from her family and friends in Russia and worldwide. Digitizing them has been a massive, ongoing project that began with her correspondence from the 1920s, including notes from her *Kherson* friends exiled in Malta.

Official Documents: Birth, Marriage, and Death Certificates are vital and hold much essential data. Beyond dates, they often list parents' names (sometimes including the mother's maiden name) and locations. Finding a maiden name is like winning the genealogy lottery.

Unfortunately, we have no original birth records for my grandparents. As they fled their homeland, they likely didn't bring them or may never have had them in the first place. As far as I know, our birth dates for relatives who immigrated to the United States were given verbally. It is reassuring that the *Kherson* crew member list confirms my grandfather Dimitri's date of birth, which is the same one we have. I've even scanned my grandmother's torn, crumpled notes, hoping they might reveal a hidden clue one day. She even recorded the exact time of her parents' deaths on one of those scraps.

Researching Names in Their Native Language: If your ancestors come from non-English-speaking countries, try to identify and use the native-language spelling of surnames. For instance, my family name, Buzyna, is spelled Бузина in Russian. Searching with both versions online has helped uncover records I never would have found otherwise. Be open to variation, also. Our surname has been translated as Buzina, Busina, and Buczyna – so I search using all versions. If you don't have a keyboard for your research language, simply use Google Translate to type the name in English and copy the original language spelling directly into your search.

In the end, genealogy is a puzzle. The more organized you are, the easier it becomes to fit the pieces together. Often, the biggest break-throughs come not from faraway archives but from the hidden clues already in your hands. This has happened to me numerous times!

CHAPTER 22
Walking in Lydia's Footsteps

Whether you know your ancestors' exact birthplace or simply a place they once lived in, traveling there, if possible, can deepen your connection to your roots and bring their stories to life. Although I have never visited my grandmother's hometown of Odessa, I hope to one day.

Even without knowing every detail, exploring places your ancestors once called home can spark a profound sense of belonging. The very first entry in Lydia's diary mentioned a specific location, and I couldn't resist pulling out a map to find it. Instantly, I imagined myself retracing her steps! Just visualizing myself there, standing in that spot, helped me feel more connected to her, but standing there in person? That would be transformative.

Boka Kotorska. Bay of Kotor. Boka.

Before reading my grandmother's diaries, I had never heard of this picturesque region filled with medieval towns and mountain views. It sounded so distant, so exotic. Would I ever be lucky enough to explore this part of the world that created such a lasting imprint on her? What was it about this corner of the world that she carried with her throughout her life? I was about to find out.

As if my grandmother were nudging me from beyond, a friend asked if I would like to join her group of friends on a cruise through the Adriatic Sea. "Send me the itinerary and I'll take a look," I said. Venice, Split, Dubrovnik, Kotor, Corfu, Olympia, Athens. It all sounded incredible.

Wait a minute, Kotor? I frantically searched for it on Google Maps. There it was. The very place my grandmother spent time ashore while living on the *Kherson*. I wrote back without hesitation: a resounding YES to my friend and YES to the cruise.

We made our plans in the summer of 2022, with an October departure in mind. My cousin, Donna, would be my roommate. I eagerly anticipated the Adriatic Coast's beauty that fall, ready to feel closer to my grandmother. But that euphoria quickly turned into crushing disappointment – an emotional rollercoaster! The cruise wasn't until October 2023 – fifteen months away! I immediately messaged my friend and cousin. "Did you know the cruise isn't *this* October?" Their calm reply: "Of course."

The wait felt torturous! Impatient but determined, I channeled my energy into researching my grandmother's connection to the Bay of Kotor. I revisited her diaries with a renewed focus, combing through her entries for references to places, experiences, and emotions she deemed worthy of recording. What would she have seen and done during her time there? What local foods might she have tasted? What sights moved her? I also began researching modern-day tourist excursions. Would I develop the same affinity for this place as she did? I didn't know, but I was thrilled to make my own memories in the place that meant so much to her.

My mother, always an enthusiastic trip planner, jumped in to help me. Just days after booking the cruise, she printed a map of the Kotor region, circling the towns her mother had visited. She gathered tourist brochures, historical notes, and even old photographs of her mother aboard the ship. I've often said that my mother must have been a travel agent in a past life, as she's always thrived on planning trips.

A seasoned world traveler herself, my mother found great joy in helping piece together this journey. Though her days of globetrotting are behind her, we were now, in a way, retracing her mother's footsteps together. I would be physically walking the streets of Kotor, while she would follow my progress from home, tracking me religiously on "Find Friends."

Imagining the journey ahead and envisioning each step alongside my grandmother, I grew more emotionally connected to the experience. Every imagined footstep brought me closer to Lydia and her remarkable life.

Although I visited a different coastal town than my grandmother, my cruise ship sailed the same waters the *Kherson* navigated just over a century ago. I would breathe the same crisp ocean air and marvel at the same dramatic cliffs and stunning views as she did. I felt butterflies stirring in my stomach with a mix of anticipation, nervousness, and excitement. I couldn't help but wonder if Lydia felt the same way as she approached the Bay of Kotor for the first time all those years ago?

As our ship silently glided through the Bay of Kotor in the early morning of our fourth cruise day, I was excited. Finally, I was about to walk in Lydia's footsteps! The forecast, however, called for rainstorms, and I couldn't help but worry, just as Lydia had written in her diary that the day's excursion might be canceled.

We had heard that a larger cruise ship had been forced to cancel its stop in Dubrovnik the day before due to the weather. The thought of that happening to us in Kotor was almost too much to bear. I felt my inner child crying out in frustration. After coming so close to realizing my dream of visiting this ancestral land, I couldn't imagine being turned away by forces beyond my control. This was not just a port stop; it was part of a personal trek.

I held my breath with every announcement over the ship's intercom. Would it be safe to dock? Would our long-anticipated tours be delayed, or worse yet, canceled? Those butterflies in my stomach hadn't left; they danced nervously as we sat at round tables on the upper deck, eating our breakfast. Floor-to-ceiling windows revealed the gloomy outdoor conditions, mirroring my rising anxiety and uncertainty.

Phew! The intercom announced that we were clear to dock and allowed us to begin our day as planned. A wave of relief washed over me. We quickly finished our breakfast and started disembarking, eager to join our tour group on land. This time, the butterflies in my stomach were buzzing with pure elation. The moment I eagerly awaited had finally arrived.

As I stepped on Montenegrin soil, I grabbed a big red umbrella provided by the cruise line. I paused, closed my eyes, and took a deep breath. I imagined my grandmother doing the same, stepping ashore for the first time after leaving everything behind. Would I feel what she felt? Would this place connect me to her even more deeply?

Rain poured down my shoulders and soaked my backpack as I reached the entrance to Old Town Kotor. The possibilities for the day ahead were endless. I opened my umbrella against the steady drizzle. The sky was grey; cobblestones were slick beneath my feet. The clouds played peek-a-boo with the mountains above, as if hesitant to reveal their dramatic backdrop to me. My gaze fixed on the weathered stone archway into the medieval town. I was ready to immerse myself in Kotor's rich history and see what stories were waiting beyond it.

With Lydia in my thoughts, I was fully present, listening closely to our guide, absorbing every detail. After our 90-minute tour, we treated ourselves to a well-earned pastry and coffee at a quaint café in the heart of the Old Town. For reasons I cannot explain, in that moment, I felt compelled to post on Instagram in real time. We continued our exploration of the medieval streets, admiring the stone buildings and narrow alleys.

I envisioned Lydia wandering these paths, perhaps selecting fabric for future sewing projects, choosing a pastry for a picnic in the field, or simply enjoying carefree window shopping. I instinctively felt the urge to buy a postcard, just as Lydia had done in every new town she visited. I spent ten euros on a postcard and magnet, carefully tucking them into my backpack for safekeeping. I entered a jewelry shop and bought myself a pair of earrings and a pendant crafted from the gemstone zultanite. I also bought a souvenir t-shirt featuring a Montenegrin landscape. Every moment here felt like a treasure to me.

Standing reverently in the historic St. Nicholas Serbian Orthodox Church in the center of Old Town Square, I crossed myself, lit a candle, and offered a silent prayer for Lydia and all the ancestors who came before me. In that moment of quiet reflection, I felt deeply connected to both past and present. My thoughts drifted back to Lydia's experience, perhaps squirming beside her parents during those long, formal church services that stretched for hours.

In that quiet moment of reflection, my phone buzzed. I received a message from my paternal third cousin. She saw my post on Instagram and asked how long I would be in Kotor, as she now lives nearby. Before I knew it, we sat face to face at another café, chatting away as if we'd known each other our whole lives. Was it a mere coincidence? Divine intervention? Or was the universe aligning to guide me toward yet another discovery?

We had only learned about each other a few years earlier, and I certainly never imagined we'd meet in person, especially not here. I was struck by the power of these unexpected familial connections as we exchanged stories and pieced together threads of our shared family history. Sitting with her felt like reuniting with a long-lost relative, because truthfully, that's exactly what she was, a piece of my family puzzle I hadn't even known was missing.

As always, whenever I make a mind-blowing genealogical discovery, my first instinct is to share the news with my mother. Without thinking about the time difference, I quickly FaceTimed her, eager for my parents, especially my father, to meet our newly discovered cousin. They were thrilled by the unexpected connection with her, and we were amazed at the technology that allowed us to share such a meaningful moment together, live and across continents.

My time in Kotor exceeded all expectations. While I had come to feel closer to my maternal grandmother, I unexpectedly uncovered a new connection to my paternal grandmother's side as well. The once sparse and tangled branches of my family tree were beginning to take shape, revealing newfound relatives and stories waiting to be told. I felt a thrill as I prepared to add a photo next to her name on my expanding family tree. When I began my genealogy research years ago, I never imagined it would lead me here, literally and figuratively. Who knows what other incredible surprises lie on this path through the Bay of Kotor?

Kotor was a blend of breathtaking views, rich history, and storybook architecture. The dramatic landscapes with their rugged "black mountains," true to the meaning of Montenegro, emerged from the mist as our visit drew to a close. As I walked back toward the ship, a deep sense of peace washed over me. Leaving was bittersweet. I vowed to return one day and to continue tracing Lydia's footsteps through this land she so loved.

As our cruise ship navigated back through the Bay of Kotor and into the Adriatic Sea, I compared my grandmother's old photos from the *Kherson* to the views unfolding before me. Sporting my new Kotor souvenir t-shirt, I made my way to the ship's top deck. The sky was a deep, vivid blue, and a crisp, cool breeze drifted in as the sun began to set, casting a golden glow over the horizon. Standing alone on the deck, I felt a comforting presence beside me – my grandmother's spirit. In that still, sacred moment, I reflected on the emotional journey of reconnecting with my family's past.

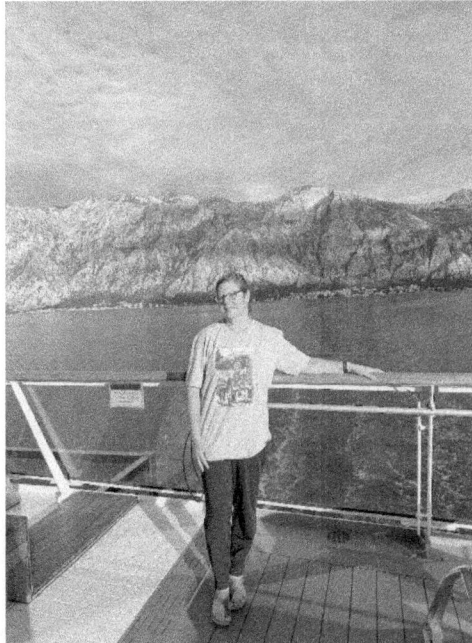

Figure 52: Tamara aboard a Viking cruise in the Bay of Kotor, wearing a souvenir Kotor shirt. October 2023. Courtesy of the Adams Family.

The contrast between the old black and white photograph from 1921 displayed on my iPhone and the vibrant landscape before me was utterly breathtaking. I couldn't help but compare the two. My eye gaze shifted back and forth like a tennis match – I first looked at the historic photo, then at the silhouette of the black mountains, and back again. Photo, mountains. Photo, mountains. Absolutely astonishing. I had to remind myself to breathe.

I believe I pinpointed the exact location using Lydia's diary entries, the vintage photo, and satellite maps. Holding my phone up to the horizon once again, I traced the silhouette of the black mountains, aligning them with the image of the past. I was convinced I had found it! I quickly captured a screenshot of the Google Maps location as a reminder to study it later and forever remember the significance of that moment.

Once again, I silently vowed to return to this place and immerse myself in the beauty of the Bay of Kotor in a way that echoes my grandmother's adventures. Perhaps I will stay at a beachside resort and swim in the same body of water Lydia swam for the first time. Or maybe I'd rent and anchor a boat, just as she did aboard the *Kherson*. In that moment, I fully understood Lydia's lifelong affection for the water and her deep connection to this rugged corner of the world. An overwhelming feeling of gratitude inundated me as I reflected on my brief but unforgettable visit here.

Lydia's experience living on the ship for a year and a half created an indelible mark, shaping her lifelong bond with the water and coastal landscapes. My mother often recalled their many family camping trips to Lake George in New York. She, her parents, and brother would load up their gear onto their beloved Lyman wooden boat, which had a white hull, red cushions, a foldable canopy, and an Evinrude outboard motor. Perhaps, as the boat gently rocked on the lake, Lydia was transported back to the rhythm of the waves lapping against the *Kherson*.

Growing up surrounded by the waters of Florida, I took that beauty and accessibility for granted, unaware of just how much it meant to my grandmother each time she visited. Summers at Panama City Beach were magical, especially our crossings to Shell Island in the many small boats we owned over the years. One vivid image remains etched in my mind of my grandmother in her seventies, bravely riding in a small kayak rigged with a sail built by my father. It was a testament to her adventurous spirit and deep, abiding love for the water. This was a test of her resilience, which she undoubtedly inherited from her ancestors and the life she so bravely lived.

CHAPTER 23
Earthshattering Discoveries

With the increased accessibility of online records, the abundance of hard copy records in archives, and my ongoing dedication to our family history research, we uncovered several discoveries that I can only describe as truly earth-shattering.

How I Found a Living Descendant of Another Passenger on the *Kherson*: The Full Identity Discoveries of Lydia's Two Closest Friends, Zhenia and Katya.

In her diaries, Lydia frequently wrote about two children: Zhenia and Katya. With each mention, I kept wondering - who were these children? What did they look like? What became of them after they left the *Kherson*? And most intriguing of all, could any living descendants of Zhenia and Katya hold more pieces of the puzzle? We were captivated by their presence in Lydia's life.

Whenever my mom and I discussed the LDK Diaries, Zhenia and Katya were always in our conversations. We often said, "If she only had written their last names." It would mean everything in figuring out the missing part of the story.

From Lydia's descriptions, I guessed that Zhenia was about her age and had two younger brothers, Kolya (Nikolai) and Alyosha (Aleksey).

But beyond that, their parents' names and the family's surname remained a mystery. Katya, on the other hand, was much younger, likely three or four years old, and Lydia often looked after her. It is clear from the entries that Lydia cared deeply for both girls, and the feeling was mutual. Their presence brought her comfort and joy. I also identified some of the other children in our photographs using her descriptions. I felt a deep sense of pride and validation when I later confirmed that I correctly identified them.

As my mother translated the diaries, she often skipped ahead, eager to uncover whatever secrets her mother had recorded. She became just as immersed in the process as I was.

We developed a system. My mother translated each diary entry from Russian to English as best she could, then emailed it to me in sections. I would review and lightly edit before sending it to our distant relative, a native Russian speaker, for further review. Once she made corrections and notations, she sent it back to me for final revisions. In the end, the task of organizing all the information ultimately fell to me.

We are both naturally impatient. Often, she would text me key details - such as a location or a name - before completing that portion of the translation so I could dive right into the research. Every time my phone dinged with a text from my mother, a surge of excitement ran through me. I never knew what new clue might be coming through. That same thrill struck every time I opened my inbox and saw a message from our distant relative after she read the latest translation segment.

Just when I was about to give up hope of ever learning Zhenia's last name, my mother texted me, brimming with excitement:

"OMG – you won't believe this! My mother *finally* wrote Zhenia's last name!"

Not only had we discovered Zhenia's surname, but we also learned that, after arriving in the United States, her family had stayed with Lydia's family for a week before settling in Detroit, Michigan. This detail had been completely unknown to us! It felt like a hidden gem, a gift we hadn't expected.

In the entry for August 1, 1923, in Volume D, page 34, Lydia *finally* reveals the surname of her best friend on the ship, Zhenia *Anikeeff*. The entries that follow recount their time spent together in New York City, offering a rare glimpse into their continued friendship after the *Kherson*.

Wednesday, August 1, 1923

Today when I came from the [piano] teacher I stopped at Aunt Liza's and there was a letter from Kruchik, he wrote that the Anikeeffs arrived yesterday in New York on the ship "President Adams" [written in English], after dinner we immediately went to South Ferry [written in English], stopped at the office to obtain a pass to go to the ship, but we were told that it was too late that we should come tomorrow at 10 o'clock. We were so disappointed but could do nothing...

Thursday, August 2, 1923

This morning at 11 o'clock we went to Broadway [written in English] to obtain a pass to go to Zhenia on the ship, i.e. to the pier. We had to go to Brooklyn [written in English], we then crossed over on a boat and walked to the ship, at first we did not see them, but then papa saw Anna Ivanovna and started calling to her, right away the rest of them came and we were all happy, we were talking all the time. It seems that Zhenia, Kolya and Alyosha did not grow at all. We stood there for a very long time and said we would return tomorrow...

Friday, August 3, 1923

I had lunch with mama and we went to the ship, we took some fruit and Russian newspapers. We were given the pass, of course. When we arrived on the ship we saw all the Anikeeffs again, gave them the fruit and newspapers and again talked for a long time. We were told that they will be taken to Ellis Island [written in English] tomorrow and we decided to meet them there. When we came home it was already 5 o'clock. I spent the evening as always.

Saturday, August 4, 1923

Today after eleven o'clock I went with mama and papa again on Broadway to obtain a pass to go to "Ellis Island" [written English], and to meet the Anikeeffs. We were given the pass right away and went by boat to "Ellis Island' [written in English]. We went to the building where they announced the names of the families who have come to meet those who have arrived but our name was not read because we were not listed. We were told to go to the hall where the passengers are. When we came there the Anikeeffs were not there, we looked for them and could not find them. Then we went to the boat that goes to New York [written in English] and saw them there. Immediately we greeted each other and were talking with each other. And that is how we unnoticeably arrived in New York [written in English], got on the elevated train and went to our place. Of course, we helped carry their luggage. When we came home we had dinner right away. After, Zhenia and Kolya described how they lived in Malta, we had a very joyous time and sat for a very long time and only at 12 o'clock did we go to bed.

Sunday, August 5, 1923

Today when everyone had drunk coffee, we all, except papa, went to Bronx Park [written in English]. There we looked at many different animals for a long time, later ate, I was with Zhenia the entire time. Finally at 7 o'clock we went home, got lost a little, but arrived home successfully. At home we had supper, drank tea, Zhenia, Kolya and I were sitting in my room telling scary and funny stories and had a wonderful time and went to bed as late as we did yesterday.

Monday, August 6, 1923

I went to the [piano] teacher's. Today mama and I were home and the Anikeeffs went to the aquarium by themselves. When they came back, after dinner and tea we went to Coney Island [written in English], it was 9 o'clock when we left. It was very interesting and fun there, we laughed so much, rode on the roller coaster and only at 2 o'clock in the morning did we come home. Everyone was very tired and went to bed immediately.

Tuesday, August 7, 1923

Today we spent all day at home. Only the Anikeeffs went to find out when the train to Detroit leaves. We were noisy all day telling many interesting and funny stories. We played many different games in the evening. The Anikeeffs plan to leave for Detroit tomorrow at 10 o'clock.

Wednesday, August 8, 1923

Today we all got up at 7 o'clock in the morning because the Anikeeffs leave for Detroit today. Having drunk our coffee we went with them to say good-bye at the railroad station. I was not long at the farewell with the Anikeeffs and then went to my music teacher's.

Discovering that Lydia and Zhenia's families had remained connected, and that the Anikeeff family also immigrated to the United States, gave me hope. I felt it was truly possible to track down the living descendants of those who had shared the *Kherson* journey. It felt like a tangible reality. I *knew* I could find them.

Within seconds of learning their name, I frantically typed "Anikeeff" into Ancestry.com. I could hardly believe what popped up: a family tree owned by a direct descendant! I stopped dead in my tracks, overcome with awe. I found Zhenia's family. I felt an adrenaline rush, like I had just run a marathon. I was getting closer to finding the answers to my grandmother's life before she came to America.

On that very family tree was the *exact* same photo of the steamship *Kherson* that my grandmother had, the one labeled "Feodosia 1920," along with photos of the children on the ship, identical to ours. My eyes locked onto the caption below the duplicate photo, reading it again and again, trying to absorb the reality of what I was seeing:

> *Michael Anikeeff and crew stole this ship [the Kherson] from the Russian Navy. His family had 2 hours to prepare for the departure, and they left Sevastopol with just a few belongings like the Singer Sewing machine, samovar, and icons...*

This was a completely different version of the story from what I had heard. Could this family hold more details than we did? Could they finally shed light on my grandmother's life aboard the *Kherson*? I soon discovered that they had even less information and even more questions. What began as a flicker of curiosity quickly became a significant research project I became fully immersed in, obsessed with, and committed to pursuing.

Without skipping a beat, I composed an email to the owners of both Anikeeff trees I had found, Michele (Kolya's daughter) and Susan (Zhenia's granddaughter). I could not believe I found not one, but two living descendants. I hoped they would share my excitement.

After ten long days, a message from Kolya's daughter arrived. Then, after another agonizing thirteen days, Susan *finally* responded. I later learned that Michele had reached out to Susan ahead of time to prepare her, explaining that a descendant of a fellow *Kherson* passenger might be contacting her. Susan, known within the family as the historian, was the perfect person to receive my inquiry. To my relief, Susan was thrilled and eager to join the search. Her passion and enthusiasm matched mine, and together, we began piecing together our family's escape from Russia.

Just when it seemed like we had uncovered every possible clue, more began to emerge. When I eventually met fourteen descendants of the Anikeeff children in person, new details about the Anikeeff family surfaced, stories that had never been written down.

One story came from Pam, Alyosha's daughter. She remembered hearing that Michael Anikeeff had contracted pink eye while aboard the steamship to America, which led to the family being detained at Ellis Island. Because he failed the medical inspection, the entire family had to remain there until he was treated and cleared to enter the United States. I had always wondered why they were not allowed to leave on the same day they arrived, as Lydia's family did. Now, with this new information, it all made sense.

Discovering Katya's last name was far less dramatic than uncovering Zhenia's but was equally satisfying. Unlike Zhenia, Lydia never recorded Katya's patronymic or surname in her diaries, leaving us puzzled for quite some time. It was one of those classic cases where the answer had been right before us all along.

After reviewing the photos and letters from the *Kherson* for what felt like the millionth time, I noticed something I had somehow missed before. On the back of one of the photos of Katya, there appeared to be a last name written in Russian: Malyavin(a). That moment was a powerful reminder that sometimes, it's worth reviewing what you already have, no matter how many times you've seen it. Also, often, you must answer a dozen other questions before the answer finally reveals itself.

How I Uncovered the Name of the *Kherson's* Captain.

When we first began this project, we had no idea who else traveled on the *Kherson* with Lydia and her family, aside from the few people she mentioned in her diaries. I never expected a crew member list to exist, much less preserved in an archive, so I had long given up hope of ever finding one. Even though the *Kherson* was part of a larger organized evacuation, we assumed it had departed in a state of panic. Under such chaotic circumstances, who would have had the time or presence of mind to document a complete crew list?

Since connecting in August 2020, Susan and I wondered who commanded the ship. Her family tree included a note that her great-grandfather, Michael, had "stolen" the *Kherson* from the Russian Navy. Was *he* the captain? We didn't think so, but we had nothing to go on either way. Lydia never once mentioned the captain in her writings.

Just as my mom had gone "digging" in her mother's memorabilia during the COVID-19 pandemic, Susan began doing her own search. After one of our conversations, she unearthed a collection of photos from her grandmother's time aboard the *Kherson*, from Malta, and several old documents that had belonged to Michael Anikeeff. Though they had been handed down to her years earlier, they had never been translated. She hadn't fully known what they were. Remarkably well preserved, they were still legible to anyone fluent in Russian.

Among them was a document that changed everything: a certificate verifying that the *Kherson* was docked in Sevastopol on November 7, 1920. At this time, we hadn't yet come across any official documentation confirming the ships involved in the Crimean evacuation. In the bottom right corner of the certificate, written in pencil, were the words "8 северная сторона," or "8th pier North Side of Sevastopol Bay." This certificate confirmed that the *Kherson* was indeed docked in Sevastopol from November 7 until its departure on November 14, 1920. Since then, we have located additional supporting documents in the Russian Archives. Knowing the exact pier where the ship moored makes me long to stand on that very spot.

Figure 53: Document issued for Michael Anikeeff, dated November 4, 1920.
Courtesy of the Anikeeff Family.

Translation of document:

Dated 4 November 1920

The bearer of this, Mikhail Kononovich Anikeeff, is the 2nd mechanic of the Volunteer Fleet steamer "Kherson" serving on the designated steamer from November 24, 1919, that is certified by the signatures and the ship's seal attached.

Captain of the steamer Schmelz [Viktor Franzevich]
Commandant of the steamer: Pilar [Nikolai Adolfovich]

The stamp on the left of the certificate, vertically:

VERIFIED 25 October 1920 (old calendar date; November 7 is the new calendar date)

Chairman of the Sevastopol verification commission of draft age

Lieutenant General
Colonel Skalsky

This single document marked a breakthrough we could only describe as earth-shattering. It became one of the most pivotal moments in our research, adding another critical piece to the *Kherson* puzzle. Perhaps more remarkably, it revealed the name of the ship's captain, Viktor Franzevich Schmelz, and the commandant, Nikolai Adolfovich Pilar, details we never imagined finding.

Even more satisfying was what came next: we found an actual crew list for the *Kherson*. And not just one, but five! Knowing the name of the captain and some of the officers aboard *before* laying eyes on that list was immensely gratifying, to say the least.

The Russian Archives held crew lists from April, May, July, September, and December 1920. For the purposes of this book, I have included only the December 1920 crew list in the Appendices, since by then, the *Kherson* was in Constantinople and had permanently left Russia. This particular list felt the most relevant, as it offers a glimpse into the lives of the people who surrounded Lydia while she was actively documenting her experiences.

These earthshattering kinds of discoveries – unexpected, hard-won, and deeply revealing – are what I love most about family history research. While the process can be frustrating and even disheartening at times, there's nothing more rewarding than the pieces coming together and finally seeing the fuller picture.

CONCLUSION

Even as we reach the conclusion of my grandmother's story and have fit together more pieces of the puzzle than I ever imagined possible, many questions remain unanswered. My number one question is, who on earth took the photos aboard the *Kherson*? Who had access to a camera in the year 1921? And perhaps more puzzling, where were those photos developed? As a photographer and someone who feels incredibly fortunate to possess these historic images, I feel this question is particularly relevant.

Another pressing mystery I hope to unravel is the specific role and responsibilities of the crew members, especially my great-grandfather Dimitri. He was listed as "Буфетчик,"[87] which literally translates to "buffet-keeper," though it is often interpreted as "purser," especially considering my grandmother always insisted he was the ship's purser. Lydia frequently mentioned her father going ashore to procure supplies, particularly meat, for the ship. From this description, he clearly managed the ship's provisions – an essential role aboard the steamship. I can't help but picture someone like Gopher from *The Love Boat* – efficient, personable, and always in motion.

I wish I had a detailed description of the cabin they stayed in. Although we have a vague description of the interior of the "largest steamship of its time," the *Kherson*, from an article from an Engineering magazine from 1896, it would have been fascinating to know Lydia's

---

87   Буфетчик, pronounced "Bufetchik"

personal impressions of their living quarters. She often mentions spending time in her room, but never any details about the room itself. And knowing cameras were being used on the ship, it would be incredible to uncover a photograph of the interior of a cabin!

While I may never find all the answers to these questions, that will not stop me from continuously searching; each time I add another piece to the puzzle, the thrill is unmatched. Despite the "*Kherson* research puzzle" having infinite pieces, every discovery brings me one step closer than I was before. Each finding, no matter how small, has encouraged me to keep pushing forward with this research project.

Throughout the process of this multi-dimensional project, my passion for uncovering my family history has deepened, sparking a desire to help others explore their own roots. Understanding your own family history contributes to a healthy sense of self-worth and grounding of your identity. Knowing your ancestors' stories, struggles, and values can give you a sense of belonging and community. For fun, I like delving into my friends' family history trees to see what nuggets of information I can muster up and share with them.

Discovering that my maternal great-grandfather also had an affinity for photography immediately made me feel a deep connection to him and my family, even though he died years before I was born! It affirmed I truly belong. This love of photography is a trait that my mother and children also carry.

My paternal grandfather had a deep passion for music and played in a mandolin orchestra both in his homeland and in Chicago upon his immigration. He even wanted to pursue music as a career, but his father discouraged him. Instead, he encouraged a more practical career, insisting there will always be wars that destroy buildings, and engineers are crucial for reconstruction.

My father followed in his father's footsteps by becoming an engineer as well as playing the mandolin throughout his life. I can still hear their duets as my aunt accompanied them on the piano. Although I participated in band classes at the middle school level, I never developed a passion like my predecessors. I appreciated music but never participated. Music was a central part of my children's school experiences, and I was the token "band mom" attending each performance and photographing and/or videotaping these incredible memories. Both my children have continued to pursue music as a leisure activity as well. I can't help but think of my father and grandfather and their passion for music and how it was passed down to my children.

The grandmother I knew as an adult and the grandmother I came to know as a child, through her diaries, gave me a complete picture of who she truly was. I have a newfound appreciation for her and wish I could have seen her in this light while she was still alive. I realized that she and I are much more alike than I ever imagined! Discovering these likenesses was the icing on the cake for this project and something I did not expect. I can proudly say I got my maternal grandmother Lydia's traits of diligence, resilience, perseverance, positive attitude, and sense of adventure, just to name a few!

Lydia's story is only a part of who I am. I am eager to explore other ancestors in my family tree to uncover the connections and commonalities we share. Although I will always seek out more details from her remarkable life, my focus will now shift to other genealogical pursuits within the family. There are no shortages of stories to explore!

Perhaps I will revisit my great Aunt Sonya's vivid memoirs of her life in pre-Revolutionary Russia, which she carefully documented in installments for my mother in the 1970s. Or I might delve into my father's dramatic escape from Poland, fleeing with his family on the last train out as their village faced imminent destruction at the start of World War II. And yet another possibility, the memoirs of a distant cousin who documented his time as a Don Cossack and arrest during World War II.

In 1989, Lydia experienced another significant upheaval, this time voluntarily, for the first time since her monumental journey from Russia in 1920. She left the family home where she lived for 50 years with her husband, children, parents, and in-laws to relocate near my parents in Tallahassee, Florida. Unlike her earlier escape from her war-torn homeland, this move was a far more pleasant transition, but no less transformative.

She was now 80 years old and remarked how all her friends were dying and there was no point in staying in Schenectady, NY anymore. Every New Year's celebration that I remember was held in this house and carries sentimental value to me. I could not believe she was selling this house, and that New Year's 1989 would be our last time together in this house. I knew it was "for the best," as my grandmother often explained when things did not go as planned.

It is this very house I smell when I open the "Lydia and Vladimir's Family Memorabilia" containers stored at my parents' house. It brings me back to those years as a kid sitting at the elegantly decorated dining room table holding our noise makers getting ready to yell, "HAPPY NEW YEAR!" and I find myself spontaneously smiling. Growing up in Florida, I always wanted a house with two stories to have a nice set of stairs to climb every day! This is the first thought that comes to mind, besides the festive celebrations with family and friends, when reminiscing about this house.

Lydia moved into an assisted living facility in her late 80's. My mother offered her to move in with us at our home, but she graciously refused. Her reasoning, we surmised, was that since, as a newlywed, both her parents and in-laws lived with her at some point in their house on Regent Street. She did not want to put her daughter through this kind of stress. She was stubborn and that was just the way it was. She purchased a lovely small townhome about a mile from our house on Lake Killarney in Tallahassee, Florida. I wonder if it was a coincidence that again she was residing near a body of water? Or was it purposeful? I never thought of it at the time. Our house was on the same lake. Water always reminded her of her time on the *Kherson* so many years ago and the wonderful memories of her childhood.

I can picture her sitting in her rose-colored La-Z-Boy in her tiny but cozy room at the Sterling House Assisted Living Facility, reading glasses perched on her nose, flipping through the delicate pages of her diary, feeling content with the life she lived. A sense of calmness travels through her aged body. The phone rings. Lydia picks up the receiver and says hello. My mother is on the other end, calling on her way home from work as she did every day.

"Hi Mom, what are you doing?"

Lydia responded jovially, "I am re-reading my diaries from the ship."

I wonder what images filled her mind as she reflected on her time on the *Kherson*? Although her body was frail and mobility was challenging, she envisioned herself carefree, strolling in town, window shopping, and purchasing some souvenir postcards.

Sadly, the diaries were never mentioned again after this conversation…until March 2020. Did my grandmother have a hand in this? It was clear that it was time for these stories to be shared.

❦ The End ❦

EPILOGUE

When I initially sat down to write this book, my goal was simply to tell my grandmother's story of her life aboard the *Kherson*. However, as I delved deeper into her character and how her pre-teen experiences shaped her, I realized how transformative this writing journey had been for me. Through this highly personal process, I discovered more about my grandmother and gained profound insights into myself and my family.

In addition to gaining a deeper understanding of why I am the way I am, discovering traits I share with my grandmother confirms a sense of belonging and closeness to her. Diligence, resilience, perseverance, and adventurous. These words describe my grandmother, which could also apply to my mother, me, and my daughter.

Many examples of her diligent nature are revealed in her diaries. The first thing that stood out was her unwavering commitment to making daily entries, without fail, for three and a half years straight. Each entry was titled the same way, with the day of the week, month, and number date, usually taking up to one-third to one-half of the composition notebook page. Her later entries incorporated new English words as she acclimated to her new life in America. Her descriptions are short and not very detailed, yet you still feel like you are there with her on this adventure. As I read her diary, I felt her joy and sadness when she felt it. Occasionally, she expanded on her emotions and described something that worried her or her parents.

She surely did not write these diaries for publication; instead, they seem to have been a means of coping with the daily traumas of life as a refugee. Perhaps her parents observed her struggling mentally and suggested journal writing to deal with the difficult situation at hand, subconsciously providing for her daughter what we call therapy today.

Throughout her entire adult life, Lydia maintained an unwaveringly positive attitude. She endured no matter what challenges she faced, and her cup-half-full mentality always prevailed. She always responded by saying, "It's for the best," and never dwelled on the past. I always attributed this cup-half-full mentality to my mother, but I have since traced it further back to my grandmother and possibly even her parents. From the very beginning, when Dimitri suggested that his wife and daughter move on to the ship in January 1920, he showed remarkable optimism, believing the situation would improve and that they would return to Odessa. When it became clear they were not returning, Dimitri and his family embraced their new life in the United States with the same positive spirit.

Why did she write these diaries in the first place? Was it out of obligation or custom? Did her parents make her do this? Had her mother kept a diary as a child? Perhaps this was self-driven? Is this what girls her age did in Russia?

Perhaps Lydia's diligence was instilled in her by her mother from a young age. The touching poem she wrote in her daughter's poetry book emphasizes how she must read and complete her lessons prior to playing. Despite her non-traditional schooling years on the ship and in Serbia, I considered her a committed and focused student. Lydia often noted how she would work on her lessons almost daily during the first part of the day, before she could interact with the other children. Sometimes she studied alongside them. One thing was clear: she could not fully enjoy playtime with her friends unless she felt her academic efforts had met her own standards.

In her later adult years, the Lydia I was familiar with thrived in a structured and disciplined environment. Dinner was served promptly at 5:30 pm daily, her belongings were meticulously organized, and everything in her home was kept "just as it should be." One detail I remember vividly from my childhood is that improper table manners, like not holding your fork correctly, were simply unacceptable. She could be firm, even stubborn at times, and certainly did not hesitate to enforce standards she believed in.

My mother shares similar memories from her own childhood. Lydia's son George describes her as warm, loving, caring, and firm when needed. This was the grandmother I knew, not the carefree young girl laughing and picking flowers in the fields with her friends, as she so often portrayed herself in her diaries.

Another possible reason Lydia sought order in her life may have been rooted in those uncertain pre-teen days living aboard the steamship. Amid the chaos of not knowing where they would ultimately settle, she likely craved structure, something her parents attempted to provide. Writing in a diary consistently every day offered predictability and stability in an otherwise unpredictable world. The pressing question that loomed over their lives was constant – would they one day return to their homeland, Russia, or be forced somewhere completely new and foreign? I believe Lydia was intrinsically motivated to remain disciplined in her studies, chores, and daily routines, but I am also certain she was encouraged and guided by her parents.

My mother, my youngest daughter, and I all share this same diligence that defined my grandmother, though each of us expresses it uniquely.

My mother began her first diary around the same age her own mother had started hers. I've often wondered – was this merely a coincidence or a conscious choice? Did her mother encourage her to write, or was she drawn to it on her own? Or perhaps a dear family friend, having heard stories of my grandmother writing in her diary aboard the *Kherson*, gifted my mother a small journal with a lock, hoping to carry on the tradition? Thanks to Lydia's diaries, my mother has recently enjoyed going back to reread her personal diaries from the 1950s. There are so many structural similarities with the entries. My mother dated each entry with the day of the week, month, and date. Contrastingly, she started each entry with

"Dear Diary." Other similar topics included whether she completed her assignments for school, what time she went to bed, and any other interesting events of the day. Again, with not much emotion but enough so you could feel her expressions of happiness, sadness, or disappointment.

The ancestral tradition of keeping a diary was broken with me. My mother always encouraged me to write a diary, and I think I tried around the same age Lydia began, but I was never consistent and eventually lost interest. As I dig deep into my memories of that time, I believe I contributed to the "Alaska Diary" my mom kept. I recall an elementarily designed cactus, which I so carefully drew, nestled among my mom's daily descriptions. My mother had a few books from her graduate art school days, with blank pages we used for our travel diaries. Naturally, she documented every moment of our trip, down to the exact mileage and number of gallons of gas we pumped into the van... *every single time.* And we were gone the entire summer of 1981. Now *that* was diligence. She took great joy in the process, while I just rolled my eyes. Despite her disappointment in my lack of enthusiasm, she was confident that one day I would appreciate it...and she was right!

The one-million-dollar question many ask me when they hear about my grandmother's diaries is whether I kept a diary too. My initial response is no; I never kept a traditional diary. But after I gave it some thought, I realized that I did keep a diary - but not in the conventional sense, but in the visual form of a scrapbook! I have always loved photography and began my first Creative Memories scrapbook in 1999, documenting my life in pictures each year up until 2011, including two baby books, a wedding album, and even a few travel scrapbooks from our earlier adventures.

When my grandmother's resilience comes to mind, I think of the struggles my great-grandparents and their parents experienced during the Russian Revolution, World War I, and World War II. Lydia always exhibited stability and steadfastness. Perhaps this was learned behavior from her parents, grandparents, great-grandparents, and great-great-grandparents. Leaving her beloved homeland as a young girl and never returning had to contribute to her resilient characteristics. Not only did she leave her country and all she had known, but she also maintained a positive attitude throughout her life. She never once expressed negative feelings towards their difficult times aboard the *Kherson*. I now know things were not as rosy as she made them seem in her diaries.

Reflecting on my own childhood, I think back to my piano lessons. When the other children teased me about my name, singing "Tomorrow" repeatedly because of its similar pronunciation. My teacher compared me to a "rock." I felt distraught inside, yet outwardly I remained calm in the face of adversity, and my teacher admired this strength. Perhaps this personality trait stems from Lydia and my other ancestors who escaped Russia under extraordinary circumstances? Does the immigrant mindset burn deep inside me by default because of what my family endured centuries ago?

Living on a large steamship for a year and a half with an uncertain future would be difficult for anyone. Lydia didn't just endure the challenges of her situation, but rather appreciated any life experience she was given. She missed her extended family back in Odessa terribly, yet could enjoy her here-and-now moments aboard the steamship she called home.

Despite the difficult conditions living aboard the *Kherson*, Lydia had a way of describing her days with such joy and appreciation of the simple things of life. Something as basic as running through a meadow of flowers in a field excited her to no end. She did not let the difficult living conditions of the steamship interfere with her ability to appreciate the little things in life.

Her perseverance carried on into adulthood as well. My mother recalls how, after her father's passing, Lydia continued to take her and her brother camping to Lake George - often accompanied by their family friend, Harry. She must have disliked it, but never complained. Perhaps she felt it was simply "for the best." It may have also been her way of feeling close to her late husband, with whom she shared many summer camping trips together as a family. Or maybe it rekindled that early sense of adventure she had once known living aboard the *Kherson* so many years before.

Could my resourcefulness come from my grandmother? Lydia continued to sew many of her clothes well into adulthood, including her bathing suits. During her visits to us in Florida, she wore a white one-piece bathing suit with red floral designs. It was her signature look, appearing in all our beach photos. At the time, I had no idea she had made it herself.

I never took an interest in sewing and often took the clothes Lydia made for granted. After a few half-hearted attempts to learn, I became uninterested. My daughter, however, has picked it up on her own. She taught herself basic sewing techniques, altering dresses that were too big, sewing on buttons, and patching up holes. It is very clearly in her genes!

In many ways, I see a glimmer of Lydia in Kristina, especially when it comes to sewing. Kristina did not ask me to help alter her clothes; she knew I didn't have the skill or the time to figure it out. So, she did what Lydia might have done: she figured it out herself. If you want something, you make it happen. That spirit runs strong in our family.

Despite loving to swim in the Bay of Kotor as a child, Lydia was never a strong swimmer. Still, she enjoyed all aspects of being in or near the water. Her one caveat was that she needed to be able to "touch the bottom" of whatever body of water she entered.

Growing up in Florida, I developed strong swimming skills. My parents introduced me to the warm waters of the Gulf of Mexico when I was a baby, and I've loved the water ever since, just like my grandmother. My mom shares that love of water, too. Unlike my grandmother, I did not always need to touch the bottom. As long as the water was crystal clear and free of sharks or alligators…I was in! Those were *my* caveats.

I end my thoughts here with a touch of sentiment and two photographs that bring me a deep sense of connection to my mother and my grandmother. In the spirit of my grandmother's resourcefulness, these images serve as a heartfelt tribute to the creativity, skill, and legacy she passed down through generations. The dresses we're wearing were sewn either by my grandmother or my mother.

Figure 54: Lydia, Tamara, and Helen, all wearing dresses sewn by Lydia (her own), and by my mom Helen (Tamara's & Helen's), 1974. Courtesy of the Buzyna Family.

Figure 55: Helen, Tamara, and Lydia wearing matching dresses sewn by Lydia, with Tamara's brother in the background. Panama City Beach, Florida, 1981. Courtesy of the Buzyna Family.

APPENDICES

APPENDIX A

Timeline

August 18, 1895 (old calendar)
The *Kherson* was built in Newcastle, England, for the Russian Dobroflot.

May 27, 1896 (old calendar)
The *Kherson* completed shipbuilding and sailed its maiden voyage to the Far East.

March 8, 1897 (old calendar)
The *Kherson* arrived in Odessa from Vladivostok.

September 1903
Renamed *Lena* after being bought by the Naval Department for the Pacific Squadron. It functioned as an auxiliary cruiser, delivered artillery, and was transferred to Vladivostok.

1904
The *Kherson* participated in the Russo-Japanese War.

September 5, 1904 – October 17, 1905 (old calendar)
American authorities detained the ship in San Francisco due to the boilers' failure.

1906
Returned to the Russian Dobroflot Fleet and reclaimed the *Kherson* name.

1907

The *Kherson* underwent major repairs, removing one of the three smokestacks.

1907-1908

The *Kherson* transferred emigrants from Libau, Russian Empire (present day Liepāja, Latvia) to New York City. The ship passenger lists can be found on the Ellis Island website.

October 1908

Returned to the port of Odessa from the Baltic.

November 25, 1909 (old calendar)

Lydia Dimitrievna Komarkoff was born in Odessa.

December 17, 1910

Evgenia "Zhenia" Mikhailovna Anikeeff born in Odessa.

1915

Took part in WWI as Transport N 73.

June 27, 1918

Captured by the German Army in Novorossiysk, then returned to the Dobroflot Volunteer Fleet on December 3, 1918.

1918 until November 14, 1920

Served in the Volunteer Fleet, transporting supplies, wounded soldiers, and civilians to different ports within the Black Sea.

November 24, 1919

Michael Kononovich Anikeeff reports for duty on the *Kherson* as Second Engineer.

December 6, 1919

As a purser, Dimitri Ivanovich Komarkoff, Lydia's father, reports to duty on the *Kherson*. Lydia and her mother joined Dimitri on the ship sometime between December 6, 1919, and January 3, 1920.

December 6, 1919

The local Odessa newspaper advertised that the *Kherson* would depart from Platonovsky pier in Odessa for Novorossiysk on November 10, 1919.[88] Michael Anikeeff and Dimitri Komarkoff worked on the ship for this voyage.

Sometime before January 3, 1920 (but after December 6, 1920)

The Komarkoff family boards the *Kherson* in Odessa.

Sometime between January 3 and 12, 1920

The *Kherson* departs the port of Odessa for Feodosia sometime after January 3 and reaches Feodosia.

January 1920

January 12: The *Kherson* arrives in Novorossiysk.

February 1920

February 3-5: * The *Kherson* was in Novorossiysk.

February 8: Odessa is overtaken by the Bolsheviks; several ships are involved in the evacuation.

March 1920

March 1, 4: The *Kherson* was in Novorossiysk.

March 15: The *Kherson*, adapted as a hospital ship, transported 1042 wounded and sick from Novorossiysk to Piraeus. Lydia mentioned, in a letter to her daughter on October 5, 1967: *"When we were in Piraeus, I saw very little of it."*

About March 20: The *Kherson* brought Russian refugees to Famagusta, Cyprus, then to Alexandria, Egypt.

---

88   Одесский листок : [Газ. полит., науч., лит., обществ. и коммер.]. Г.46 1919,
      № 186 (23 нояб.). С.1 / Odessa Leaflet: [Polit., scient, lit., soc. and comer.
      newspaper]. Y [of publication] 46th 1919, No. 186 (23 Nov.). P.1.

March 26: Russian doctors and nurses disembarked from the *Kherson* in Chanak.[89]

March 27: The White Army is defeated by the Red Army in Novorossiysk. No ships of the White Army returned here after this date.

March: Lydia fell ill with Typhus sometime this month.

April 1920

The *Kherson* was stationed in Feodosia (exact dates unknown).

April 20: * The *Kherson* was in Constantinople.

April 28: * The *Kherson* was in Sevastopol.

May 1920

May 21-25: The *Kherson* was in Sevastopol.

May 21-22: A fight between two stokers, Nikifor Chernikov and Nikolay Burkhanov (76).

June 1920

June 3: Michael Anikeeff received permission for his wife (and children) to live with him aboard the *Kherson*.

June 6: The *Kherson* was in Sevastopol, confirmed by an incident report of Grigory Vsevoldovich Yalovikov's (5) bullet in the face.

June 10: * The *Kherson* was in Sevastopol (I believe the Anikeeff family joined Michael sometime after June 3rd before the ship headed to Constantinople).

June 28: * The *Kherson* was in Constantinople.

July 1920

July 6: * The *Kherson* left Sevastopol on this date, having returned from Constantinople sometime after June 28th.

July 8: * The *Kherson* arrived in Constantinople.

---

89   Чинаки, or Chanak, the present day Çanakkale on the shore of the Dardanelles in Turkey.

July 10-12: * The *Kherson* was in Constantinople.

July 24: * The *Kherson* departed Constantinople, most likely headed to Sulina, Romania.

August 1920

August 1: The *Kherson* was headed to Sulina, Romania.

August 10: Many ships, including the *Kherson*, entered the port of Feodosia.

August 30: * The *Kherson* was in Constantinople.

September 1920

September 1, 4, 7-8, 10: * The *Kherson* was in Constantinople.

Also in September, the *Kherson* transported cadets from the island of Lemnos to Egypt.

October 1920

October 4: * The *Kherson* was in Alexandria, Egypt.

October 16-19: The *Kherson* transported the White Army officers from the island of Lemnos to Sevastopol, who were evacuated there in March 1920.

End of October: The *Kherson* arrived in Feodosia with 4,000 refugees.

November 1920

The *Kherson* was back in Sevastopol. We are unsure exactly when they arrived at the port, but the steamship remained here, preparing for the historic evacuation on November 14.

By November 7: The *Kherson* docked at Pier #8 on the north side of the Sevastopol big bay.

November 14: At about 2 am, the *Kherson* left the Kilen-Bay and anchored in the outer roadstead of the Sevastopol port, where it was delayed until about 8 pm when it finally, almost the last one, went out to sea.

November 15: Several other ships departed from Streletskaya Bay.

November 16: The *Kherson* reached the Bosphorus.

November 17: The *Kherson* arrived in Constantinople at night.

November 17-20: The *Kherson* was anchored at the roadstead of Constantinople.

November 20: The *Kherson* departed Constantinople.

November 21: The *Kherson* reached Gallipoli.

November 22-26: Units of the Russian Army of General Wrangel disembarked from the *Kherson* to the shores of Gallipoli.

December 1920

December 1, 4, 6-8: * The *Kherson* was in Constantinople.

*These dates do not represent the ship's arrival or departure (unless specified as such), but the dates it was officially documented as being in port. The ship may have stayed longer or shorter, but it was certainly present on these specific dates.[90]

December 23: The *Kherson* entered the Bay of Kotor.

December 31: The *Kherson* was redirected to the port of Bakar, stood there in the roadstead for three weeks, waiting for the end of the quarantine, then refugees disembarked.

January 1921

January 29: Lydia writes her first entry in her diary in Bakar, Croatia.

January 30: The *Kherson* arrived in the Bay of Kotor.

February 1921

February 2: Celebration for Chief Engineer Truen (6).

April 1921:

April 5: Lydia's Name Day Celebration.

April 14: The *Kherson* crew refused to work until they were given food.

---

90   The Russian State Historical Archives. F.98. Inv.7. File 23. P.7, 8, 9, 10, 18, 19. 21.

End of April: The *Kherson* was transferred to the London Steamship and Trading Company.

May 1921:

May 1: The *Kherson* crew and family celebrated Easter.

May 10: All the children were photographed.

May 15: First of 4 weddings.

June 1921

June 15: The *Kherson* is renamed *Raetoria*, and the British flag was flown on the mast.

July 1921

July 30: Dimitri Komarkoff received his paycheck.

August 1921

August 2: Lydia and her family moved off the ship into a hotel in Castelnuovo (current day Herceg Novi, Montenegro).

September 1921

September 16: The Komarkoff family received a letter from Uncle Kostya urging them to join him in New York.

October 1921

October 6: The *Kherson* departed the Bay of Kotor for Malta.

November 1921

November 11: The Komarkoff family decides to meet Uncle Kostya in America.

December 1921

December 8: Lydia turned 12 years old in Novi Sad.

February 1922

February 13: The *Kherson* crew won the court case against the British shipping company. The court ordered the sale of the ship.

March 1922
March 18: General Peter Wrangel visited Lydia's classroom in Novi Sad.

April 1922
April 4: Lydia watched King Alexander I and Queen (then Princess) Maria pass by in a car on the streets of Novi Sad.

May 1922
May 12: The Komarkoff family boarded a train in Novi Sad to begin their journey to America.

June 1922
June 5: The Komarkoff family arrived in New York City.

1923
January: Seven crew members remained in Malta.

1924
The *Kherson* was dismantled and turned into scrap metal in Venice, Italy.

APPENDIX B

Kherson Crew Members and Others Traveling Aboard the *Kherson*

Volunteer Fleet: List (muster roll) of the crew of the ship "Kherson." December 4, 1920

The Russian State Historical Archives. F.98. Inv.7. File 23. P.14-14back, with information added from P.94-99.

All crew members were Russian citizens unless otherwise specified.

Information gathered about the crew members who immigrated to the United States is from Ancestry, Family Search, or MyHeritage websites.

Photographs belong to either the Komarkoff or the Anikeeff descendants, unless otherwise specified.

Birthdates of the crew members are according to the Julian Calendar (old style). All other dates are according to the Gregorian Calendar (New Style).

This photo depicts the crew members aboard the *Kherson*. The lifebuoy has *Kherson* written in Russian displayed on it. The man sitting on the far right is Michael Anikeeff (7), with a child in front of him, who appears blurred due to movement. The man sitting, wearing the hat is the chief engineer Truen (6). Perhaps these are the engineers of the ship.

Figure 56: Crew members on the deck of the steamship Kherson.
Courtesy of the Anikeeff Family.

(1) Captain: Viktor Franzevich Schmelz
Boarded the *Kherson*: October 1, 1919

Captain Schmelz was born on February 26, 1878, in Simferopol, Russia.[91] He was in service with the Russian Volunteer Fleet from May 20, 1899. Lydia Pavlovna Kolosova was Viktor's second wife and accompanied him on the voyage. Their son, Alexander "Sasha," was born on the ship on August 27, 1920. Lydia describes how she would push "Little Sasha" in his carriage on the ship's deck. On the next page is a photo of Sasha on deck. The Schmelz family stayed on the *Kherson* until the ship was sold in Malta, then in 1922, they moved to Serbia before immigrating to Australia in 1950. The daughter of "Little Sasha" is Abbess Elizabeth, born in Melbourne, Australia, who is currently the abbess in the Convent of St. Mary Magdalene in the Garden of Gethsemane in Jerusalem. The second son of Schmelz, Nikolai, was born in Malta.

*Figure 57: Captain Schmelz.
Courtesy of the Schmelz Family
(Abbess Elizabeth).*

---

91 Российский государственный архив военно-морского флота (РГА ВМФ). Ф. 933. 2-й Балтийский флотский экипаж г. Петроград. Оп. 2. Д.179. Шмельцев Виктор Францевич. Прапорщик по морск. части. 1905. Л.25 / The Russian State Archives of the Navy. F.933. 2nd Baltic Fleet Crew, Petrograd. Inv. 2. File 179. Schmelzev Victor Franzevich. Ensign for the naval unit. 1905. P.25. Российский государственный исторический архив (РГИА). Ф.98. Пароходное общество "Добровольный флот". Оп.2. 1879-1920 гг. Д.516. Пароходное общество "Добровольный флот". Личные дела. Шмельц В.Ф. 1900-1919 / Шмельц В.Ф. 1900-1919 гг. / The Russian State Historical Archives (RSHA). F.98. Inv.2. File 516. The Shipping company "Volunteer fleet". Personal files. Schmelz V.F. 1900-1919.

Figure 58: Alexander Viktorovich Schmelz, son of the Kherson's Captain Schmelz. Courtesy of the Anikeeff Family.

(2) Chief Mate: Orest Vladimirovich Semenopulo
Boarded the *Kherson*: October 10, 1919

Semenopulo, born on March 9, 1887, enlisted in the Russian Volunteer Fleet in 1906 and moved ships frequently, often a result of a conflict with either the captain or other personnel. He was very eager to rise in the ranks and would become disgruntled if he was demoted. Finally, in November 1915, he was employed in the position of chief mate of the steamship *Suchan*.[92] This vessel sailed to the port of New York City picking up a full load of supplies for the army. On its return to Russia, around the North Cape near the northern Norway Coast on October 6, 1916, a German submarine captured the ship and the entire crew. Orest and the crew survived terrible hunger in a prisoner of war camp and many crew members died from exhaustion and disease.[93] He remained here until January 1919.

Orest traveled on the *Kherson* with his wife Maria, and their children Mary "Manya" and Irene "Ira." Lydia mentions the children in her diaries,

92   РГИА. Ф.98. Оп.2. Д.465. Пароходное общество "Добровольный флот". Личные дела. Семенопуло О.В. 1911-1919 гг. / RSHA. F.98. Inv.2. File 465. Shipping Company "Volunteer Fleet". Personal files. Semenopulo O.V. 1911-1919.

93   Бочек Александр Павлович. Всю жизнь с морем. Гл.VIII. Война: / Bochek Alexander Pavlovich. All life with the sea. Ch.VIII. War: https://biography .wikireading.ru/hMvCeXf94Y

and they also appear in photographs. This family continued their voyage on the *Kherson* to Malta in the latter part of 1921, as many other crew members did, eventually immigrating to London, England and becoming a naturalized citizen in 1927. There was a third child, also named Orest, born in 1920. Lydia does not mention him, and I do not know if he was born on the ship or prior to sailing.

Orest died in 1951 with his wife dying one year earlier. The children, Manya died in 1982, Ira in 1996, and son Orest in 1961. All are buried in Chelsea, London, and England. The youngest Orest was an actor known as "Orest Orloff" and appeared in three films, "Oh…Rosalinda!!" (1955), "The Divided Heart" (1954), and "The Four Just Men" (1959).[94]

(3) Second Mate: Vissarion Dimitrievich Malyavin
Boarded the *Kherson*: March 8, 1920

Malyavin, born on July 13, 1892, joined the Russian Volunteer Fleet in 1919. His commanders repeatedly noted his excellent abilities and love for naval service.[95] He traveled on the *Kherson* with his wife Elizaveta Ivanovna, and their young daughter Katya. Lydia spent much of her time with Katya on the ship and recalled how her mother took them on excursions to shore for picnics in the Bay of Kotor. Like many other refugees aboard the *Kherson*, the Malyavin family stayed in Malta until the ship was sold. After leaving Malta they relocated to Harbin, China in exile. Lydia received several postcards from the family after their departure from the ship and kept a photo of Katya from 1930 in her collection. She spoke very warmly of Katya.

---

94 https://www.film.ru/person/orest-orloff?ysclid=m2t6gpdzif530485168

95 РГА ВМФ. Ф.406. Послужные и формулярные списки чинов морского ведомства (Коллекция). Оп.9. Послужные списки офицеров. Д. 2504М / The Russian State Archives of the Navy. F.406. Service records and service forms of the ranks of the naval department (Collection). Inv.9. Service records of officers. File 2504M.

Figure 59: Katya Malyavina in Harbin, China.
Courtesy of the Buzyna Family.

Figure 60: Elizaveta Malyavina
with her son, Dimitri - Katya's
mother and brother. Courtesy of
the Buzyna Family.

Figure 61: Katya on the shores of Zelenika, with trains visible along the coastline - perhaps the very ones Lydia described in her diaries. Courtesy of the Buzyna Family.

Figure 62: Elizaveta Ivanovna, Katya, and Vissarion Dimitrievich Malyavin, aboard the steamship Kherson. Courtesy of the Anikeeff Family.

Diary entry from Wednesday, January 3, 1923, when she learned that Katya and her family will immigrate to China. She must have been sorely disappointed she was not joining her in the United States.

> *"Today, when I came home from school, I was very, very happy since I received a letter from Katyusha and a photograph where she is photographed alone and another where she is with Elizaveta Ivanovna, Visarion Dimitrievich, and Katyusha. Soon they will leave for Harbin [China], I am so sorry but cannot do anything about it. I kissed Katyusha, her mama and papa tightly, tightly and cannot not look at the photos enough. Mama said that I would also have a photo taken to send to Katyusha. Katyusha grew a lot and looks like a lovely doll. I looked at the photos of her all day and fear that they will not have rough seas."*

(4) Third Mate: Eduard Christoforovich Berg
Boarded the *Kherson*: September 15, 1919
Berg was born on April 28, 1894, and joined the Volunteer Fleet in 1914. He previously sailed on steamships of private owners and the Russian East Asian Company.

(5) Fourth Mate: Grigory Vsevolodovich Yalovikov
Boarded the *Kherson*: December 24, 1918.
Yalovikov was born on November 28, 1891,[96] and joined the Volunteer Fleet on October 5, 1908. When he boarded the *Kherson* on December 24, 1918, he held the position of senior navigator's apprentice, and on December 19, 1919, he was promoted to Fourth Mate.[97]

---

96 РГА ВМФ. Ф.432. Морское училище. Петроград (14 января 1701 г. - 09 марта 1918 г.). Оп.2. Аттестационные тетради. Д.2505. Яловиков Григорий Всеволодович. 1907-1908. Л.1 / The Russian State Archives of the Navy (The Naval Archives). F.432. Naval School. Petrograd (January 14, 1701 – March 9, 1918). Inv.2. Certification notebooks. File 2505. Yalovikov Grigory Vsevolodovich. 1907-1908. P.1.

97 The Russian State Historical Archives. F.98. Inv.7. File 23. P.65.

On June 6, 1920, he sustained an accidental gunshot wound to the face that required medical treatment, while the *Kherson* was docked in Sevastopol.

(6) Chief Engineer: Alfred Viktor Martinovich Truen
Boarded the *Kherson*: November 12, 1919

Truen was born on January 4, 1859,[98] and joined the Volunteer Fleet on November 12, 1896. Unlike most of the crew, he was Roman Catholic. Born to a French father, he had French citizenship and became a Russian citizen in 1898. At his request, the Tsar granted him personal honorary citizenship (a status close to nobility) for his long-term service. He is listed in the 1914 Odessa directory as a nobleman. This social class possessed more acknowledged privilege and higher social status than most other classes in society. He was also awarded foreign orders. He participated in the Russo-Japanese War as an assistant to the chief ship engineer aboard the auxiliary cruiser *Dnieper* from November 1904 to 1905. Lydia describes a party on the ship to celebrate his 25th anniversary with the Volunteer Fleet on February 2, 1921.

Figure 63: Alfred Viktor Martinovich Truen aboard the steamship Kherson. Courtesy of the Anikeeff Family.

---

98   РГА ВМФ. Ф.417. Главный Морской Штаб. Оп.3. Статистическое отделение (1885-1917 гг.). Мобилизационное отделение (1893-1917 гг.). Учебное отделение (1911-1917 гг.). Д.3119. Труэн А., прпщ. 1904-1912. Л.1 / The Russian State Archives of the Navy. F.417. General Naval Headquarters. Inv.3. Statistical Department (1885-1917). Mobilization Department (1893-1917). Educational Department (1911-1917). File 3119. Truen A., ensign. 1904-1912. P.1.

(7) First Assistant Engineer: Michael Kononovich Anikeeff
Boarded the *Kherson*: November 24, 1919

Anikeeff was born on September 1, 1882,[99] and joined the Volunteer Fleet on June 1, 1915. He was stationed in the cities of Odessa, Arkhangelsk, and Sevastopol. All three of his children, Evgenia "Zhenia," Nicholas "Kolya," and Alexis "Alyosha," and his wife Anna Ivanovna Tishkovsky, were born in Odessa, and in 1917, moved to Sevastopol. It is possible that his brother, family, and both sets of parents also resided there. Zhenia was Lydia's best friend on the ship, and they shared many memories together. I am now in contact with the descendants of this family.

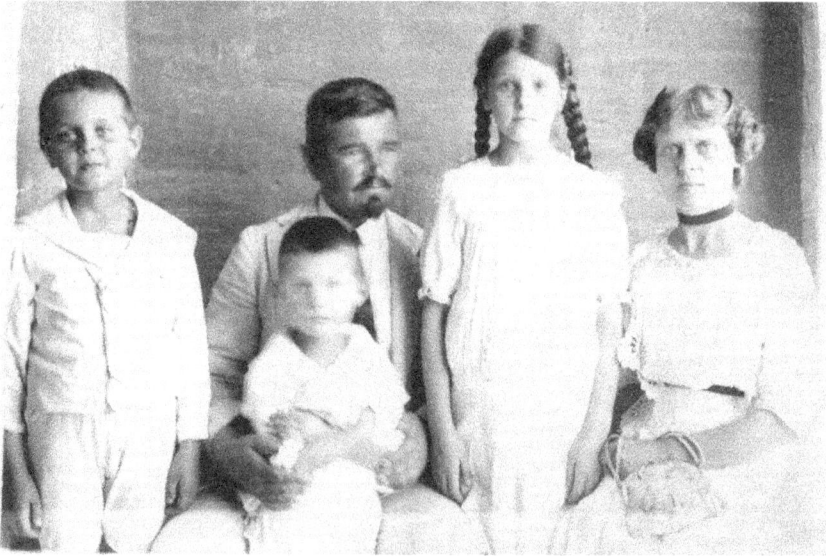

Figure 64: The Anikeeff family in Malta. Courtesy of the Anikeeff Family.

---

99   Scanned extract from the metric book on birth of Michail Anikeeff, received from Anikeeff family, and РГИА. Ф.98. Оп.2. Д.1491. Пароходное общество "Добровольный флот". Личные дела. Аникеев М.К. 1917-1919 гг. Л.1об / The Russian State Historical Archives. F.98. Inv.2. File 1491. Shipping Company "Volunteer Fleet". Personal files. Anikeev M.K. 1917-1919. P.1back.

(8) Second Assistant Engineer: Stepan Milentievich Vlasichenko

Boarded the *Kherson*: December 6, 1919

Vlasichenko was born on August 1, 1868, and was found in the 1897 Census living in Odessa. He joined the Volunteer Fleet in 1915.

(9) Third Assistant Engineer: Pavel Pavlovich Guibner

Boarded the *Kherson*: December 6, 1919

Guibner was born on July 25, 1889, and joined the Volunteer Fleet on the same day he boarded the *Kherson* on December 6, 1919.

(10) Ship Doctor: Mikhail Alexandrovich Bayev

Boarded the *Kherson*: March 1, 1920

Dr. Bayev (also spelled Baev, Baeff) was born on August 28, 1884, in Orel, Russia, and joined the Volunteer Fleet on the same date he boarded the *Kherson* on March 8, 1920. Dr. Bayev succeeded Dr. Slavsky as the ship's doctor after Slavsky resigned from the position in March 1920 while the steamship *Kherson* was in Novorossiysk. He served as the ship's doctor for two and a half years before immigrating to the United States on January 15, 1923, traveling from Constantinople via Malta. On the passenger list for the steamship *Madonna*, he stated his person of contact and destination as "friend, Dimitri Komarkoff at the Restaurant Petrograd on East 145th St." He married in 1928 and died in Michigan in 1968.

(11) Wireless Operator/Radiotelegraph Operator: Konstantin Mikhailovich Pytkovsky

Boarded the *Kherson*: May 16, 1919

Pytkovsky was born on November 16, 1891, and joined the Volunteer Army on December 6, 1915. His wife Nina must have accompanied him on the Crimean evacuation voyage aboard the *Kherson*, as their daughter was born in the former Yugoslavia in January 1923 (unknown exactly when they disembarked the *Kherson*, but it had to have been prior to October 1921 since that is when the ship departed for Malta), two days prior to her father immigrating to America. Nina and daughter Tatiana immigrated one year later.

(12) Radiotelegraph Operator: Vasily Ivanovich Vlasov
Boarded the *Kherson*: July 11, 1919

Vlasov was born on December 29, 1888, and joined the Volunteer Fleet on February 4, 1914.

(13) Junior Navigator Student: Evgeniy Klimentievich Stadnikov
Boarded the *Kherson*: December 21, 1918

Stadnikov was born on January 27, 1899 (new calendar), in Odessa and attended the Rostov Nautical School. He joined the Volunteer Fleet on December 21, 1918. After leaving the *Kherson*, he frequently traveled to the United States as a crew member aboard various ships. Eventually, he finally immigrated to the United States, arriving aboard the Steamship *Westernland* on October 13, 1937, the same year his first wife, Emilie, passed away. He had married her in Antwerp, Belgium, in 1928. Stadnikov remarried in New York City in 1946. He passed away on August 24, 1960, at the age of 61. To the best of my knowledge, he did not have any children.

(14) Junior Navigator Student: Vasily Nicholayevich Kurinsky
Boarded the *Kherson*: August 14, 1919

Kurinsky was born on March 11, 1896, and joined the Volunteer Fleet on July 11, 1918.

(15) Junior Navigator Student: Marian Osipovich Vengrovsky
Boarded the *Kherson*: November 7/20, 1919

Vengrovsky was born on May 8, 1897, and joined the Volunteer Fleet on November 20, 1919. He was a Polish citizen.

(16) Junior Navigator Student: Leonid Ivanovich Nechiporenko

Boarded the *Kherson*: December 1 or 10, 1919

Nechiporenko was born on August 4, 1892, and joined the Volunteer Fleet on the same day he boarded the *Kherson*. He previously sailed on the training sailing ships in the Caspian, Azov, and Black Seas, also on the steamships of the Russian Steam Navigation and Trading Company.[100]

(17) First Aid Man: Boris Gavrilovich Kazantsev

Boarded the *Kherson*: December 6, 1919

Kazantsev was born in 1896 and joined the Volunteer Fleet on the same date he boarded the *Kherson*, December 6, 1919.

(18) Orderly: Ivan Ivanovich Petrov

Boarded the *Kherson*: May 9, 1920

Petrov was born on February 15, 1888, and joined the Volunteer Fleet on the same date he boarded the *Kherson*, May 9, 1920.

(19) Boatswain: Evgeniy Petrovich Sukovatykh

Boarded the *Kherson*: December 3, 1918

Sukovatykh was born in approximately 1871 and joined the Volunteer Fleet on March 1, 1887. From 1891 to 1897, he served in the military. Lydia frequently mentions how the boatswain, likely Sukovatykh, who was listed as Boatswain on the crew list, took the kids for rides on the tender. She also writes how the boatswain poured water over her on a particularly hot day to cool her off. These events occurred in spring 1921 as they were anchored in the Bay of Kotor.

(20) Leading Seaman: Efim Galaktionovich Pavlenko

Boarded the *Kherson*: July 9, 1919

Pavlenko was born on January 20, 1891, and joined the Volunteer Fleet on June 5, 1914. He previously sailed on warships.

---

100   The Russian State Historical Archives. F.98. Inv.7. File 23. P.55.

(21) Carpenter: Karp Fedorovich Repeshko
Boarded the *Kherson*: August 26, 1919

Repeshko was born on October 13, 1883, and joined the Volunteer Fleet on August 26, 1919. Previously sailed on the training ship *Titania*. Possibly his wife is Anastasia I. Repeshko (99), who was the Emigrants' Stewardess.

(22) Senior Helmsman: Nicholai Kallistratovich Lukianchikov
Boarded the *Kherson*: March 3, 1920

Lukianchikov was born in 1865 and joined the Volunteer Fleet in 1892. He previously sailed on the ships of the Russian Steam Navigation and Trading Company.

(23) Helmsman: Konstantin Stepanovich Gorozhankin
Boarded the *Kherson*: August 26, 1919

Gorozhankin was born on May 12, 1896, and joined the Volunteer Fleet on the same date he boarded the *Kherson*, August 26, 1919. He previously sailed on the ships of the Russian Steam Navigation and Trading Company, the Caucasus and Mercury Company, and the Ministry of Trade and Industry.

(24) Helmsman: Alexander Timofeyevich Rudenok
Boarded the *Kherson*: March 2, 1920

Rudenok was born on October 6, 1897, and joined the Volunteer Fleet on the same date he boarded the *Kherson*, March 2, 1920. He previously sailed on the ships of the Merchant Navy and the Ministry of Trade and Industry.

(25) Helmsman: Daniil Ivanovich Teslya
Boarded the *Kherson*: April 27, 1920

Teslya was born on December 11, 1870, and joined the Volunteer Fleet in 1894. He previously sailed on the ships of the Russian Steam Navigation and Trading Company.

(26) Helmsman Supernumerary: Leonty Alexeyevich Spisovsky

Boarded the *Kherson*: After September 1920

Lydia mentions a "Mr. Spesovsky" in her diary. We assume this is whom she meant.

Entry for: Friday, April 22, 1921

> *"Today I studied and then strolled on the deck. After dinner Mr. Spesovsky took the children for a ride on the tender and I rowed, the children played hide-and-seek on the ship. In the evening I washed dishes and that is how I spent the day."*

(27) Able Seaman: Yusup Islyatulin Muceyev

Boarded the *Kherson*: December 3, 1918

Muceyev was born on November 2, 1892, and joined the Volunteer Fleet in 1916. He previously sailed on the steamships of the Caucasus and Mercury Company.

(28) Able Seaman: Alexey Petrovich Kurnosov

Boarded the *Kherson*: June 1, 1919

Kurnosov was born on September 28, 1887, and joined the Volunteer Fleet on the same date he boarded the *Kherson*, June 1, 1919. He previously sailed on warships and sailing vessels.

(29) Able Seaman: Grigory Mikhailovich Marchenko

Boarded the *Kherson*: April 26, 1920

Marchenko was born on April 17, 1895, and joined the Volunteer Fleet on April 1, 1905.

(30) Ordinary Seaman: Peter Antonovich Avgis

Boarded the *Kherson*: April 4, 1919

Avgis was born on November 2, 1891, and joined the Volunteer Fleet on the same date he boarded the *Kherson*, April 4, 1920. He was a Lithuanian citizen.

(31) Ordinary Seaman: Alexander Ivanovich Petrov
Boarded the *Kherson*: January 27, 1920

Petrov was born in November 1899 and joined the Volunteer Fleet on the same date he boarded the *Kherson*, January 27, 1920.

(32) Ordinary Seaman: Alexander Fomich Mezhero
Boarded the *Kherson*: August 28, 1919

Mezhero was born in June 1896 and joined the Volunteer Fleet on the same date he boarded the *Kherson*, August 28, 1919. He previously sailed on the steamships of the Caucasus and Mercury Company.

(33) Ordinary Seaman: Evgeniy Efimovich Zaporozhchenko
Boarded the *Kherson*: December 6, 1919

Zaporozhchenko was born on November 15, 1898, and joined the Volunteer Fleet on the same date he boarded the *Kherson*, December 6, 1919. He previously sailed on military transports and ships of the Russian Steam Navigation and Trading Company.

(34) Ordinary Seaman: Mikhail Aronovich Stamboly
Boarded the *Kherson*: August 19, 1919

Stamboly was born in January 1890 and joined the Volunteer Fleet on May 1, 1919. He previously sailed on ships on the Kuban River.

(35) Ordinary Seaman: Grigory Petrovich Sutyrin
Boarded the *Kherson*: January 10, 1920

Sutyrin was born on November 14, 1886, and joined the Volunteer Fleet on the same date he boarded the *Kherson*, January 10, 1920. He previously sailed on the ships of the Vladivostok Transport Fleet.

(36) Ordinary Seaman: Vladimir Ivanovich Proskuryakov
Boarded the *Kherson*: June 1, 1920

Proskuryakov was born on July 15, 1902, and joined the Volunteer Fleet on the same date he boarded the *Kherson*, June 1, 1919.

(37) Ordinary Seaman: Silvester M. Levchenko
Boarded the *Kherson*: July 3, 1920[101]

(38) Ordinary Seaman: Mikhail M. Talanov
Boarded the *Kherson*: July 4, 1920[102]

(39) Ordinary Seaman: Fedor Gordeyevich Mamchich
Boarded the *Kherson*: July 6, 1920[103]

(40) Ordinary Seaman: Sergei M. Lakisov
Boarded the *Kherson*: July 16, 1920[104]

(41) Ordinary Seaman: M. E. Apukhtin
Boarded the *Kherson*: Between September 10 and December 4, 1920

(42) Ordinary Seaman: O. P. Peresypkin
Boarded the *Kherson*: Between September 10 and December 4, 1920

(43) Ordinary Seaman: A. I. Anreyev
Boarded the *Kherson*: Between September 10 and December 4, 1920

(44) Ordinary Seaman: I. Z. Vyrypayev
Boarded the *Kherson*: Between September 10 and December 4, 1920

(45) Baker: Nicholai D. Kalashnikov
Boarded the *Kherson*: July 11, 1920[105]

(46) Deck Crew Cook: M. A. Sitnikov
Boarded the *Kherson*: Between September 10 and December 4, 1920
On page 129 of Inna Grubmair's book *Emigrants from Russia in Zagreb*, Michael Sitnikov is mentioned as a graduate of the Faculty of Veterinary Medicine at the University of Zagreb in 1932. There is insufficient

---

101   The Russian State Historical Archives. F.98. Inv.7. File 23. P.49.
102   Ibid.
103   Ibid.
104   Ibid P.49back.
105   Ibid.

evidence to confirm that M. A. Sitnikov listed in the *Kherson* is the same person mentioned in the book, however it is a possibility.

(47) Cook's Mate: Theodosy A. Zen'kovsky
Boarded the *Kherson*: August 12, 1920[106]

(48) Mechanic 1st Class: Franz Georgievich Burbool
Boarded the *Kherson*: January 12, 1915

Burbool was born on August 4, 1866, and joined the Volunteer Fleet in 1896. On Sunday, July 24, 1921, Lydia mentioned in her diary that he took her and Zhenia to the engine room, and it was *"very interesting."*

(49) Mechanic 1st Class: Mikhail Ivanovich Klimenko
Boarded the *Kherson*: December 6, 1919

Klimenko was born in September 1887 and joined the Volunteer Fleet in 1906. He previously sailed on the ships of the Russian Steam Navigation and Trading Company and the Danube Company and on private ones.

(50) Mechanic 1st Class: Anatoly Nicholayevich Skochemaro
Boarded the *Kherson*: April 16, 1919

Skochemaro was born on September 12, 1898, in Kerch, Russia, and joined the Volunteer Fleet on February 26, 1919. He previously sailed on the transport ship *Lukull*.

Lydia frequently mentioned him in her diaries and even received a photo of him with a handwritten message on the back. She affectionately referred to him as "Dyadya Skochemaro," meaning "Uncle Skochemaro," despite not being related. Children commonly use the term to address adults as a sign of respect.

His marriage records[107] from 1932 in Paris named his parents as Nicholas Skochemaro (spelled Skoutchemaro on the document) and Eudoxie Koupidonoff. He married Victoire Porcelli, who was born in Berdiansk, Ukraine.

---

106 Ibid.

107 Paris archives, 1923-1932. Marriages 15 arrondissement V11E 504

Figure 65: Skochemaro sent Lydia this photo with a handwritten note on the back, dated 1922, Malta. Courtesy of the Buzyna Family.

Figure 66: Skochemaro sent this photo from France, where he was living at the time, with a note on the back addressed to Michael and Anna Ivanovna Anikeeff. Dated April 11, 1927. Courtesy of the Anikeeff Family.

(51) Mechanic 1st Class: Filimon Andreyevich Shcherboon
Boarded the *Kherson*: December 3, 1919

Shcherboon was born on December 14, 1883, and joined the Volunteer Fleet in 1907. He previously sailed on the ships of the Volunteer Fleet.

(52) Mechanic 2nd Class: Ivan Grigorievich Kruchek
Boarded the *Kherson*: April 4, 1919

Kruchek was born in 1898 and joined the Volunteer Fleet on the same date he boarded the *Kherson* on April 4, 1919. He remained on the *Kherson* as they sailed to Malta in October 1921 and remained there until he immigrated to the United States on January 18, 1923. He moved to Detroit, Michigan, where he married his wife Nina (who was also born in Russia) in 1926 and had two children, Alexander and Valentine. (Information taken from his Petition for Citizenship in 1929). Lydia also mentions "Mr. Kruchek" in her diaries. She describes his arrival in New York City, which corresponds with the ship passenger list I discovered on Ancestry.

Lydia's entry dated Friday, January 19, 1923:

> *"...Later, Mr. Kruchek came at 5 o'clock. He arrived in New York City yesterday. He brought photographs from Zhenia [Anikeeff] and Uncle Skochemaro [(50)]. I, of course, was very happy. He sat with us a rather long time and told us about our "Kherson" people. He left at 9 o'clock and I went to bed soon after."*

As you can imagine, Lydia was especially excited to see "Uncle Vanya" (as she referred to him later in the diaries. Vanya, or Ivan, can be translated to John in English) because he brought a letter from her best friend Zhenia from the *Kherson*. Her family remained in Malta for the time being.

(53) Mechanic 2nd Class: Vasily Andreyevich Perevalov
Boarded the *Kherson*: April 16, 1919

Perevalov was born in approximately 1860 and joined the Volunteer Fleet in 1879. He previously sailed on the ships of the Russian Steam Navigation and Trading Company.

(54) Mechanic 2nd Class: Nicholai Mitrofanovich Shmelev
Boarded the *Kherson*: September 15, 1919

Shmelev was born on July 27, 1891, and joined the Volunteer Fleet on the same date he boarded the *Kherson* on September 15, 1919.

(55) Mechanic 2nd Class: Vladimir Nicholayevich Nasonov
Boarded the *Kherson*: August 25, 1919

Nasonov was born on June 23, 1894, and joined the Volunteer Fleet on May 15, 1919. He previously sailed on the steamships *Titania* and *Ekaterinodar*.

(56) Mechanic 2nd Class: Nicholai Antonovich Rachkov
Boarded the *Kherson*: December 8, 1919

Rachkov was born in October 1893 and joined the Volunteer Fleet on the same date he boarded the *Kherson* on December 8, 1919.

(57) Mechanic 2nd Class: Policarp Alexandrovich Meitus
Boarded the *Kherson*: December 8, 1919

Meitus was born on Feb 23, 1866, and joined the Volunteer Fleet in 1890. During the Russo-Japanese War he was sent to a floating workshop in Libava (current day Liepaja, Latvia, on the Baltic Sea).

(58) Mechanic 2nd Class: Mikhail Eduardovich Pavlovsky
Boarded the *Kherson*: May 13, 1920

Pavlovsky was born in October 1883 and joined the Volunteer Fleet on the same date he boarded the *Kherson* on May 13, 1919.

(59) Mechanic 2nd Class: V. K. Verzhbovsky
Boarded the *Kherson*: Between September 10, 1920, and December 4, 1920

(60) Mechanic 2nd Class: A. I. Galuza
Boarded the *Kherson*: Between September 10, 1920, and December 4, 1920

(61) Mechanic 2nd Class: Adolf Gansovich Kigo
Boarded the *Kherson*: August 28, 1919

Kigo was born on May 30, 1896, and joined the Volunteer Fleet on the same date he boarded the *Kherson* on August 28, 1919. He was an Estonian citizen.

(62) Electrician: Prokhor Kirillovich Yantchook
Boarded the *Kherson*: March 4, 1919

Yantchook was born on July 28, 1889, and joined the Volunteer Fleet on January 2, 1912. Yantchook was in military service from December 1913 to March 19, 1919, when he joined the Volunteer Fleet. Yantchook was found on the same passenger list as the Anikeeff family on August

1, 1923, arriving in New York City. His wife, Glikeria, and daughter Nadezhda (born August 1920) followed him to the United States later. They lived in Detroit, Michigan and had 2 more children after Nadezhda (Nadine) - Vera and Paul.

(63) Electrician: Nicholai Vladimir Pavlovich Gazenbush/ Hasenbusch
Boarded the *Kherson*: December 9, 1919

Gazenbush/Hasenbusch was born on December 4, 1862, in what is now Chişinău, Moldova. He joined the Volunteer Fleet in 1891 and is recorded as a crew member on the Volunteer Fleet steamship *Tambov* sailing from Murmansk, Russia to New York City in 1916 and from Arkhangelsk, Russia to New York City in 1917. It appears his family stayed behind in Odessa, as his father, Paul Konstantin (born in Estonia), and one of his siblings were laid to rest at the Odessa Second Cemetery.[108] Gazenbush died in Malta on March 3, 1922.

(64) Mechanics' Cook: Andrey Ivanovich Gureyev
Boarded the *Kherson*: October 1, 1919

Gureyev was born on October 16, 1882, and joined the Volunteer Fleet on the same date he boarded the *Kherson* on October 1, 1919.

(65) Messman: Boleslav Adolfovich Chernetsky
Boarded the *Kherson*: December 12, 1919

Chernetsky was born on December 13, 1887, and joined the Volunteer Fleet on December 7, 1913. On August 1, 1921, the day before Lydia and her family bid farewell to the *Kherson*, she mentioned that all the children were treated to a ride on the tender with "Boleslav." Given that Chernetsky is the only Boleslav listed among the crew, it is likely he was the one she was describing.

(66) Stoker First Class: Nikita Nicholayevich Zhigulin
Boarded the *Kherson*: May 18, 1919

---

108 https://sites.google.com/view/2cmentarz/

Zhigulin was born in May 1879 and joined the Volunteer Fleet on the same date he boarded the *Kherson* on May 18, 1919. He previously sailed on the ships of the Regir Company.

(67) Stoker First Class: Ignaty Ivanovich Ivanov
Boarded the *Kherson*: July 11, 1919
Ivanov was born in December 1871 and joined the Volunteer Fleet on March 27, 1918.

(68) Stoker First Class: Samuel Sidorovich Gryzun
Boarded the *Kherson*: July 19, 1919
Gryzun was born about 1878 and joined the Volunteer Fleet in 1904.

(69) Stoker First Class: Nikiphor Ivanovich Korsun
Boarded the *Kherson*: February 5, 1920
Korsun was born about 1875 and joined the Volunteer Fleet on the same date he boarded the *Kherson* on February 5, 1920. He previously sailed on private ships.

(70) Stoker First Class: Ilia Osipovich Afanasiev
Boarded the *Kherson*: July 16, 1919
Afansiev was born on July 18, 1897, and joined the Volunteer Fleet on the same date he boarded the *Kherson* on July 16, 1919. He previously sailed on the steam scows on the Sea of Azov.

(71) Stoker First Class: Ivan Ivanovich Kolesnichenko
Boarded the *Kherson*: December 20, 1919
Kolesnichenko was born on June 1, 1886, and joined the Volunteer Fleet on February 11, 1913. He previously sailed on the ships of the Russian Steams Navigation and Trading Company and of the ships of the Northern Shipping Company.

(72) Stoker First Class: Ivan (Iosif) Iosifovich Sinkevich
Boarded the *Kherson*: March 4, 1920

Sinkevich was born on March 27, 1896, and joined the Volunteer Fleet on the same date he boarded the *Kherson* on March 4, 1920. He previously sailed on the ships of the Russian Company.

Lydia was a bridesmaid at his wedding and described the day beautifully. From her entry for Sunday, May 22, 1921 (they were still residing on the *Kherson* in the Bay of Kotor):

> *Today was another wedding. Getting married was Sinkevich and Lydia Stepanovna and Zhenia and I were bridesmaids again. We went to the church at 6:30, my mama also came, my best man, Skacheomaro, mama and I and Skacheomaro and the groom were the first to leave to buy flowers. Having bought the flowers everyone went to the church, after the groom and bride were married, we went to the restaurant. It was very joyous there, everyone drank champagne, wine and beer and ate ice cream. Mama and I, the doctor [Dr. Michael Alexandrovich Bayev], Aunt Liza, Constantine and Uncle Kolya [nickname for Nicholai] left earlier by carriage at 11 o'clock, having arrived at the pier we hired a tender and went to the ship.*

(73) Stoker First Class: Fedor Gerasimovich Filatov
Boarded the *Kherson*: March 4, 1920
Filatov was born on February 8, 1888, and joined the Volunteer Fleet on the same date he boarded the *Kherson* on March 4, 1920.

(74) Stoker First Class: Nikita S. Lysenko
Boarded the *Kherson*: July 5, 1920[109]

(75) Stoker First Class: Fedor Ignatievich Alexeyev
Boarded the *Kherson*: March 3, 1920
Alexeyev was born in 1884 and joined the Volunteer Fleet on the same date he boarded the *Kherson* on March 3, 1920.

---

109   The Russian State Historical Archives. F. 98. Inv.7. File 23. P.49.

(76) Stoker First Class: Nicholai Christophorovich Burkhanov

Boarded the *Kherson*: August 28, 1919

Burkhanov was born on March 12, 1898, and joined the Volunteer Fleet on the same date he boarded the *Kherson* on August 28, 1919. He previously sailed on the steamship *Shilka*.

(77) Stoker First Class: Gavriil Emelianovich Kuznetsov

Boarded the *Kherson*: March 4, 1920

Kuznetsov was born on March 26, 1891, and joined the Volunteer Fleet on the same date he boarded the *Kherson* on March 4, 1920.

(78) Stoker First Class: I. S. Bogomolov

Boarded the *Kherson*: Between September 10 and December 4, 1920

(79) Stoker First Class: B. M. Cherevatenko

Boarded the *Kherson*: Between September 10 and December 4, 1920

(80) Stoker First Class: Vsevold Isidorovich Vasilevsky

Boarded the *Kherson*: Between September 10 and December 4, 1920

According to his Petition for Citizenship to the United States in October 1927, he was born in St Petersburg, Russia on November 3, 1882. He immigrated to the United States aboard the steamship *Legie* on October 18, 1922. His last foreign residence was Malta, which confirms he sailed on the *Kherson* with the remaining crew members in October 1921 to Malta. He married Glikeria on October 4, 1923, in New York City.

Lydia mentions "Vsevold Isidorovich" and "Mr. Vasilevsky" several times in her diary. Her family received a letter from him on December 11, 1921, suggesting he was likely in Malta at the time. He sent news that he would send their letters to Odessa (from Malta).

Lydia's entry from Thursday, December 28, 1922: [Lydia and her family had been in the United States since June of 1922)

> *...In the evening suddenly Mr. Vasilevsky came over. He had arrived from Malta very recently [October 18]. He told us*

about Katyusha [Katya Malyavina] and about everyone,
everyone. We, of course, were very happy to see such a good
fellow from "Kherson". He left rather late…

She last mentions him on Sunday, May 13, 1923. He came over for a
visit during dinnertime.

Figure 67: This photo[110] of
Vsevold Isidorovich Vasilevsky
was taken during his studies
at St. Petersburg University
(1911-1914). From the Central
State Historical Archives of
St Petersburg.

110   Центральный государственный исторический архив Санкт-Петербурга.
Ф.14. Императорский Петроградский универсет. Петроград. 1819–1918.
Оп.3. Дела правления и правления по хозяйственному столу. Личные
дела студентов за 1831, 1870-1916 гг. Д. 58919. Василевский Всеволод
Исидорович. 1911 Л.94 / Central State Historical Archives of St. Petersburg.
Fund 14. Imperial Petrograd University. Petrograd. 1819–1918. Inv.3. Affairs of
the board and the economic board. Personal files of students for 1831, 1870-1916.
File 58919. Vasilevsky Vsevolod Isidorovich. 1911. P.94.

(81) Stoker First Class: Alexander Ivanovich Gorelov
Boarded the *Kherson*: December 8, 1919

Gorelov was born on August 30, 1896, and joined the Volunteer Fleet on the same date he boarded the *Kherson* on December 8, 1919. He previously sailed on the steamships *Kornilov* and *Konstantin*.

(82) Stoker First Class: Alexander Grigorievich Derkachev
Boarded the *Kherson*: April 19, 1920

Derkachev was born on April 10, 1897, and joined the Volunteer Fleet on the same date he boarded the *Kherson* on April 19, 1920. He sailed previously on the steamships *Ekaterinodar, Engineer Avdakov*, and *Titania*.

Lydia describes participating as a bridesmaid in the first of several weddings that occurred after Easter in 1921. She thoroughly enjoyed taking part in the weddings of the *Kherson* crew members, which became a cherished memory of her time aboard the ship. How wonderful the adults thought to include the children in the experiences. Derkachev, along with other stokers from the *Kherson,* participated as well. Lydia's entry from Sunday, May 15, 1921:

> *Today is Nata's wedding and because of this Zhenia [Anikeeff] and I are bridesmaids, and my Best Men are Slobodianik (85) and Derkachev (82), and Zhenia's are Petrov-Tokarev (87) and Sazonovich (86), we went at 3 o'clock by train for the flowers. On the way we stopped at Maria Martinovna's, and having bought the flowers we got in the carriage and went to meet the bride. Having arrived at the church the groom and bride were married, and we went to the restaurant. There were many guests including my mama and papa, we ate and drank and later danced and were also photographed. We arrived on the ship at 1 o'clock at night and we welcomed the bride and that is how I had a very fun day.*

(83) Stoker Second Class: Stephan Kirikovich Malchevsky
Boarded the *Kherson*: August 26, 1919

Malchevsky was born in 1888 and joined the Volunteer Fleet on the same date he boarded the *Kherson* on August 26, 1919. He previously sailed on the steamship *Titania* and the icebreaker *Petrovsk* in the Caspian Sea.

(84) Stoker Second Class: Dmitry Semenovich Andreyev
Boarded the *Kherson*: August 28, 1919

Andreyev was born on March 26, 1895, and joined the Volunteer Fleet on the same date he boarded the *Kherson* on August 28, 1919. He previously sailed on the Russian Steam Navigation and Trading Company ships.

(85) Stoker Second Class: Alexander Nicholayevich Slobodyanik
Boarded the *Kherson*: December 6, 1919

Slobodyanik was born on June 10, 1900, and joined the Volunteer Fleet on the same date he boarded the *Kherson* on July 6, 1919. He previously sailed on ships No. 142 and No. 67. Lydia mentions him in her diaries, participating in a wedding together.

(86) Stoker Second Class: Leonty Vasilievich Sazanovich
Boarded the *Kherson*: December 6, 1919

Sazanovich was born on April 12, 1896, and joined the Volunteer Fleet on December 1, 1915. Lydia mentions him in her diaries, participating in a wedding together.

(87) Stoker Second Class: Vikenty Vikentievich Petrov-Tokarev
Boarded the *Kherson*: April 19, 1920

Petrov-Tokarev was born in May 1896 in Odessa and joined the Volunteer Fleet on the same date he boarded the *Kherson* on April 19, 1920. He previously sailed on motorboat No. 25 of the head of the road works department of the Bessarabian region.

I discovered him in the 1897 Odessa census at eight months old, living with his father, also named Vikenty Vikentievich, and his mother.

His brother Nicholai was born in 1898. Vikenty Vikentievich Senior also served with the Volunteer Fleet on numerous steamships, including the *Kherson* at one point.[111] After serving as Captain (Petrov-Tokarev, Senior) on the steamship *Batum* in 1927, he was arrested and banned from living in 6 cities of the border regions for three years. Nicholai was also a victim of repression and was arrested on July 15, 1938, and executed on November 2, 1938.[112]

Lydia references Petrov-Tokarev twice in her diaries. The first mention occurs at a wedding on May 15, 1921 (refer to the description under First Stoker Alexander Grigorievich Derkachev (82). The second instance was on May 14, 1923, when she received a registered letter from him. However, she did not elaborate on the letter's contents.

After he left the steamship *Kherson*, Petrov-Tokarev settled in Zagreb, Croatia, where he worked as a railway employee. On August 25, 1944, at the age of 48, he died of tuberculosis and was buried in Zagreb's Mirogoj Cemetery, where the grave has been preserved.[113]

(88) Stoker Second Class: Peter Grigorievich Vystorop
Boarded the *Kherson*: May 16, 1920
Vystorop was born on June 29, 1896, and joined the Volunteer Fleet on the same date he boarded the *Kherson* on May 16, 1920. He previously sailed on the yacht *Titania* and the transport *Ekaterinodar*.

---

111   Российский государственный исторический архив. Ф.98. Оп.1. 1865-1922 гг. Д.751 Пароходное общество "Добровольный флот". Комитет. Личный состав. Дело Петрова-Токарева В.В. 1915 г. / The Russian State Historical Archives. Fund 98. Inv.1. 1865-1922. File 751. Shipping Company "Volunteer Fleet". Committee. Personal files. The file of Petrov-Tokarev V.V. 1915.

112   From the Victims of Political Terror in the USSR, website https://base.memo.ru/person/show/2897145, https://base.memo.ru/person/show/2897146

113   Пушкадия-Рыбкина Т.В., Грубмайр И.И. Эмигранты из России в Загребе. Жизни и судьбы. - Изд. 2-е, испр. и доп. Загреб, 2019. С.320 / Pushkadia-Rybkina, Tatiana, and Inna Grubmair. Emigrants from Russia in Zagreb: Lives and Destinies. Second edition, corrected and supplemented. Zagreb, 2019. P.320.

(89) Stoker Second Class: A. N. Slezhinsky
Boarded the *Kherson*: Between September 10 and December 4, 1920
Madame Vera Matveyevna Slezhinsky, who Lydia describes as her tutor on the ship, could be his wife.

(90) Stoker Second Class: P. N. Melnikov
Boarded the *Kherson*: Between September 10 and December 4, 1920

(91) Stoker Second Class: A. M. Pokrovsky
Boarded the *Kherson*: Between September 10 and December 4, 1920

(92) Stoker Second Class: A. A. Dyatlov
Boarded the *Kherson*: Between September 10 and December 4, 1920

(93) Stoker Second Class: V. G. Zubov
Boarded the *Kherson*: Between September 10 and December 4, 1920

(94) Stoker Second Class: M. D. [Michael Dmitrievich?] Udovichenko
Boarded the *Kherson*: Between September 10 and December 4, 1920

(95) Stoker Second Class: A. A. Orlov
Boarded the *Kherson*: Between September 10 and December 4, 1920

(96) Stoker Second Class: N. S. Vlasichenko
Boarded the *Kherson*: Between September 10 and December 4, 1920
Perhaps a relative of Stepan Milentievich Vlasichenko (8).

(97) Emigrants' Lacquey: Grigory Vasilievich Bityutskikh
Boarded the *Kherson*: December 6, 1919
Bityutskikh was born in 1886 and joined the Volunteer Fleet on the same date he boarded the *Kherson* on December 6, 1919.

(98) Emigrants' Lacquey: Alexei Vasilievich Kondratov
Boarded the *Kherson*: March 6, 1920

Kondratov was born on June 17, 1897, and joined the Volunteer Fleet on the same date he boarded the *Kherson* on March 6, 1920. He previously sailed on the steamship *Regir*.

(99) Emigrants' Stewardess: Anastasia I. Repeshko
Boarded the *Kherson*: July 25, 1920
She is possibly the wife of Carpenter Karp Fedorovich Repeshko (21)

(100) Cook: Lev Pavlovich Tsvekanov
Boarded the *Kherson*: September 1, 1919[114]
Tsvekanov was born on February 18, 1886, and joined the Volunteer Fleet on the same date he boarded the *Kherson* on September 1, 1919. He previously sailed on the ships of the Northern Company and the East Asiatic Company and private vessels.

Tsvekanov brought Lydia a torte on her Name Day. She describes this in her entry for Tuesday, April 5, 1921:

> *Today, 23rd of March, is my Name Day [Old Calendar], in the morning after I got ready, Katya [Malyavina] came over and gave me figs, then Zhenia [Anikeeff] came and gave me a portrait of herself, and after that I went on the deck. Elizaveta Ivanovna [Malyavina] gave me beads, Elizaveta Vasilievna a pastry, Maria Aleksandrovna a napkin, Manya some cocoa and Vera Matveyevna some chocolate. Lydia Pavlovna [Perhaps this is Captain Schmelz' wife Lydia Pavlovna Kosolova] treated the children to a torte. I spent the day very well, in the evening Lev Pavlovich [Tsvekanov] brought a torte and later all the children came over. I spent the day happily and at 8:30 went to bed.*

(101) Purser: Dimitri Ivanovich Komarkoff
Boarded the *Kherson*: December 6, 1919

---

114   The Russian State Historical Archives. F.98. Inv.7. File 23. P.49back.

Komarkoff was born on May 4, 1874, and belonged to the Volunteer Fleet since June 1893. He was in military service from 1895 to 1899. He is my great-grandfather and Lydia's father.

(102) Lacquey: Ivan Stepanovich Suk
Boarded the *Kherson*: October 4, 1919

Suk was born in November 1876 and joined the Volunteer Fleet in 1901. He was in the military from 1915 to 1919.

(103) Lacquey: Anton Aloisovich Lipnitsky
Boarded the *Kherson*: December 6, 1919

Lipnitsky was born on January 17, 1887, and joined the Volunteer Fleet in 1911. He was in military service from 1914 until November 23, 1919.

(104) Lacquey: Pavel Georgievich Lambov
Boarded the *Kherson*: December 20, 1919

Lambov was born on May 8, 1894, and joined the Volunteer Fleet in 1915. He previously sailed on the steamship *Dnieper*.

(105) Lacquey: Nicholai Evstafievich Zazulya
Boarded the *Kherson*: March 17, 1917

Zazulya was born on April 21, 1895, and joined the Volunteer Fleet on the same date he boarded the *Kherson* on March 17, 1917. He previously sailed on the steamship *Dnieper*.

(106) Lacquey: Nicholai Ivanovich Bogolepov
Boarded the *Kherson*: December 6, 1919

Bogolepov was born on December 3, 1888, and joined the Volunteer Fleet on the same date he boarded the *Kherson* on December 6, 1919. He previously sailed on warships.

Lydia describes a funny incident that occurred when she was ashore with her father and Bogolepov in her entry for Tuesday, February 22, 1921:

> *Today after breakfast I went to town with my father and*
> *Nikolai Bogolepov came with us. In town we went to stores,*

*papa bought nuts, figs and pastry for mama, later we went
to a restaurant where papa and Nikolai drank beer, and
afterwards wine, I also had a shot of wine. But when we
were drinking wine a large, fat sausage fell on the counter,
everyone was frightened at first but later laughed. We were
in town until 3 o'clock and then went to the dock where the
tender was, boarded the tender, sat down, and went [to the
ship]. On the ship I went outside on the deck, in the evening
I read and then went to bed.*

(107) Lacquey Supernumerary: Ya. A. Shmorgun
Boarded the *Kherson*: Between September 10 and December 4, 1920

(108) Dishwasher: Konstantin Nicholayevich Perakis
Boarded the *Kherson*: October 14, 1919

Perakis, a Greek citizen, was born on October 25, 1899, and joined the
Volunteer Fleet on the same date he boarded the *Kherson* on October 14,
1919. He previously sailed on warships.

(109) Pot Cleaner: Anton Augustinovich Bolchunas
Boarded the *Kherson*: April 19, 1919

Bolchunas was born in approximately 1892 and joined the Volunteer Fleet
on the same date he boarded the *Kherson* on April 19, 1919. He previously sailed on the ships of the Russian Steam Navigation and Trading
Company and on the steamship *Regir*.

(110) Stewardess: Maria K. Rachkova
Boarded the *Kherson*: August 15, 1920[115]

Perhaps she is the wife of Nicholai Antononvich Rachkov (56).

(111) Laundress: Feodosia Abramovna Kurnosova
Boarded the *Kherson*: December 6, 1919

---

115   Ibid.

Kurnosova was born approximately April 1886 and joined the Volunteer Fleet on the same date she boarded the *Kherson* on December 6, 1919.

(112) Laundress: Maria I. Brutary

Boarded the *Kherson*: June 1, 1920[116]

Brutary is listed as the Laundress, along with Kurnosova (111) in the September 10, 1920, Crew List.[117]

Commandants of the *Kherson*:

The Commandant of the ship was in a vital, high-ranking position. He was responsible for all vessel operations. Neither one was listed on the Crew Member lists.

Senior Lieutenant Nikolai Adolfovich Pilar (A)

The identity of Pilar is still uncertain and requires further research. However, several coincidences in his biography suggest he may have been Baron Nikolai (full name: Gustav Adolf Nikolai) Adolfovich Pilar von Pilchau from the Baltic German nobility. The first coincidence is that he graduated from the Naval Corps in 1907, the second is the year of graduation from the Officer's Navigator's Class in 1914, and receiving the rank of Navigator First Class in 1915. The third coincidence is the rank of senior lieutenant, and the fourth is that he later emigrated to Yugoslavia.[118]

Pilar served as the commandant of the *Kherson* from June 7 until December 6, 1920, when Borsuk assumed the role. Notably, Pilar signed the certificate dated November 4, 1920, as commandant under Captain

---

116   Ibid.

117   Ibid. P.5back.

118   The Russian State Historical Archives. F.98. Inv.7. File 23. P.7, 19-22. Историк С.В. Волков. База данных «Участники Белого движения в России» / Historian S.V. Volkov. Database "Participants of the White Movement in Russia": https://swolkov.org/2_baza_beloe_dvizhenie/2_baza_beloe_dvizhenie _abc-01.htm; Website Русская Эстония. Пилар фон Пильхау Николай Адольфович / Russian Estonia. Pilar von Pilchau Nikolai Adolfovich: http:// russianestonia.eu/index.php?title=Пилар_фон_Пильхау_Николай _Адольфович&oldid=68865; Известия Русского генеалогического общества. Выпуск 39. Санкт-Петербург, 2022. С.132 / Proceedings of the Russian Genealogical Society. Issue 39. Saint Petersburg, 2022. P.132.

Schmelz - a document held by the family of Michael Anikeeff. This certificate was particularly significant because it revealed the captain's name before the crew member list was obtained. On December 7, 1920, Pilar assumed the duties of senior navigator's apprentice while remaining on the *Kherson*.[119]

Figure 68: Nikolai Adolfovich Pilar's signature appears at the bottom of this certificate, along with Captain Schmelz's signature, also seen in Figure 53. Courtesy of the Anikeeff Family.

Viktor Nikolaevich Borsuk (B)

Born in 1877, Borsuk graduated from the Naval Cadet Corps in 1897 and later served as the senior officer of the minelayer *Dunai* beginning on December 17, 1907. On August 18, 1908, he took the role of senior officer of the cruiser *Memory of Mercury*. From 1911-1914, he served as the flagship miner of the headquarters of the commander of the Black Sea naval forces. According to various sources, he was promoted to Captain 1st

---

119   The Russian State Historical Archives. F.98. Inv.7. File 23. P.7.

rank in 1916 (for distinction in actions against the enemy, in the Russian Imperial Navy) or in 1920, in the Armed Forces of the South of Russia.[120]

Appointed on June 28, 1920, he commanded the battleship *General Alekseyev*, a position he held until he arrived in Constantinople following the Crimean Evacuation. After departing from the *Kherson* in October 1921, he lived in exile in Belgrade, where he became the chairman of the department of the Naval Union in Yugoslavia. He passed away on December 4, 1950, in Belgrade.[121]

Borsuk assumed the role of commandant of the *Kherson* in Constantinople on December 5, 1920.[122]

Crew Members added to the *Kherson* in Constantinople:
Several crew members joined the *Kherson* after evacuating Sevastopol aboard a different ship. These men joined the crew on the *Kherson* in Constantinople on December 6, 1920.

Nicholai Meldizon and Kirill Levanevsky
Boarded the *Kherson*: December 6, 1920, Constantinople
Meldizon and Levanevsky evacuated from Sevastopol on November 14, 1920, aboard the destroyer *Captain Saken.*

Meldizon and Levanevsky, both born in Sumy, had joined the Armed Forces of South Russia (White Army) on October 6, 1919. Having both sailed on the icebreaker ship *Gaidamak,* from April to October 1920, they transferred to the destroyer *Captain Saken* to evacuate Sevastopol. They had written a letter to the assistant managing director of the Volunteer Fleet, General Vasily Aleksandrovich Shtenger, desperately requesting his

---

120   https://www.korabel.ru/persones/detail/82.html?ysclid=m0w9r2sabz421577449; Список офицерских чинов русского императорского флота. Царствование императора Николая Второго. Составитель В. Ю. Грибовский: http://petergen.com/publ/omsn202.shtml

121   Историк С.В. Волков. База данных «Участники Белого движения в России» / Historian S.V. Volkov. Database "Participants of the White Movement in Russia": https://swolkov.org/2_baza_beloe_dvizhenie/2_baza _beloe_dvizhenie_abc-01.htm

122   The Russian State Historical Archives. F.98. Inv.7. File 23. P.10.

help in getting them work on a ship. They reminded him that during their time in Polish captivity (possibly during World War I), they had shown kindness by delivering a letter to him from Warsaw from his relative.[123]

They received an answer to their request on December 7, 1920:[124]

> *"By order of Mr. Managing Director of the Voluntary Fleet 4/XII, you should report to the captain of the SS Kherson, currently located in Constantinople, where you will be given positions in the deck crew, about which the captain of the SS Kherson has been instructed."*
>
> *Signed: Sergei Domozhirov [Chief of the Marine Department of the Voluntary Fleet]*

Because of this act of kindness, Meldizon and Levanevsky were ordered to work on the *Kherson* starting on December 6, 1920, while it was still at the port in Constantinople.

Former Helmsman Alexander Andreevich Zvyagin[125]

Boarded the *Kherson*: December 6, 1920, Constantinople

Zvyagin was evacuated from Sevastopol on November 14, 1920, aboard the battleship *General Alekseyev*.

Prior to finding refuge aboard the *Kherson*, Zvyagin endured a series of misfortunes and tragic events. Captured during his service on the steamship *Suchan* in 1916, Zvyagin was taken as a prisoner to Germany, but managed to escape to England in 1917. From there, he was sent to Arkhangelsk with Russian Army units stationed in France, where he remained until February 1920. He was captured yet again, this time by the Bolsheviks, on his way to the Finnish border on February 26, 1920, and was taken to Petrozavodsk. He was mobilized, enlisted in the navy, and later transferred to Mariupol in July 1920. However, on September 1,

---

123 Ibid. P.23-27 (Information on both Meldizon and Levanevsky)

124 Ibid. P.11.

125 Ibid. P.17-18.

1920, he was arrested again by the Bolsheviks, not because of his actions but because of his family's political affiliations. His father, mother, brother, and sister had already been executed for these allegations, and Zvyagin faced an uncertain fate.

The situation turned around in his favor, as the White Army unexpectedly occupied Mariupol on September 15, 1920, resulting in his release. He fought with the White Army until the Crimean evacuation on November 14, 1920. Although now out of danger, he faced another hardship; his identification papers had been taken from him by the Bolsheviks, resulting in a lack of proof for identity or service. Only through the testimony of his former colleague of the *Suchan*, and current crew member on the *Kherson*, Orest Semenopulo (2), was his past service confirmed. He was accepted to work as a supernumerary sailor on the *Kherson*.

Despite pressure from the Volunteer Fleet to reduce the ship's crew, Captain Schmelz of the *Kherson* nevertheless enrolled Zvyagin, recognizing this as Zvyagin's last chance of survival. This provided a glimpse of hope after suffering such hardships.

Definition of Crew Member Duties:

A sample of the ship's crew roster was drawn up for the steamship "*Kherson*" for guidance in drawing up crew rosters on the steamships of the Volunteer Fleet. Saint Petersburg, 1897. P.4-7:[126]

The chief mate supervises the general order on the vessel; he is directly in charge of all the crew's living quarters and passenger cabins, as well as hold No. 1.

The second mate oversees the forecastle and the bow of the upper deck to the spar deck, the provisions and refrigerator rooms, and hold No. 2.

---

126 Book Title in Russian: Образец расписания судовой команды, составленный применительно к пароходу "Херсон", для руководства при составлении расписаний команд на пароходах Добровольного флота. Санкт-Петербург. 1897. С.4-7

The third mate oversees the poop deck and deckhouses to the spar deck, the wheelhouse, and hold No. 3.

The fourth mate oversees the spar deck, the chart room and bridge, the quarterdeck corridors, and hold No. 4.

The chief engineer carries out general supervision of all the mechanisms and mechanical devices on the vessel. He is directly in charge of the main engine and boilers.

The second engineer controls the working boiler, all steam machinery outside the main engine room, and electric lighting and ventilation.

The third engineer oversees the water drainage and fire systems, with their steam and hand pumps; ballast and other systems with their water pipes; sanitary water supply and fire hydrants.

The fourth engineer is attached to the chief engineer in charge of the main engine and boilers and is separately in charge of the screw shaft tunnels and the steam launch engine.

The ship's doctor oversees the hospital, pharmacy, and all the ship's premises with regard to the cleanliness of the air in them.

The Helmsman is someone who steers the boat.

The Messman cleans the command staff's cabins, corridors, and dining room, distributing food, dishes, and bed linen.

The purser (steward):[127] I was particularly interested in the specific job duties of my great-grandfather, Dimitri Ivanovich Komarkoff (101). The *Kherson* crew lists from April, September, and December 1920 indicate that he served as the ship's buffet-keeper, translated as "purser" or "steward." As I discovered, his duties closely align with those of a "steward."

The buffet-keepers on Volunteer Fleet ships, including the *Kherson*, were responsible for overseeing the buffet and closely supervising the

---

127 Положения о денежном, пищевом и других довольствиях служащих на судах Добровольного флота и штат администрации и береговых служащих. Санкт-Петербург. 1897. С.11-13 / Regulations on monetary, food and other allowances for employees on ships of the Volunteer Fleet and the staff of the administration and shore employees. St. Petersburg, 1897. PP.11-13. (book)

servants. The restaurateur was required to have an experienced purser, who would properly instruct the servants in carrying out their duties and ensuring they complied with all orders from the captain, his assistants, and the restaurateur himself. The purser was also responsible for reporting any negligence, sloppiness, rule violations, or failure to perform duties to the restaurateur.

The purser keeps a queue of servants on duty and ensures that the cabins are never left without servants, especially at night.

When night falls, the purser must order the extinguishing of unnecessary lighting fixtures, and only those intended to burn all night remain. Without doing this, he has no right to leave the passenger compartment.

Before any steamship embarked on a voyage, the Odessa office of the Volunteer Fleet would contract with a restaurateur to provide food service for the passengers.

APPENDIX C

Other Travelers on the *Kherson*

On November 14, 1920, the ship *Kherson* embarked on its final departure from Sevastopol. Most of its travelers were evacuees from various military units or desperate civilians fleeing the advancing Red Army. Of the 7,200 people aboard, only around 100 were crew members, and just a few had their families traveling with them, and three of those were my grandmother and her parents. Who were these other people on the ship? What led them to board the *Kherson* instead of other vessels docked at the port? Did their commanders assign them to specific ships? Or was it sheer chaos, scrambling to board whatever vessel they could?

Upon reaching Constantinople, many disembarked and began a life in exile there, while others dispersed throughout Europe. The Main Information Bureau compiled a list in Constantinople that Countess Varvara Nicholayevna Bobrinskaya organized. In 1922, the Bureau had 1,000 lists, 162,000 forms with names and details of each refugee, but at the end of 1922, the central part of the Bureau's archive was burned by order of the Russian Consulate in Constantinople.[128]

---

128 Главное справочное бюро в Константинополе, 1920–1922 гг. : именные списки беженцев и чинов Русской Армии : Сборник документов. Выпуск 1 / Составитель А. В. Ефимов. — М.: Институт Наследия, 2022. С.5 / Main Information Bureau in Constantinople, 1920-1922: Lists of Names of Refugees and Officers of the Russian Army: Collection of Documents. Issue 1 / Compiled by A.V. Efimov. – Moscow: The Institute of Heritage, 2022. P.5.

I wonder if my grandmother and her family were among those recorded and lost in these archives? Or were they omitted entirely because their journey continued aboard the *Kherson*?

Everyone listed evacuated from Sevastopol aboard the *Kherson* on November 14, 1920. The information is presented as it was recorded in February or March 1922:

Vasily Dimitrievich Talalayev[129]

Occupation: Sotnik (lieutenant in the Cossack troops). Orthodox. 34 years old in 1922.

Born in 1886, Talalayev took part in the White Army movement, including being a part of the Don Army from March 1918 to March 1920, and in General Wrangel's White Army from April to early November 1920. As of March 1922, he lived in exile at the Dolmabahçe Palace stables in Constantinople, then in Bulgaria. In 1923, he was a member of the "Union of Repatriation" in Varna,[130] which encouraged Russians who fled the country after the Revolution to return by promising amnesty. Unfortunately, many were arrested and shot upon their return. He may have returned to Russia, as there is a "Talalayev Vasily Dimitrievich" arrested in 1932 listed as one of the victims of political repression.[131]

---

129 Главное справочное бюро в Константинополе, 1920–1922 гг. : именные списки беженцев и чинов Русской Армии : Сборник документов. Выпуск 2 / Составитель А. В. Ефимов. — М.: Институт Наследия, 2022. C.173 / Main Information Bureau in Constantinople, 1920-1922: Lists of Names of Refugees and Officers of the Russian Army: Collection of Documents. Issue 2 / Compiled by A.V. Efimov. – Moscow: The Institute of Heritage, 2022. P.173.

130 Историк С.В. Волков. База данных «Участники Белого движения в России» / Historian S.V. Volkov. Database "Participants of the White Movement in Russia": https://swolkov.org/2_baza_beloe_dvizhenie/2_baza_beloe_dvizhenie_abc-01.htm

131 https://base.memo.ru/person/show/3071771

Jacob Gotlieb Lays[132]

Occupation: Private. Lutheran. 25 years old in 1922.

Upon arriving in Constantinople, he lived at the Yeni Kuey Mennonite Home.[133] As of March 1922, he was planning on moving to Germany. Born in about 1897.

Leo Samoilovich Golobel[134]

Occupation: Tailor. Hebrew. 41 years old in 1922.

Leo traveled with his wife, Sonya Davidovna (30 years old), and son David (8 years old). We believe he boarded the *Kherson* at some point in 1920 when the ship was docked in Feodosia. The family disembarked in Constantinople and stayed in the "Nora" Hotel just north of the historic Galata district. By September 1922 the family had immigrated to the United States.

Nicholay Georgievich Dontsev[135]

Occupation: Ooryadnik (Sergeant in the Cossack Troops). Orthodox. 25 years old in 1922.

132　Главное справочное бюро в Константинополе, 1920–1922 гг. : именные списки беженцев и чинов Русской Армии : Сборник документов. Выпуск 2 / Составитель А. В. Ефимов. — М.: Институт Наследия, 2022. C.177 / Main Information Bureau in Constantinople, 1920-1922: Lists of Names of Refugees and Officers of the Russian Army: Collection of Documents. Issue 2 / Compiled by A.V. Efimov. – Moscow: The Institute of Heritage, 2022. P.177.

133　From September 27 to July 1, 1922, an American Mennonite Relief (AMR) unit administered relief in Constantinople to Russian refugees, particularly Mennonites. In February 1921 the home was moved to Yeni Kuey, six miles north of Constantinople. There was a group of 62 men who had been serving in the White Army that stayed there at some point after evacuating from the Crimea. https://gameo.org/index.php?title=Constantinople_(Turkey)

134　Главное справочное бюро в Константинополе, 1920–1922 гг. : именные списки беженцев и чинов Русской Армии : Сборник документов. Выпуск 1 / Составитель А. В. Ефимов. — М.: Институт Наследия, 2022. C.379-380 / Main Information Bureau in Constantinople, 1920-1922: Lists of Names of Refugees and Officers of the Russian Army: Collection of Documents. Issue 1 / Compiled by A.V. Efimov. – Moscow: The Institute of Heritage, 2022. P.379-380.

135　Ibid. P.388.

Dontsev lived in San Stefano, current day Yeşilköy, located seven miles west of Constantinople's historic city center. This information is as of February 10, 1922.

Vassily Vassilievich Vassilieff[136]

Occupation: Lieutenant. Orthodox. 25 years old in 1922.

Koda Bultukovna Tavunova[137]

Occupation: unknown. Buddhist. 21 years old in 1922.

She lived in the Selimiye Barracks, located on the Asian side of Constantinople. Details as of February 21, 1922.

Arion Nikiforovich Borisoff[138]

Occupation: Fisherman. Orthodox. 41 years old in 1922.

Details as of February 26, 1922.

Lev Pavlovich Tsvetkanoff[139]

Occupation: A Private, Cook. Orthodox. 37 years old in 1922.

Tsvetkanoff is recorded as the ship's cook aboard the *Kherson,* and Lydia even mentions him in her diary on April 5, 1921. Perhaps he returned to Constantinople after leaving the *Kherson?* Details as of March 1, 1922.

---

136   Ibid. P.390.

137   Ibid.

138   Ibid. P.398.

139   Ibid. P.405.

List of the personnel of the Red Cross on the ship *Kherson*, sent from Crimea and arrived in Constantinople on November 15, 1920:[140]

Gavriil Vasilievich Shirokorad[141]

Occupation: Doctor

He was in the Armed Forces of South Russia and the Russian Army in the service of the Red Cross until the evacuation of Crimea. He had a daughter, Larissa.

Leonid Dlusky

Occupation: Doctor

Konstantin Ivanovich Zobnin[142]

Occupation: Assistant Manager

Zobnin was born in 1873 and was in the Armed Forces of South Russia. In the Russian Army, he was assistant manager of the Red Cross service until the evacuation of Crimea. His wife is listed below.

Evdokia Mikailovna Zobnina[143]

Occupation: Hospital Nurse

Zobnina, born in 1885, was the wife of Konstantin Ivanovich.

---

140 Ibid. Issue 3. P.506

141 Волков С.В. База данных № 2: «Участники Белого движения в России» / Volkov S.V. Database No. 2: "Participants of the White Movement in Russia" https://swolkov.org/2_baza_beloe_dvizhenie/2_baza_beloe_dvizhenie_abc-01.htm

142 Историк С.В. Волков. База данных «Участники Белого движения в России» / Historian S.V. Volkov. Database "Participants of the White Movement in Russia":https://swolkov.org/2_baza_beloe_dvizhenie/2_baza_beloe_dvizhenie_abc-01.htm

143 Ibid.

Count Ivan Viktorovich Kankrin[144]

Occupation: Clerk

Kankrin was the Governor of the Bessarabian Province of the Russian Empire and later a senator. His wife is listed below.

Countess Vera Petrovna Kankrina

Occupation: Medic

Kankrina, nee Strukova, was born in either 1862 or 1864. She was the daughter of Major General Peter Ananiyevich Strukov.

Count Ivan Ivanovich Kankrin

Occupation: Military Sergeant Major

Kankrin, born in 1892, was the son of Ivan Viktorovich and Vera Petrovna. He was a Cossack from the Don Cossack village of Mariinskaya, and was a Cossack Staff Captain of the Life Guards Cossack Regiment. Eventually retired as a military sergeant major on May 25, 1920. In the Russian Army, he was a secretary in the Red Cross service until he evacuated Crimea on the *Kherson*. He lived in exile in Yugoslavia in 1929 and eventually immigrated to the United States. He died in 1961 in Denver, Colorado. His wife died in March 1920 in Sevastopol.

Konstantin Maleyev

Occupation: Aidman

Dimitri Shirokorad

Occupation: Aidman

---

144 Волков С.В. Офицеры российской гвардии. Опыт мартиролога. М.: Русский путь, 2002. С.217 / Volkov S.V. Officers of the Russian Guard. Experience of a Martyrologist. Moscow: Russian Way, 2002. P.217

List of the personnel of the Volunteer Fleet with their families who arrived in Constantinople on the ship *Kherson* on November 16, 1920:[145]

Sergey Petrovich Domozhirov[146]

Varvara Domozhirov, wife

Nicholai Domozhirov, son

Marine Corps 1884. Captain of the 2nd rank of the Guards Crew, retired. State Councillor. In the Armed Forces of the South of Russia and the Russian Army, he was the head of the naval department of the Directorate of the Volunteer Fleet before the evacuation of Crimea. Evacuated on the *Kherson* ship. In exile in France, by 1930 he was a member of the Association of the Guards Crew. He died on August 1, 1954, near Paris. Wife Varvara, son Nikolai (May 6, 1906 – August 13, 1932).

Edward Degrofe[147]

Anna Degrofe, wife

Occupation: Marine Engineer.

In the Armed Forces of the South of Russia and the Russian Army in the Volunteer Fleet before the evacuation of Crimea. Evacuated on the *Kherson* ship. Wife Anna.

Listvennikova Alexandra[148]

Occupation: Clerk of the Volunteer Fleet

145　Главное справочное бюро в Константинополе, 1920–1922 гг. : именные списки беженцев и чинов Русской Армии : Сборник документов. Выпуск 3 / Составитель А. В. Ефимов. — М.: Институт Наследия, 2022. С.507 / Main Information Bureau in Constantinople, 1920-1922: Lists of Names of Refugees and Officers of the Russian Army: Collection of Documents. Issue 3 / Compiled by A.V. Efimov. – Moscow: The Institute of Heritage, 2022. P.507.

146　Волков С. В. Офицеры флота и морского ведомства: Опыт мартиролога. — М.: Русский путь, 2004. С.152 / Volkov S.V. Naval and Maritime Officers: The Experience of Martyrology. Moscow: Russian put, 2004. P.152.

147　Ibid. P.140.

148　Ibid. P.277.

In the Armed Forces of the South of Russia and the Russian Army, a clerk in the Volunteer Fleet before the evacuation of Crimea. Evacuated on the *Kherson* ship.

Alexander Kalenkovsky[149]

Alexandra Kalenkovskaya, wife

Occupation: agent of the Volunteer Fleet located in Sevastopol

Kalenkovsky was in the Armed Forces of South Russia and the Russian Army in the Volunteer Fleet (agent in Sevastopol) until the evacuation of Crimea.

Innokenty Zenzinov[150]

Occupation: agent of the Fleet, located in Moscow

Zenzinov was an agent of the Volunteer Fleet in Moscow. He was in the Armed Forces of South Russia and the Russian Army in the Volunteer Fleet until the evacuation of Crimea. He lived in exile in France and died on July 17, 1935, in Paris.

Nicholai Prokhorov[151]

Occupation: Assistant to the Chief Representative

Prokhorova Maria, wife

Prokhorov was in the Armed Forces of South Russia and the Russian Army, assistant to the chief representative of the army in the Volunteer Fleet until the evacuation of Crimea. Wife Maria.

Afanasieva Elena[152]

The Chief Agent's Wife

---

149 Волков С.В. База данных № 2: «Участники Белого движения в России» / Volkov S.V. Database No. 2: "Participants of the White Movement in Russia": https://swolkov.org/2_baza_beloe_dvizhenie/2_baza_beloe _dvizhenie_abc-01.htm

150 Ibid.

151 Ibid.

152 Ibid.

Afanasieva was in the Armed Forces of South Russia and the Russian Army in the Volunteer Fleet until the evacuation of Crimea. Wife of the primary agent of the Volunteer Fleet.

Other people evacuated on the *Kherson*:

George Alekseyevich Orlov[153]

Lydia does not mention Orlov in her diaries, perhaps because he disembarked before her first entry in her diary. Thanks to his diary, we know the movements and details of the *Kherson* from November 14 to November 26, 1920, as it evacuated Sevastopol. He provides a detailed account of their departure from Sevastopol, arrival in Constantinople, and eventual journey to Gallipoli, where he disembarked.

Orlov was born February 10, 1895, in the Varvarino farm of the Mogilev Province, currently Belarus. Just before boarding the *Kherson*, Orlov was enlisted in the 3rd separate division of light artillery of Colonel Drozdovsky. With the remaining members of the Drozdovskaya Division, he boarded the *Kherson* in the evacuation of Crimea led by General Wrangel.

In 1921, Orlov left Gallipoli for Prague and became one of the founders of the Russian Gallipoli community. He married and had a son. In 1944, the family moved to Bern, Switzerland. He died on April 19, 1964.

---

153 Орлов Г.А. Дневник добровольца : хроника гражданской войны 1918-1921 / Георгий Орлов ; [предисловие и комментарий С. В. Волкова, доктора исторических наук]. - Москва: Посев, 2019 / Orlov G.A. Diary of a Volunteer : Chronicle of the Civil War 1918-1921 / Georgy Orlov: [foreword and commentary by S. V. Volkov, Doctor of Historical Sciences]. - Moscow: Posev, 2019.

Vladimir Alexeyevich Moshin[154]

Occupation: Russian Historian. Byzantologist. Archpriest

Moshin, born October 9, 1894, in St Petersburg, Russia, evacuated Crimea on November 14, 1920, from Feodosia on the steamship *Askold*. He boarded the *Kherson* in Constantinople. On January 3, 1921, he went ashore in Bakar and boarded a train to Koprivnitsa, Croatia (on the border of Hungary). He was one of the most prominent representatives of the White émigrés in Yugoslavia. Moshin died Feb 3, 1987, in Skopje, North Macedonia. His wife was Olga Yakovlevna Kiryanova. Dates he was on the *Kherson:* November 20, 1920 – January 3, 1921

---

154 Information from an unpublished autobiography of Moshin cited in: Пушкадия-Рыбкина Т.В., Грубмайр И.И. Эмигранты из России в Загребе. Жизни и судьбы. - Изд. 2-е, испр. и доп. Загреб, 2019. С.20 / Pushkadia-Rybkina, Tatiana, and Inna Grubmair. Emigrants from Russia in Zagreb: Lives and Destinies. Second edition. Zagreb, 2019. P.20; Священник Игорь Иванов. Протоиерей В.А. Мошин как византолог и славист в Югославии / Priest Igor Ivanov. Archpriest V.A. Moshin as a Byzantologist and Slavist in Yugoslavia: https://old.spbda.ru/publications/ svyaschennik-igor-ivanov-protoierey-v-a-moshin-kak-vizantolog-i-slavist -v-yugoslavii/

APPENDIX D

Others Mentioned in Lydia's Diaries

The Barkovsky Family[155]

Grigory Barkovsky and Lyubov Sokolov-Borodkin had two children, Konstantin (born in 1909) and Kirill (born in 1911). The family left the Crimean Peninsula in July 1920 for the Kingdom of Serbs, Croats, and Slovenes and settled in Sremska Kamenica, a community within Novi Sad, where Lydia's family lived for nine months. Grigory died in 1926.

Lydia attended school in Novi Sad, Yugoslavia, with the two boys. She received a postcard[156] from Lyubov Barkovsky on October 26, 1922: Translation:

> *Dear Lyda, I am sending you a view of Prague. Thank you for writing to the boys and sending views of New York, it gave them great pleasure. Tomorrow I'm going to the gymnasia to see Kotik and Kika, I took them there 3 months ago and haven't been there since. I'm worried about Kika, he's been in the infirmary for 5 weeks now. The Moscow Art Theater was recently in Prague, and now it is going to America. Be sure, [???] dear Lyda, [to???] ask your mother and go see*

---

155 Василенко А.С. Любовь наша, Отечество! : Барковские, Прохоровы. Соколовы-Бородкины в памяти и истории / Анатолий Василенко. — Изд. 2-е — Кировоград : Имэкс-ЛТД, 2011 / Vasilenko A.S. Our love, Fatherland! : Barkovskys, Prokhorovs. Sokolovs-Borodkins in memory and history / Anatoly Vasilenko. - 2nd ed. - Kirovograd: Imex-LTD, 2011.

156 Šetelik, Jaroslav. Prague Watercolors. Postcard featuring Svatopluk Čech Bridge.

"Tsar Fyodor Ioannovich" You will have great pleasure.
Maya Veinb.[157] *[Veinberg?] wrote to you and is waiting for*
an answer she is at home in Belgrade and will take an exam
at gymnasia.

I kiss you warmly
L. Barkovskaya

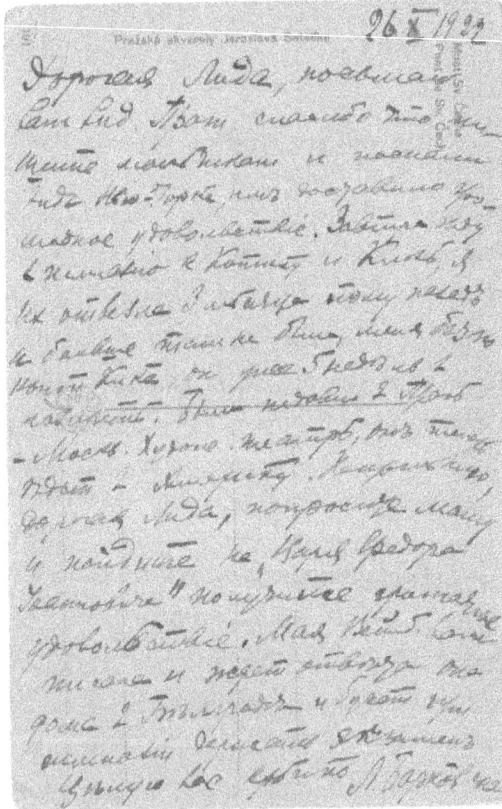

Figure 69: Reverse side of a postcard from the Barkovsky family in Serbia.
Courtesy of the Buzyna Family.

---

157   As noted in her diaries, Lydia has a friend Maya in Novi Sad who she often would
play with at the Barkovsky's as well as at school. This is possibly who Lyubov
Barkovsky is referring to in this postcard.

Written on the front of the postcard:

I'm sending regards to your mom and dad.
Please write the boys how you live and study.

Figure 70: Front of a postcard from the Barkovsky family in Serbia.
Courtesy of the Buzyna Family.

Masha Kamarovskaya

Masha was Lydia's classmate in Novi Sad and wrote this note on her last day of school there.

She wrote a message to Lydia in her cherished *Album of Poetry* she carried with her from Odessa all the way to the United States. Today, it sits in a container at my mother's house, well preserved.

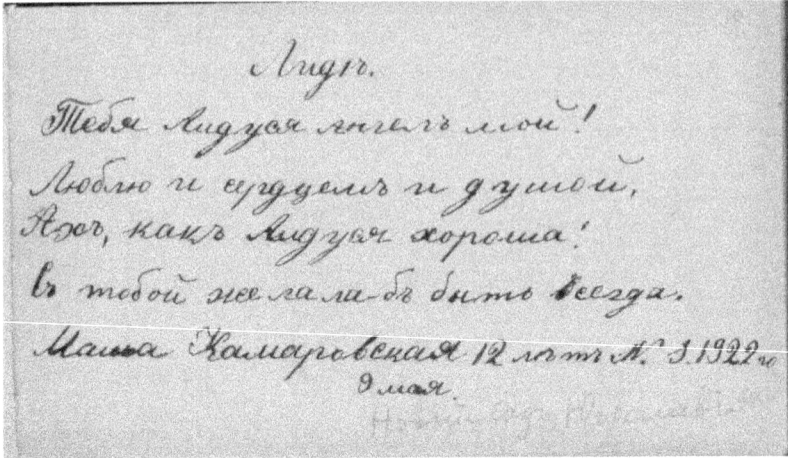

Figure 71: A note from Masha Kamarovskaya in Lydia's "Album of Poetry."
1922. Courtesy of the Buzyna Family.

Translation

> *Lidoosya, my angel,*
> *I love you with my heart and soul!*
> *Oh, how good Lydoosya is!*
> *I'd like to be with you always.*
> *Маша Камаровская 12 years old, N.S. [=Novi Sad] 1922,*
> *May 9*

[written in pencil:] *Novi Sad, Yugoslavia*

Sergei Rudolfovich Mintslov,[158]

Principal of the Realschule in Novi Sad at the Orphanage of the All-Russia Union of Cities, where Lydia attended school in 1921 to 1922. His original signature is on Lydia's report cards. He was born in 1870 in Ryazan, Russia to a noble Lithuanian family. He died in Riga, Latvia in 1933.

---

158 Хомякова И. Г. МИНЦЛОВ СЕРГЕЙ РУДОЛЬФОВИЧ // Большая российская энциклопедия. Том 20. Москва, 2012, стр. 418 / Khomyakova I. G. MINTSLOV SERGEY RUDOLFOVICH // The Great Russian Encyclopedia. Volume 20. Moscow, 2012, p. 418.

Vera Fedorovna Shkinskaya[159]

She was the Realschule inspector and Lydia's class form-master[160] (see Report II). A colonel's daughter, she was born on June 6, 1880. She graduated from the Smolny Institute for Noble Maidens in St. Petersburg and, according to the word of one of her former students in Novi Sad, later worked as a (form-master) tutor in the Smolny Institute.

Vera Dimitrievna Chaleyeva-Gortynskaya[161]

Chaleyeva-Gortynskaya (1901-1985, ballerina, teacher) is mentioned by Lydia as her teacher of rhythmic gymnastics at the Russian Real Gymnasium (Realschule) of the Union of Cities in Novi Sad. She is buried in Belgrade.

Raisa Mitrofanovna Kondratieva

Kondratieva was Lydia's gymnastics teacher at a high school in Novi Sad.

---

159 Центральный государственный исторический архив Санкт-Петербурга. Ф.2. Воспитательное общество благородных девиц и Александровский институт (Смольный институт). Петроград. 1764–1918. Оп.1. Дела общего характера, дела Совета, личные дела служащих и воспитанниц 1764-1917. Раздел описи 1892 год / Общие дела. Д.13933. Личное дело Шкинской Веры Федоровны 23.05.1898–без даты / The Central State Historical Archive of St. Petersburg. F.2. Educational Society for Noble Maidens and the Alexander Institute (Smolny Institute). Petrograd. 1764–1918. Inv.1. General affairs, Council affairs, personal affairs of employees and pupils 1764-1917. Inventory section year 1892. File 13933. Personal file of Vera Fedorovna Shkinskaya. May 23, 1898 – no date. Виноградов Леонид. Надеялись вернуться в Россию. 22.20.2013 / Русский век Портал для российских соотечественников: https://ruvek.mid.ru/publications/nadeyalis_vernutsya_v_rossiyu_8486/

160 Form-Master refers to a class teacher. This term was typically used in European schools.

161 https://rosgenea.ru/familiya/chaleeva-gortinskaya

Chaleyeva-Gortynskaya and Kondratieva are listed in the article by the outstanding historian of Russian emigration Alexey Borisovich Arsenyev.[162]

---

162 Алексей Арсеньев. Русские педагоги в Воеводине (1920-1950-е гг.) / Alexey Arsenyev. Russian teachers in Vojvodina (1920-1950s): https://maznew.narod.ru/maznevtur/etap10/dn10_11/ars_13.htm

APPENDIX E

Evacuated Ships from Sevastopol on November 14, 1920

Source for the list of ships and number of passengers (given in brackets): Кузнецов, Н.А. Русский флот на чужбине. Москва: Вече, 2009 C.403-406 / Kuznetzov N.A. Russian fleet in foreign lands. Moscow: Veche, 2009. P.403-406.

Explanations for the names of the vessels are made by the author of this book.

1. Steamship *Modig* (604) - Norwegian (translated as "brave")
2. Dispatch-Boat *Yakut* (299) - Towing:
   - Boat *Captain 2nd Rank Medvedev* (formerly English *M1-204*, and *SK-1*) (60) - Named in honor of the commander of the naval landing company, Captain 2nd Rank S. I. Medvedev, who was killed on the bridge of the schooner *Pericles* in the port of Genichesk on June 18, 1919, by a fire from a Red Army armored train.
   - Boat *Crimea* (formerly Turkish) (180)
3. Rescue tug *Chernomor* (34) – The name is derived from the Russian name of the Black Sea – Chernoye more. Chernomor is the commander of the thirty-three knights in Alexander Pushkin's "Tale of the Tsar Saltan." Towing:
   - Transport *Sarych* (formerly No. 131) (4500) - Sarych is the name of a cape on the southern coast of Crimea.

4. Steamship ***Doob*** (271) - Doob is the name of a cape on the Black Sea in the Tsemess Bay (opposite Novorossiysk).

5. Transport ***Zarya*** (formerly No. 141) (34) - Zarya means "Dawn." Submarine division base.

6. Submarine ***Burevestnik*** (39) - Means "storm petrel," a type of bird. My grandmother's best friend's husband in Schenectady, New York, Alexis Ivanovich Diakoff, was the Chief Engineer on this submarine and evacuated on this vessel.

7. Submarine ***Utka*** (28) - Means "duck"

8. Submarine ***Tyulen*** (15) - Means "seal"

9. Submarine ***A.G. 22*** (14) - An AG-class (the American Holland class) submarine, designed by the American Holland Torpedo Boat Company/Electric Boat Company and fabricated in Canada.

10. Steamship ***Beshtau*** (960) - Beshtau comes from the Turkish word "bes," meaning "five," and "tau," meaning "mountain; It is a five-domed mountain (volcano) in the vicinity of Pyatigorsk in the Northern Caucasus.

11. Steamship ***Lazarev*** (1200) – Supposedly named in honor of one of the prominent naval commanders, the three Lazarev brothers. The most famous of them was Admiral Michael Petrovich Lazarev (1788-1851), an outstanding seafarer and chief commander of the Black Sea Fleet and ports from 1833.

12. Steamship ***Grand Duke Alexander Mikhailovich*** (743) - Named after the cousin of Emperor Tsar Nicholas II.

13. Icebreaker ***Ilya Muromets*** (300) - Ilya Muromets is one of the main characters of an ancient Russian epic.

Towing:

- Fire guard tug (formerly battleship) ***George the Pobedonosets*** (3,400) - Meaning George the Victorious
- Destroyer ***Tserigo*** (290) - Named in honor of Admiral Feodor Feodorovich Ushakov's victory over the French, who

captured the island of Cerigo (in Italian, Kythira in Greek) during his 1798-1799 campaign in the Ionian Islands.

◦ Transport *Ostorozhny* (22) - Means "cautious".

14. Steamship *Saratov* (7350)

Towing:

◦ Boat *Lazar Kiryako* (sank from a collision) - Named after Lazar Kiryakovich Kiryako, captain of one of the ships of the Special Purpose Expedition that made multiple voyages along the Danube River to Serbia during WWI.

◦ Boat *Sevastopol* (formerly Shatt-al-Arab) (20) - Shatt-al-Arab is the name of a river in Iraq, on the border with Iran. It flows into the Persian Gulf.

15. Hydrographic vessel *Kazbek* (358) - Mount Kazbek is a dormant volcano and one of the major mountains of the Caucases.

Towing:

◦ *Minesweeper Baklan* (58) - Baklan means "Cormarant," an aquatic bird.

16. Steamship *Khersones* (764) - Khersones was an ancient Greek colony founded about 2,500 years ago on the Crimean coast. The ancient city was located on the outskirts of present-day Sevastopol. In Greek, the name means "peninsula."

Towing:

◦ Minesweeper *Berezan* (26) - Berezan is an island in the Black Sea located five miles from the city of Ochakiv.

17. Transport *Moryak* (2700) - Moryak means "sailor"

18. Transport *Ararat* (2030) - Mount Ararat is a dormant volcano in Eastern Turkey. Formerly it was part of the territory of the Russian Empire. Although lying outside the borders of modern Armenia, the mountain is the principal national symbol of Armenia.

19. Steam scow *Adjader* (230)

    Towing:

    ◦ Steam Schooner *Lebed* (diving base) (147) - Lebed means "swan."

20. Steamship *Kherson* (7200) - sailed to Bay of Kotor after Constantinople.

    Towing:

    ◦ Boat *Typhoon*
    ◦ Patrol boat *Kyiv* (formerly *Mine Boat No.1*)
    ◦ A barge – this barge was lost at sea on the night of November 14, the next morning the *Kherson* had to return some distance to retrieve it.

21. Messenger ship *Kitoboy* – Means "Whaler"

22. Messenger ship (yacht) *Lukull* (106) – There is a cape called Lukull to the north of Sevastopol, on the coast of Crimea.

23. Tugboat *Hippolai* (36) – Hippolai was probably derived from the name of Cape Hippolaus mentioned by Herodotus.

24. Tub boat *Belbek* (35) - Belbek is a river in the Crimea.

25. Messenger ship (boat) *Ataman Kaledin* (formerly *Gorgippia*) (110) - Alexey Maximovich Kaledin (1861-1918) was a Don Cossack Cavalry General during WWI. He also led the Don Cossack White Movement in its beginning and committed suicide after the Volunteer Army's retreat. Gorgippia was an ancient city on the site of the present-day Anapa on the Black Sea coast that existed in the 4th century BC - 3rd century AD as part of the Bosporan Kingdom.

26. Steamboat *Neozhidanniy* – Means "unexpected"

27. Steam scow *Surozh* (320) - Surozh is the ancient name of the city of Sudak on the Crimean coast.

28. Steam schooner *Peter* (34) - In 1921 this vessel returned to Russia.

29. Sailing schooner **Donets** (12) - Donets is a river in the Ukraine.
30. Sailing Schooner **Orlik** (54)
31. Patrol Boat **SK-6** (formerly **No. 317**) -

    Towed by:

    ◦ **Typhoon,** then the **Kherson**.

32. Transport **Psezyuapye** (85) - Named after the river Psezuapse in Sochi on the Black Sea coast.

    Towing:

    ◦ Yacht **Zabava** (formerly **Gyacinth/Hyacinth**) - it was abandoned at sea on November 16. Zabava means fun.

33. Motor vessel **Livathos** (94) - The region of Livathos lies on the central south coast of Kefalonia, the largest of the Ionian Islands in Greece.
34. Tugboat **Typhoon** - it initially towed Patrol Boat SK-6
35. Sailing Schooner **Margarita** (15)
36. Sailing Motor Schooner **Peter the Great** (22)
37. Steamship **Polonia** (921) - Polish
38. Steamship **Sphinx** (214) - Greek
39. Motor Sailing Schooner **Fata Morgana** - Means a mirage at sea (or desert) on the horizon.
40. Motor Sailing Schooner **St. George**

MAPS

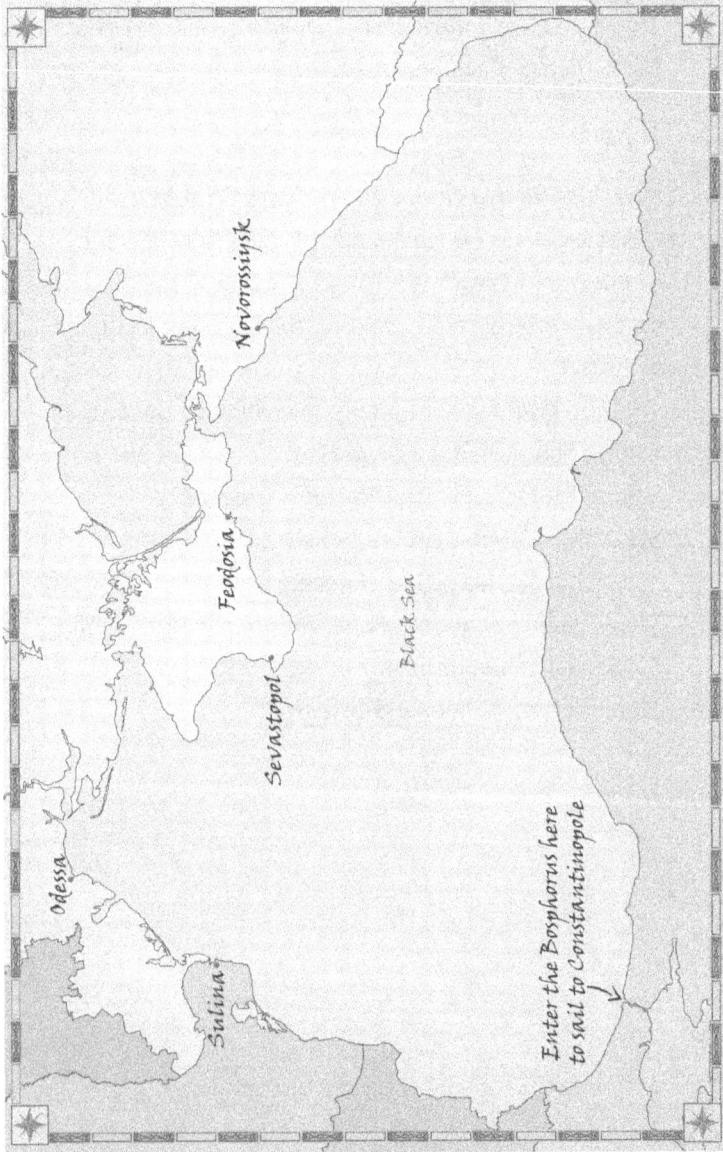

Figure 72: The Black Sea. Custom illustration created by Milica Stamenković, commissioned by the author.

Labels on map: Novorossiysk, Feodosia, Sevastopol, Odessa, Sulina, Black Sea, Enter the Bosphorus here to sail to Constantinople

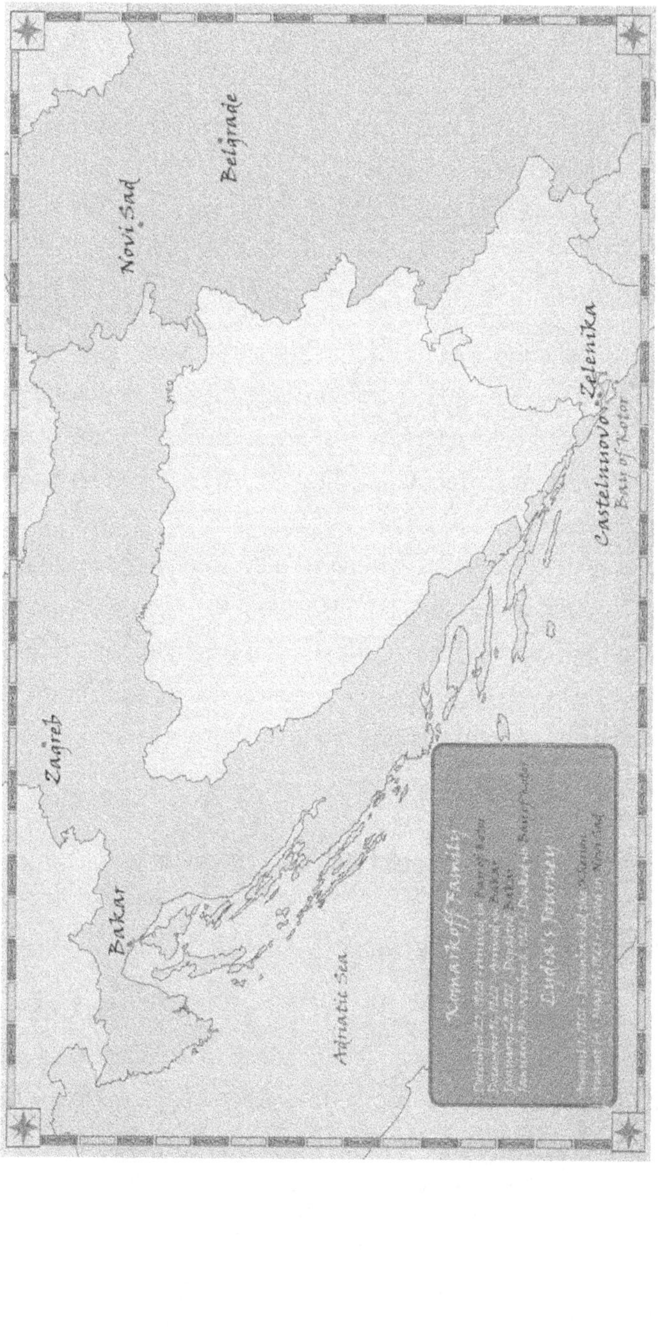

Figure 73: The Adriatic Sea and Bay of Kotor. Custom illustration created by Milica Stamenković, commissioned by the author.

RECIPES

ydia's diaries mention various Eastern European dishes, some of which were passed down several generations, and I fondly remember them from my childhood. I enjoyed traditional meals prepared by my maternal grandmother, Lydia, my paternal grandmother, Anna, my mother, Helen, and other relatives.

As you prepare these recipes, I invite you to think not only about my grandmother's cultural heritage, but also about the memories and traditions that food brings to your own life. Cooking is more than following a recipe; it is a way to connect with the past, present, and future. May these dishes bring warmth, nostalgia, and a deeper connection to your own story.

Kisel (Pureed Fruit Dessert)

Recipe from the Stupak/Buzyna Family

I have included this recipe first because it is my all-time favorite traditional dish prepared by my paternal grandmother. In her diary, when Lydia mentioned her mother making kisel with dewberries, I was immediately nostalgic, recalling the many times I sat at my (paternal) grandmother's dining room table in her brownstone in Chicago, savoring every spoonful of this treat.

Lydia's mother prepared this special dessert in the hotel on their first night after moving off the ship. Perhaps it was a comforting gesture to ease their transition from life at sea to the uncertainty of their next chapter into the unknown.

This particular recipe is a Stupak/Buzyna Family Recipe, from my father's side, and may even be the very recipe my "Babushka" made for me. Like many grandmothers from "the old country," she rarely used written recipes or measured ingredients. She instinctively knew how much to add and what to do.

Add enough water to the washed fruit to barely cover.

Cook until tender.

Put fruit and juice through a sieve and sweeten to taste.

To each cup of hot puree, allow 1 -1 ½ tsp cornstarch.

Moisten cornstarch with a little water and add to the hot puree.

Cook for five minutes, stirring constantly.

Lemon juice can be added for flavor.

Kotleti

Recipe from Helen Buzyna

This is the dish I remember both my grandmother Lydia and my mother making. It is a meat patty, much like a burger, but it has a crisp, golden crust on the outside and a tender, juicy center.

This recipe comes from my mother. One day, when my kids were little, she visited and wrote it down from memory on a scrap piece of paper. As we cooked together, she guided me through each step. I must admit, I have only made this a handful of times. After reading her diaries, I feel a deeper connection to this dish and will prepare it with greater purpose and appreciation.

1 pound of meat (either ground turkey or ground chuck)

1 egg

1-2 slices of dried bread or a roll soaked in water

Breadcrumbs

Spices to taste: salt, pepper, garlic, salt, yellow mustard

1 sautéed onion

Canola Oil

1. Combine meat, egg, sauteed onion, spices, and bread that was soaked in water
2. Make a ball and roll in breadcrumbs
3. Pat the ball into an oval and make a crosshatched design on the patty
4. Pan fry in Crisco or canola oil to a golden brown

This freezes well.

Селёдка (Schmaltz[163] Herring)

Recipe by Lydia Dimitrievna

This recipe was beautifully handwritten by Lydia and later typed by me. Throughout, she included a few side notes to my mother, which I will include *(in italics)*. Though this dish is a classic Russian delicacy, I must admit it has never been a favorite of mine. However, because it was an important recipe for Lydia and holds fond memories of my mother, I felt it deserved a place here.

On the very top, she writes (in a message to her daughter Helen): *You didn't write Селёдка correctly, as you can see.*

> *I always buy a schmaltz (I don't know how to spell this) her-ring. The name is probably Jewish. If you buy this herring in a non-Jewish store (the last time I bought it at Grand Union, they didn't know what "schmaltz" herring was, they still gave me the right kind). The herring has to be whole,*

---

163   Schmaltz is herring caught just before spawning; male herring is preferred because the fish is thicker.

usually without a head. You and Yura will probably have a good laugh when you read this. Well, here is the recipe:

Skin the herring by making a long slash with a knife on two sides of the fish: on one side, you have to take the insides out, which you throw away *(I hope Yura knows how to do it – he is a fisherman).* After taking the skin off, separate the fillet from the backbone *(I usually do it with my hands, and it is a messy job).* Rinse the fillets under cold water, just a little, and put them in a dish *(I usually use a Pyrex square pan: don't use a metal one, as it may smell like a herring, even after washing it well).*

After the herring has been placed in a pan, pour milk over it so that the herring will be covered. Then, cover the dish with a lid or aluminum foil and let it stand overnight. I keep it in the kitchen, but perhaps it is better if you put it in the refrigerator. You can do this the night before, and in the morning, you can prepare it.

Take the herring out of the pan and, under a cold faucet, wash it off a little. Then slice the herring into small pieces; while doing it, try to take some big bones out, but don't try to take out all of them; it's impossible.

In a cup, put approximately 3 Tablespoons of white vinegar, and about ¼ cup or more of salad oil *(I use Wesson),* also add about 2 Tablespoons of prepared mustard. Mix it a little. Also, slice an onion into very thin slices, and now you can put all these ingredients together in a pretty deep dish *(not metal).* Just alternate the herring with the onion and the sauce. When everything is in the bowl, it doesn't have to be completely covered by the sauce, but it should be moist. If you feel you don't have enough of it, you can always add more.

For a company of 8, you will probably need 4 herrings. It is a very messy job, but of course, Yura is your wonderful helper.

If you have a Jewish delicatessen, try to get the herring there.

Traditional Eastern Orthodox Easter Recipes

The two recipes that instantly come to mind when I think of Easter are Pascha and Kulich. I have cherished memories of enjoying every Easter for as long as I can remember. These traditional dishes are served after breaking the Lenten fast on Easter.

Pascha, made from cottage cheese or farmer cheese, is a classic dish molded into the shape of a truncated pyramid, decorated with raisins and candies. My mother has always used farmer cheese to make her Pascha, which required a special order weeks in advance from our local Publix grocery store - a process that was always quite an ordeal! But dedication to ensuring we had Pascha on our Easter table year after year was well worth it.

Since there was no Russian Orthodox Church in Tallahassee, Florida, during my childhood, our family attended the Greek Orthodox Church, despite our Russian heritage. While Greek and Russian Orthodoxy are branches of Eastern Orthodoxy and share the same core beliefs, they differ in traditions and cultural influences. For instance, on Palm Sunday, the Russian churches distribute pussy willows instead of the traditional palms, as palms were not readily available in the colder climates.

When Lydia and her mother celebrated Easter in Novi Sad on April 16, 1922, her mother used the cottage cheese version of the recipe. I am including my mother's Pascha recipe using farmer cheese.

Kulich, known as Easter bread, is a sweetened, dome-shaped yeast bread filled with raisins and nuts, topped with icing and colorful sprinkles for decoration. I never cared for the bread itself, only the parts with icing. My paternal grandmother would bake Kulich in coffee cans to get the signature tall, cylindrical shape. If she was not spending Easter with us, she would send a care package of Kulich, sausages and other Easter goodies by airplane, and I vividly remember going to the airport to pick them up from baggage claim.

Zhenia's granddaughter, Leslie and her sister Kelly, have continued to this day with the tradition of making Easter Pascha and Kulich. During our conversation about what Russian traditions we follow from our ancestors, we discovered we both own the same Russian Cooking[164] recipe book from 1967.

Pascha – Easter Cheese Pyramid with Candied Fruit

Recipe from Helen Buzyna. This is the recipe she always uses.

3 pounds Farmer Cheese (no salt)

5 egg yolks (whites can be used for meringues)

1 box confectioners' sugar – to taste

½ pound sweet butter

½ pint sweet cream (beaten)

1 teaspoon vanilla

Raisins, white or currents, or both

Candied fruit

Crushed almond

(amounts as desired)

Step 1:

Strain the farmer cheese 3 times into a large bowl through sieve or Foley's Food Mill.

Step 2:

Beat egg yolks and gradually add sugar. Then add softened sweet butter. Beat sweet cream and add to egg – sugar – butter mixture.

Step 3:

Add to egg-sugar-butter mixture 1 tsp. vanilla, raisins, or candied fruit and crushed almonds can be added to the egg-sugar-butter mixture OR / AND used as decoration (see photo). Mix the farmer cheese and egg-sugar-butter mixture thoroughly. Hang in cheesecloth (double

---

164   Papashvily, Helen, and George Papashvily. *Russian Cooking.* Edited by the editors of Time-Life Books, Time-Life Books, 1967.

thickness, about 2 yards) in the refrigerator overnight to allow some liquid to drain out. Fill the Pascha mold with the cheese mixture and place in the refrigerator.

Plan A: Hang the entire mixture in a cheese cloth (double thickness, about 2 yards) in the refrigerator overnight to allow the liquid to drain. Remove the mixture from the cheesecloth and shape into a pyramid shape with a spatula or by hand.

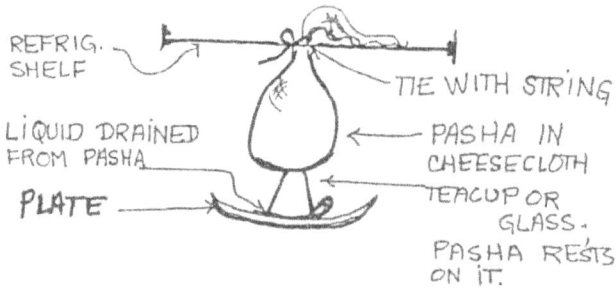

REFRIG. SHELF

TIE WITH STRING

LIQUID DRAINED FROM PASHA

PASHA IN CHEESECLOTH

PLATE

TEACUP OR GLASS. PASHA RESTS ON IT.

OR

Plan B: Line a mold with cheesecloth and place the entire mixture in the mold; on a plate, place the mold UPSIDE DOWN so liquid can drain onto the plate. A mold can be purchased online or sometimes sold at Eastern European stores.

Remove the mold from the refrigerator and place it right side up on a serving platter. Remove the mold to reveal your Pascha cheese pyramid. Decorate with raisins, candied fruit, chocolate chips with an orthodox cross, and the Cyrillic letters "XB," which stand for "Christos Voskrese," meaning "Christ is Risen." Refrigerate leftovers.

The wooden mold can be purchased at various Eastern European food stores or online.

Figure 74: Pascha and Kulich from Orthodox Easter, May 2, 2021. My mother made the two cheese Paschas with help from her grandchildren, while the Kulich – purchased from a local European grocery store - was decorated by my mother with icing and sprinkles. Courtesy of the Buzyna Family.

Kulich, also called Paska

Recipe from Ludmilla Romanenko

Yields 4 Large Paskas
Yeast Mixture (Medium Bowl)
    4 active dry yeast packets
    1 cup warm water
    3 tbsp sugar
    ¾ cup + 1 tbsp flour

Microwave water for 45 seconds, water should be lukewarm to the touch (test with knuckle). Mix water and yeast together. Mix in sugar. Mix in flour (sifted). Consistency should be like a pancake batter. Place wax paper and a dish towel on top of the bowl and set in a warm place to rise. The yeast mixture will begin to bubble up near/the top of the bowl. Once it reaches its peak, it will start to come back down. Yeast is ready for the dough mixture.

Dough Mixture (Large Mixer)

    20 egg yolks
    10 egg whites
    25 level Tbsp sugar
    ½ tsp salt
    1 packet of vanilla sugar
    1 tsp vanilla
    1 cup half and half
    ½ cup whole milk
    2 sticks of melted butter or margarine
    6 cups + 4 tbsp flour (sifted)

Whip egg yolks for 10 minutes – will turn a light yellow/whitish color. In a separate bowl, whip up egg whites with a whisk. Combine whites and yolks together for 5 minutes. Add sugar, salt, vanilla sugar, and vanilla to the mixture and whip up for an additional 5 minutes. Slowly, add in the yeast mixture. Continue whipping for 5 minutes. Combine half and half and milk and heat in the microwave for 1 minute. Pour slowly into the dough mixture. Continue whipping for 5 minutes. Add in flour (sifted) – 1 spoonful at a time. Switch to the dough hook halfway through the flour step. After all the flour is incorporated, mix for an additional 5 minutes. Transfer dough into the extra-large bowl. Place wax paper and a dish towel on top of the bowl and let rise in a warm place until the mixture reaches the top of the bowl. Melt 2 sticks of butter and knead into the dough. Repeat the rising step until it reaches the top.

Prepare coffee cans (2 lbs.). Grease with Crisco and spray with Pam. Fill each can 1/3 of the way with the dough mixture. Turn the oven to the lowest temperature (170) and keep the oven door open. Place cans on the open door and cover with wax paper and dish towels. Once the dough rises to the top of the can, it is ready for baking. Bake at 350° for 45 minutes.

Once Paskas are baked, they must be gently removed from the coffee cans. Gently slide out of a coffee can onto a pillow covered with a dishtowel. Paskas must be turned frequently for 20-30 minutes to prevent collapsing.

Decorate top with powdered sugar/milk mixture and candy sprinkles if desired.

Store in Ziploc Bags and freeze if desired.

Paskas are best when eaten slightly warm.

Borscht

I have always loved borscht, especially the hot green version my paternal grandmother used to make, not the red, cold one. As I've gotten older, I have come to prefer the red version, but only if it's hot! A dollop of chilled sour cream melting into a warm bowl of borscht was the perfect comfort food on chilly days, sitting in my Russian grandmother's kitchen. It also gave me, unknowingly at the time, a deep connection to my Russian roots.

Lydia and her family enjoyed borscht to celebrate the Name Day of her mother, Daria, on Sunday, April 1, 1922, in Novi Sad.

> *We celebrated her Name Day this way: ate delicious borscht, drank two bottles of beer and later ate apples.*

Borscht

Recipe from Ludmilla Romanenko

This is for a huge batch of Borscht and requires an oversized pot. You can scale the recipe for the size of the pot you have.

Ingredients
2 Medium Onions Chopped

3 Cloves of Garlic Chopped

3 Carrots Chopped

3 Celery Stalks Chopped

6 Medium Fresh Beets. Peeled and cut into thin strips, or use the shredding disk on the Cuisinart

1 handful of Flat Parsley Chopped Finely

1 handful of Dill Weed Chopped Finely

Salt and Pepper to taste

1 Small can of tomato Paste

1 Large Cabbage - Shredded (like for coleslaw)

1-2 quarts of Mushrooms - quartered and sautéed until golden brown

1 can of Northern Beans - rinsed and drained

3 Idaho Potatoes - Peeled and cut into small cubes

2-3 Tbs Chicken flavored Better Than Bouillon

7 Quarts of Cool Water

Vegetable Oil for sauteing

Recommend having all vegetables ready mise en place.

Fill an oversized pot with 7 quarts of water and bring the water to a simmer.

In a large frying pan, sauté chopped onions until golden, add chopped carrots and celery, and cook until tender. Add shredded beets until tender (you may need to add some more oil as you sauté, so it's a little oily looking). Then add chopped garlic and sauté for another 1-2 minutes. Add 1 small can of tomato paste and mix into the vegetables while on low heat until thoroughly combined. Bring water to a boil and add in the vegetable/tomato paste mixture.

Let the mixture continue to boil lightly for 5 minutes. Add cubed potatoes and 2-3 Tbs of chicken-flavored Better Than Bouillon. When the potatoes begin to get slightly soft and then add the shredded cabbage. Continue to cook on a low boil until cabbage is slightly crisp. Add in sauteed mushrooms, beans, parsley, and dill. Add salt and pepper to taste if needed. Turn off the heat as the borscht will continue to cook, and the cabbage will get softer as it sits.

When serving borscht, add a spoonful of sour cream to your bowl.

Pirozhki

Recipe from Ludmilla Romanenko

Traditional dishes were often prepared around holidays, and Lydia's mother's pirozhki was no exception. Christmas, according to the old calendar, is January 7. The day before, in 1922, she made pirozhki (small meat pies) while her father brought home a small Christmas tree.

> *Today mama was making pirozhki since morning and was cooking compote and kutya, although with rice, when papa returned from town, he brought a small tree [for Christmas].*

Meat Mixture Filling
    4-5 lbs of Pot Roast cooked until tender
    2 large onions, chopped and sautéed
    3-4 lbs potatoes, mashed
    Salt and Pepper to taste

Trim fat on meat after cooking. Place the meat in a food processor and mix it with onions and potatoes. Salt and Pepper to taste.

Dough
In a separate bowl, mix
    4 packages quick rise yeast with 1/2 cup warm water
    1 Tbs Sugar
    1 Tbs Flour

Let the yeast mixture rise in a warm place until it doubles

In the meantime
    2 cups of Milk
    2 sticks of Butter

Warm milk and butter slowly until the butter melts

In mixer, beat well:

　　6 medium eggs

　　1 cup sugar

　　1 tsp of salt

Then slowly add in the milk/butter mixture and the yeast mixture.

Add up to 6 cups of flour until the dough is not sticky but not dry.

Let the dough mixture rise in a warm place 2x - 30 minutes for each rise, and punch the dough down in between.

Roll the dough into small balls and cover. Roll the dough into flat disks (3-4 inches) and then fill with meat mixture, pinching close, forming into an oblong shape, setting seam side down on a tray covered with a sprinkle of flour. Cover with a towel and let rise for 30 minutes after filling it.

You can bake these at 350°F or fry them in a neutral oil in a deep-frying pan or pot, turning over when golden brown on each side. Drain on a paper towel.

These reheat nicely for 20-30 seconds in the microwave. You can also freeze once cooled off.

BIBLIOGRAPHY

Российский государственный исторический архив (РГИА). Ф.98. Пароходное общество «Добровольный флот». Оп.7. 1916-1921 гг. Д.23. Пароходное общество «Добровольный флот». Материалы по личному составу парохода «Херсон». 20 апреля - 8 декабря 1920 г. / The Russian State Historical Archives (RSHA). Fund 98. Steamship Company "Volunteer Fleet". Inv.7. 1916-1921. File 23. The Shipping company "Volunteer fleet". Materials on the personnel of the ship "Kherson". April 20 - December 8, 1920.

РГИА. Ф.98. Оп.6. 1878-1923. Д.196. Пароходное общество «Добровольный флот». Переписка с агентством Добровольного флота в городе Новороссийске о маршруте парохода «Иртыш» и о снабжении парохода «Херсон» топливом. 21 декабря 1919 г. - 2 июля 1920 г. / RSHA. Fund 98. Inv.6. 1878-1923. File 196. The Shipping company "Volunteer fleet". Correspondence with the Volunteer Fleet agency in the city of Novorossiysk about the route of the steamship "Irtysh" and about the supply of fuel to the steamship "Kherson". December 21, 1919 - July 2, 1920.

The Sale of the *Kherson*:

Государственный архив Российской Федерации (ГАРФ). Ф. Р-6817. Русский Военно-Морской агент в Королевстве Сербов, Хорватов и Словенцев. Белград. Оп.1. Русский военно-морской агент в КСХС. Белград. Д.3. Переписка с комендантом парохода белогвардейского добровольческого флота «Херсон», с белогвардейским военным

агентом в Королевстве С. Х. С. и другими о прибытии пароходов
в заграничные порты и отправке их с военными грузами в Крым
для белогвардейской армии ген. Врангеля. 1920-1922 / The
State Archives of the Russian Federation (ГАРФ, Moscow). Fund
P-6817. THE Russian Naval Agent in the Kingdom of Serbs, Croats
and Slovenes. Belgrade. Inv.1. Russian naval agent in the KSCS.
Belgrade. File 3. Correspondence with the commandant of the White
Guard Volunteer Fleet steamship "Kherson", with the White Guard
military agent in the Kingdom of S.C.S. and others about the arrival of
steamships in foreign ports and their dispatch with military cargo to the
Crimea for the White Guard army of General Wrangel. 1920-1922.

РГИА. Ф.98. Оп.6. 1878-1923 гг. Д.351. Пароходное общество
«Добровольный флот». Переписка с Лондонской пароходной
и торговой корпорацией по эксплуатации пароходов «Тверь»,
«Херсон», «Саратов». Том 1. 28 июля - 23 сентября 1921 г. / RSHA.
The Russian State Historical Archives. Fund 98. The Steamship
Company "Volunteer Fleet." Inv.6. 1878-1923. File 351. The Steamship
company "Volunteer fleet". Correspondence with the London
Steamship and Trading Corporation on the operation of steamships
"Tver", "Kherson", "Saratov". Volume 1. July 28 – September 23,
1921. Page 77.

РГИА. Ф.98. Оп.6. Д.352. Пароходное общество «Добровольный
флот». Переписка с Лондонской пароходной и торговой
корпорацией по эксплуатации пароходов «Тверь», «Херсон»,
«Саратов». Том 2. 26 сентября - 16 ноября 1921 г. / RSHA.
Ф.98. Inv.6. File 352. The Steamship company "Volunteer fleet".
Correspondence with the London Steamship and Trading Corporation
on the operation of steamships "Tver", "Kherson", "Saratov". Volume
2. September 26 – November 16, 1921.

Malta and Russia: Journey through the centuries: Hist. discoveries
in Russo - Maltese relations / Comp. a. ed. with introd. by
Elizaveta Zolina. - [Valetta], Cop. 2002 (published in Russian
in 2005 Путешествие через века : исторические открытия в

российско-мальтийских отношениях: [перевод с английского] / сост., ред. и авт. предисл.: Елизавета Золина. - Москва: ЦГО, 2005).

Personal Files:

Российский государственный исторический архив (РГИА). Ф.98. Пароходное общество «Добровольный флот». Оп.2. 1879-1920 гг. Д.1491. Пароходное общество «Добровольный флот». Личные дела. Аникеев М.К. 1917-1919 гг. / The Russian State Historical Archives (RSHA). F.98. Shipping Company "Volunteer Fleet". Inv.2. 1879-1920. File 1491. Shipping Company "Volunteer Fleet". Personal files. Anikeev M.K. 1917-1919.

РГИА. Ф.98. Оп.1. 1865-1922 гг. Д.751. Пароходное общество «Добровольный флот». Комитет. Личный состав. Дело Петрова-Токарева В.В. 1915 г. / RSHA. F. 98. Inv.1. 1865-1922. File 751. Shipping Company "Volunteer Fleet". Committee. Personal files. The file of Petrov-Tokarev V.V. 1915.

РГИА. Ф.98. Оп.2. Д.465. Пароходное общество «Добровольный флот». Личные дела. Семенопуло О.В. 1911-1919 гг. / RSHA. F.98. Inv.2. File 465. Shipping Company "Volunteer Fleet". Personal files. Semenopulo O.V. 1911-1919.

РГИА. Ф.98. Оп.2. Д.516. Пароходное общество "Добровольный флот". Личные дела.

Шмельц В.Ф. 1900-1919 гг. / RSHA. F.98. Inv.2. File 516. The Shipping company "Volunteer fleet". Personal files. Schmelz V.F. 1900-1919.

Российский государственный архив Военно-Морского Флота (РГА ВМФ). Ф.93. Оп.2. Ед.Хр.179. Шмельцев Виктор Францевич. Прапорщик по морск. Части / The Russian State Archives of the Navy (The Naval Archives). F.93. 2nd Baltic Fleet Crew, Petrograd (1906-1918). Inv.2. File 179. Schmelzev Viktor Franzevich. Warrant Officer for the Naval Division.

РГА ВМФ. Ф.432. Морское училище. Петроград (14 января 1701 г. - 09 марта 1918 г.). Оп.2. Аттестационные тетради. Д.2505. Яловиков Григорий Всеволодович. 1907-1908 / The Naval Archives. F.432. Naval School. Petrograd (January 14, 1701 – March 9, 1918. Inv.2. Certification notebooks. File 2505. Yalovikov Grigory Vsevolodovich. 1907-1908.

РГА ВМФ. Ф.432. Оп.2. Д.1290. Малявин Виссарион Дмитриевич. 1905-1909 / The Naval Archives. F.432. Inv.2. File 1290. Malyavin Vissarion Dmitrievich. 1905-1909.

РГА ВМФ. Ф.432. Оп.2. Д.1291. Малявин Виссарион Дмитриевич. 1902-1905 / The Naval Archives. F.432. Inv.2. File 1291. Malyavin Vissarion Dmitrievich. 1902-1905.

РГА ВМФ. Ф.417. Главный Морской Штаб. Оп.3. Статистическое отделение (1885-1917 гг.). Мобилизационное отделение (1893-1917 гг.). Учебное отделение (1911-1917 гг.). Д.3119. Труэн А., прпщ. 1904-1912 / The Naval Archives. F.417. General Naval Headquarters. Inv.3. Statistical Department (1885-1917). Mobilization Department (1893-1917). Educational Department (1911-1917). File 3119. Truen A., ensign. 1904-1912.

Центральный государственный исторический архив Санкт-Петербурга. Ф.14. Императорский Петроградский университет. Петроград. 1819–1918. Оп.3. Дела правления и правления по хозяйственному столу. Личные дела студентов за 1831, 1870-1916 гг. Д. 58919. Василевский Всеволод Исидорович. 1911 / Central State Historical Archives of St. Petersburg. Fund 14. Imperial Petrograd University. Petrograd. 1819–1918. Inv.3. Affairs of the board and the economic board. Personal files of students for 1831, 1870-1916. File 58919. Vasilevsky Vsevolod Isidorovich.

Центральный государственный исторический архив Санкт-Петербурга. Ф.2. Воспитательное общество благородных девиц и Александровский институт (Смольный институт). Петроград. 1764–1918. Оп.1. Дела общего характера, дела Совета, личные дела служащих и воспитанниц 1764-1917. Раздел описи 1892 год / Общие дела. Д.13933. Личное дело Шкинской Веры Федоровны

23.05.1898–без даты / The Central State Historical Archive of St. Petersburg. F.2. Educational Society for Noble Maidens and the Alexander Institute (Smolny Institute). Petrograd. 1764–1918. Inv.1. General affairs, Council affairs, personal affairs of employees and pupils 1764-1917. Inventory section year 1892. File 13933. Personal file of Vera Fedorovna Shkinskaya. May 23, 1898 – no date.

Books and Articles:

Ascherson, *Neal. Black Sea: Coasts and Conquests: From Pericles to Putin.* Revised edition, with updated foreward. Vintage, 2007.

The Russian Volunteer S.S. "Kherson" / Engineering: An Illustrated Weekly Journal. Edited by W.H. Maw and J. Dredge. Vol. LXII. – From July to December 1896. London: Offices for advertisements and publication, 35 & 36. Bedford Street, Strand, W.C. 1896. [Dec.11, 1896.] P.730-732.

The 1998 interview was conducted by Dr. Valentina Pichugin, who, at the time, was teaching Russian Language and Literature at Florida State University. Since 2001, she has been affiliated with the University of Chicago. The interview with Lydia was part of an academic research project about the Russian language of people who belong to the first wave of Russian emigration after the revolution of 1917.

Wrangel, Pyotr. *Always with Honor.* Edited by Alexandr Vatlin, translated by Sophie Lund, Russian Liberation Movement Historical Society, 1957.

Василенко А.С. Любовь наша, Отечество! : Барковские, Прохоровы. Соколовы-Бородкины в памяти и истории / Анатолий Василенко. — Изд. 2-е — Кировоград : Имэкс-ЛТД, 2011 / Vasilenko A.S. Our love, Fatherland! : Barkovskys, Prokhorovs. Sokolovs-Borodkins in memory and history / Anatoly Vasilenko. - 2nd ed. - Kirovograd : Imex-LTD, 2011.

Волков С.В. Офицеры российской гвардии. Опыт мартиролога. М.: Русский путь, 2002 / Volkov S.V. Officers of the Russian Guard. Experience of a Martyrologist. Moscow: Russian Way, 2002.

Волков С. В. Офицеры флота и морского ведомства: Опыт мартиролога. — М.: Русский путь, 2004 / Volkov S. V. Officers of the Fleet and the Naval Department: An Experience of a Martyrologist. — M.: Russian Way, 2004.

Главное справочное бюро в Константинополе, 1920–1922 гг. : именные списки беженцев и чинов Русской Армии : Сборник документов. Выпуск 1 / Составитель А. В. Ефимов. — М.: Институт Наследия, 2022 / Main Information Bureau in Constantinople, 1920-1922: Lists of Names of Refugees and Officers of the Russian Army: Collection of Documents. Issue 1 / Compiled by A.V. Efimov. – Moscow: The Institute of Heritage, 2022.

Главное справочное бюро в Константинополе, 1920–1922 гг. : именные списки беженцев и чинов Русской Армии : Сборник документов. Выпуск 2 / Составитель А. В. Ефимов. — М.: Институт Наследия, 2022 / Main Information Bureau in Constantinople, 1920-1922: Lists of Names of Refugees and Officers of the Russian Army: Collection of Documents. Issue 2 / Compiled by A.V. Efimov. – Moscow: The Institute of Heritage, 2022.

Главное справочное бюро в Константинополе, 1920–1922 гг. : именные списки беженцев и чинов Русской Армии : Сборник документов. Выпуск 3 / Составитель А. В. Ефимов. — М.: Институт Наследия, 2022 / Main Information Bureau in Constantinople, 1920-1922: Lists of Names of Refugees and Officers of the Russian Army: Collection of Documents. Issue 3 / Compiled by A.V. Efimov. – Moscow: The Institute of Heritage, 2022.

Емелин А. Ю., Кузнецов Н. А. (канд. ист. наук, историк флота) Русская эскадра. Прощание с Императорским флотом = The Russian squadron. Farewell to the Imperial fleet = L'Escadre russe. Adieu à Marine imperiale / [А. Ю. Емелин, Н.А. Кузнецов при участии В.В. Крестьянникова и др.]. - Москва : Арт Волхонка, 2015 / Emelin A. Yu., Kuznetsov N. A. (Ph.D. in History, naval historian) The Russian squadron. Farewell to the Imperial fleet = L'Escadre russe. Adieu à Marine imperiale / [A. Yu. Emelin, N. A. Kuznetsov with the participation of V. V. Krestyannikov and others.] - Moscow: Art Volkhonka, 2015.

Кузнецов Н.А. Русский флот на чужбине. М.: Вече. 2009 / Kuznetzov N.A. Russian fleet in foreign lands. Moscow: Veche, 2009.

Образец расписания судовой команды, составленный применительно к пароходу «Херсон», для руководства при составлении расписаний команд на пароходах Добровольного флота. Санкт-Петербург. 1897. С.4-7 / Sample of the ship's crew roster, drawn up for the steamship "Kherson", for guidance in drawing up crew rosters on the steamships of the Volunteer Fleet. Saint Petersburg, 1897. PP.4-7.

Орлов Г.А. Дневник добровольца : хроника гражданской войны 1918-1921 / Георгий Орлов ; [предисловие и комментарий С. В. Волкова, доктора исторических наук]. - Москва: Посев, 2019 / Orlov G.A. Diary of a Volunteer: Chronicle of the Civil War 1918-1921 / Georgy Orlov; [foreword and commentary by S. V. Volkov, Doctor of Historical Sciences]. - Moscow: Posev, 2019.

Положения о денежном, пищевом и других довольствиях служащих на судах Добровольного флота и штат администрации и береговых служащих. Санкт-Петербург. 1897. С.11-13 / Regulations on monetary, food and other allowances for employees on ships of the Volunteer Fleet and the staff of the administration and shore employees. St. Petersburg, 1897. PP.11-13.

Пушкадия-Рыбкина Т.В., Грубмайр И.И. Эмигранты из России в Загребе. Жизни и судьбы. - Изд. 2-е, испр. и доп. Загреб, 2019 / Pushkadia-Rybkina, Tatiana, and Inna Grubmair. *Emigrants from Russia in Zagreb: Lives and Destinies*. Second edition. Zagreb, 2019.

Судоплатов А. Дневник / Александр Судоплатов; вступ. статья, сост. О. Матич, подгот.

текста, послесл. и коммент. Я. Тинченко. – М.: Новое литературное обозрение, 2014 / Sudoplatov A. Diary / Alexander Sudoplatov; introduction, compiled by O. Matich, text preparation, afterword and commentary by Ya. Tinchenko. – M.: New Literary Review, 2014.

Timeline Sources:

Варнек П. У берегов Кавказа в 1920 году // Флот в Белой борьбе. М.: Центрполиграф, 2002 / Varnek P. Off the coast of the Caucasus in 1920 // Fleet in the White Struggle. Moscow: Centerpoligraf, 2022.

Беляков В.В. Гости английского короля. Воспоминания генерала Ф.П.Рерберга об эвакуации беженцев в Египет // Восточный архив. 2009. № 2 (20) / Belyakov V.V. Guests of the English King. Memories of General F.P. Rerberg about the evacuation of refugees to Egypt // Eastern Archive. 2009. No. 2 (20).

Историк С.В. Волков. База данных «Участники Белого движения в России» / Historian S.V. Volkov. Database "Participants of the White Movement in Russia":

https://swolkov.org/2_baza_beloe_dvizhenie/2_baza_beloe_dvizhenie _abc-01.htm

Кампе, Леонид. Круги ада или прибытие белой эмиграции в Котор / Русский вестник. # 97. July 1, 2018. Адаптированный перевод: Гуля Смагулова / Kampe, Leonid. The circles of the Inferno or the arrival of the white [*movement*] expatriates in Kotor / Russian Herald. # 97. July 1, 2018. Adapted translation: Gulya Smagulova

https://web.archive.org/web/20190128191510/http://rusvestnik.me/ krugi-ada-ili-pribytie-beloj-jemigracii-v-kotor-2/

Краинский Д.В. Записки тюремного инспектора. М.: Институт русской цивилизации, 2006 / Krainsky D.V. Notes of a Prison Inspector. Moscow: Institute of Russian Civilization, 2006.

Решетников Л.П. Русский Лемнос. Изд.: ФИВ. 3-е изд., 2012 / Reshetnikov L.P. Russian Lemnos. Publisher: FIV. 3rd ed., 2012.

Савич Н.В. Воспоминания. СПб.: Издательство «Logos»; Дюссельдорф: «Голубой всадник», 1993 (Историческая серия. XIX-XX век) / Savich N.V. Memories. SPb.: Logos Publishing

House; Dusseldorf: The Blue Rider, 1993 (Historical series. XIX-XX centuries).

Севастополь. 1920. Исход. На изломе : [к 95-летней годовщине исхода Русской армии генерала П. Н. Врангеля из Крыма и Севастополя] : документальный альбом / [сост.: Вадим Николаевич Прокопенков и др.]. - Севастополь : [б. и.] ; Симферополь : Салта, 2015 / Sevastopol. 1920. Exodus. At the Break: [for the 95th Anniversary of the Exodus of the Russian Army of General P. N. Wrangel from Crimea and Sevastopol]: documentary album / [compiled by: Vadim Nikolaevich Prokopenkov and others]. - Sevastopol: [publ. not spec.]; Simferopol: Salta, 2015.

Яровой В.В. Добровольный флот. СПб.: Галея-Принт, 2010 / Yarovoy V. V. The Volunteer Fleet. Saint Petersburg: Galeya Print, 2010.

Appropriation Books (Malta):

https://www.crewlist.org.uk/data/vesselsnum?officialnumber=137746& submit=searchb

https://www.crewlist.org.uk/data/appropriation?officialnumber= 137746 (in the bottom)

Websites about the Steamship *Kherson*:

https://tynebuiltships.co.uk/K-Ships/kherson1896.html

https://retroflot.com/dobrovoljnyj_flot/parohodkrejser_herson.html

ACKNOWLEDGEMENTS

First and foremost, I want to thank my mother, Helen, and my father, George, for their unwavering support and incredible ability to drop everything on a moment's notice to bring me what I needed, right away. Whether it was a photograph from our archives or simply lunch, you always delivered without hesitation and never questioned why. You just knew it was necessary for the good of the project, and for that, I am endlessly grateful.

To my uncle George, thank you for sharing your invaluable insights into your mother, my grandmother Lydia. Your reflections helped me focus on what mattered most to her, as you truly understood the kind and gentle soul she had. Like you, I look forward to seeing her again on the other side.

To all the Anikeeff descendants, especially Susan and Pam, who have supported me throughout this research project, thank you. You have not only enriched this story with your insights but have deeply touched me on a personal level. Just as Zhenia, Kolya, and Alyosha were my grandmother's family on the ship, you hold a special place in my heart as family. I genuinely believe our grandmothers are looking down on us, smiling at the bond we have formed. This connection was no accident - it was divine intervention, bringing us together across time and history.

To my incredible editor, Aubyn, for always challenging me to look beyond my grandmother's story and explore the depths of my connection to the past. Your encouragement and the high standards you set for me pushed me beyond what I thought possible.

To my amazingly talented graphic designer, Claudine, you genuinely took an interest in this story, and your artistic vision captured my grandmother's essence on the book cover.

To the Thought Leader Academy Team: Sara, Amy, Marietta, without you, this book would not have come into being. Your motivating sessions, whether through group coaching, text messages, or insightful classes on how to write a book, reignited the fire in me each time.

To Jane, Jennifer, Liz, Mike, and the fantastic team at TLA Publishing, thank you to everyone who played a role in bringing this book to fruition. Your expertise and willingness to answer my many questions were truly appreciated.

To my husband Mike, and children, Daniel and Kristina, thank you for your endless patience, love, and understanding as I poured so much of my time and energy into this book. You put up with my late nights, distractions, and constant thoughts about the story, always offering your support without hesitation.

To Valentina, who, unknowingly at the time, provided a priceless interview with my grandmother, one that would serve its true purpose over 20 years later. Your vast knowledge of the Russian language and history is truly admirable, and I am so grateful you allowed me to use this invaluable information in my book.

Thank you to all my friends and those surrounding me for your support and interest in my endeavors.

Thank you for joining me on this journey. To explore more about *Last Ship to Freedom*, scan the QR Code to visit my website, where I share updates on new findings and how you can contact me with questions about your own research.